❧ Bushwhackers ❧

THE CIVIL WAR ERA IN THE SOUTH
Brian Craig Miller and LeeAnn Whites, Series Editors

*Bushwhackers: Guerrilla Warfare, Manhood,
and the Household in Civil War Missouri*
Joseph M. Beilein Jr.

Bushwhackers

Guerrilla Warfare, Manhood,
and the Household in
Civil War Missouri

Joseph M. Beilein Jr.

The Kent State University Press
Kent, Ohio

First paperback edition
Library of Congress Catalog Number 2015036092
ISBN 978-1-60635-378-3
Manufactured in the United States of America

Search And Destroy
Written by Iggy Pop and James Williamson
Copyright © 1973 BMG Bumblebee, Strait James Music and EMI Music Publishing Ltd.
Copyright Renewed
All Rights for BMG Bumblebee and Strait James Music Administered by
BMG Rights Management (US) LLC
All Rights for EMI Music Publishing Ltd. Administered by Sony/ATV Music Publishing
LLC, 424 Church Street, Suite 1200, Nashville, TN 37219
All Rights Reserved   Used by Permission
Reprinted by Permission of Hal Leonard Corporation

Library of Congress Cataloging-in-Publication Data
Beilein, Joseph M., Jr., author.
Bushwhackers : guerrilla warfare, manhood, and the household in Civil War Missouri /
Joseph M. Beilein Jr.
pages cm. — (The Civil War era in the South)
Includes bibliographical references and index.
ISBN 978-1-60635-270-0 (alk. paper) ∞
1. Missouri—History—Civil War, 1861–1865—Underground movements. 2.
Missouri—History—Civil War, 1861–1865—Commando operations. 3.
Guerrilla warfare—Missouri—History—19th century.
4. Guerrillas—Missouri—History—19th century.
5. Missouri—History—Civil War, 1861–1865—Campaigns.
I. Title.
E470.45.B45 2016
977.8'03—dc23

2015036092

22 21 20 19 18   5 4 3 2

For my kin:
the Gums, Nilands, Rules, and Beileins,
past, present, and future.

I'm a street walkin' cheetah with a heart full of napalm

I'm a runaway son of the nuclear A-bomb

I am the world's forgotten boy

The one who searches and destroys

Honey gotta help me please

Somebody's gotta save my soul

Baby detonate for me

Look out honey, 'cause I'm using technology

Ain't got time to make no apology

Soul radiation in the dead of night

Love in the middle of a firefight

Honey gotta strike me blind

Somebody gotta save my soul

Baby penetrate my mind

And I'm the world's forgotten boy

The one who's searchin', searchin' to destroy

And honey I'm the world's forgotten boy

The one who's searchin', searchin' to destroy

—*Iggy Pop and James Williamson*
"Search and Destroy" (1973)

Contents

Author's Note

IT IS WITH MIXED EMOTIONS that I present to you *Bushwhackers*. It is a book that has given me joy and purpose and has sparked a great amount of self-discovery and growth. As it leaves my hands and enters yours, I am confronted with that anxious feeling that always accompanies the irresistible onrushing of the unknown. What will I do now? Can my next project give me as much as this study? Will I ever be able to fully emerge from the universe of the guerrilla and enter another historical world? Despite these questions that remain unanswered for the moment, it is with a deep sense of pride that I offer you this book, without apology, caveat, or qualification. I have striven to put onto the pages that follow the most intimate historical rendering of the guerrillas who fought in Civil War Missouri. In my pursuit of their identity as men, I was forced to become much more aware of myself. Along the way there were fights with a wide range of adversaries both real and metaphorical; there were victories and defeats, I lost pieces of myself, but in sacrificing a little bit I have gained much more. Most important, in the spirit of the guerrillas, I lived to fight another day and was able to produce something that will live on and keep up the fight long after I am gone.

Acknowledgments

THERE WERE A GREAT MANY INSTITUTIONS and individuals who came to my aid in the production of this book. This project, which can be traced back to my master's thesis and dissertation, could not have been possible if not for the various forms of financial support that I received from the Department of History at the University of Missouri. The James S. Rollins Slavery Atonement Endowment for Black Studies at the University of Missouri also provided support during this process. Additionally, the Filson Historical Society gave me a helpful research grant. The Southern Roundtable at the University of Georgia gave me a great opportunity to share my work, and I thank them for the opportunity to receive feedback from a wonderful set of young scholars and to make a great many new friends. Penn State Behrend has been very supportive in a number of different ways to help facilitate the research and completion of *Bushwhackers*. Finally, I would like to thank the dozens of archivists, curators, and librarians and all of the various institutions who helped me to track down so much of the material that appears in this book.

It is impossible to name all of the people who assisted or otherwise influenced the creation of this book. The list of teachers and comrades and colleagues is probably too long for me to mention everyone, but I will try. My first interest in Missouri's guerrilla conflict came during my undergraduate days at Kenyon College where Will Scott did his best to guide me through the complexities of the war "on the other side of the river," as he called it.

His biggest challenge was not so much explaining the war but rather who he was trying to explain it to (a rather distracted student with a passion for a number of extracurricular activities). Bruce Kinzer and Roy Wortman were also of great influence upon my work, but no one knew it at the time. In my graduate studies, the list of professors who taught me at the University of Missouri is a long one: Mark Carroll, Wilma King, Mary Jo Neitz, Jeff Pasley, Linda Reeder, Robert Smail, Robert Weems, John Wigger, and Laurel Wilson. I have also been very lucky to have a wide range of Civil War scholars read, comment, or otherwise shape all or pieces of this book. They are Paul Anderson, Steve Berry, Jim Broomall, Diane Mutti Burke, Vikki Bynum, Zach Garrison, Lesley Gordon, James Huston, Brian Miller, Barton Myers, Megan Kate Nelson, Ken Noe, Chris Phillips, Bill Piston, Aaron Sheehan-Dean, and Matt Stanley.

Comradery was critically important to the completion of this project. There were my friends from Mizzou who sat around the same seminar table with me, read pieces of this book, but more important were supportive both in and out of the classroom. The cast of characters from the basement of Read Hall includes but is not limited to Megan Boccardi, Dave Brock, Daniel Conner, Jonathan Dee Jones, Vernon Mitchell, Will Mountz, Josh Nudell, Jonathan Root, Leroy Rowe, Mike Snodgrass, T. J. Tomlin, Lucas Volkman, and Andrea Weingartner. My colleagues here at Penn State Behrend have also provided wonderful friendship during the final phases of writing the book, and I couldn't ask for better colleagues in the history program: Dick Aquila, Leigh-Ann Bedal, Amy Carney, Glenn Kumhera, and John Rossi. Also, I've formed relationships with many of my fellow professors in the School of Humanities and Social Sciences who have helped to foster a positive work environment. This list includes but is not limited to Joe Bookman, Teri Caruso, Eric Corty, Sharon Dale, Elizabeth Fogle, John Gamble, Steve Hicks, Jill Kambs, Matt Levy, Janet Neigh, Tom Noyes, Dan Shank, Joshua Shaw, and Craig Warren. Of special note is Matt Lesnett, a student of mine and my research assistant. His labor was incredibly valuable to me, but more than that, his observations and questions helped me to see the work in new ways. Thank you all!

There are people who have had a larger influence on this work than anyone else. The first is Andrew Fialka, who is first and foremost an old friend. You will not only see his maps in the pages of this book, but he is producing maps for this entire generation of guerrilla scholars. His own work, which deals directly with mapping the guerrilla war in dynamic ways, is some of the most fascinating scholarship out there and should lead us all to think about the guerrillas in new ways. Next is Matt Hulbert, who is my best friend in the profession and something of a partner in crime. Our shared interest in a particular region and particular men created a common bond that turned very quickly into friendship. It has been to my great benefit to have Matt read this work at various stages and offer his honest feedback in the nicest possible way. The person who has had the greatest influence on this work is my mentor, LeeAnn Whites. I was more than a little bit lucky that she let me study with her and even luckier that she believed in me and was willing to invest so much time and energy in me (as she does with all her graduate students). Under her tutelage, I learned quite a bit about the Civil War, gender, and history in general; I learned how to read works of history; I learned how to research and interpret documents. But more than anything else, she taught me how to think like a historian so that I could set about making my own contribution to the great cosmic conversation. Andrew, Matt, and LeeAnn, I am forever in your debt.

I would not be here if not for my family and longtime friends. The list of my childhood, high school, and college friends is too long to list here: you know who you are and I am ever in your debt. Daniel Miller and the rest of the Miller family, who are Missourians to the bone, have been lifelong friends who have taken great interest in my work and showed their support throughout the years in a variety of ways. Also, Greg and Maureen Schmidt have opened their door to me each and every time I've come through Kansas City for research, fun, or some other business. The next beer is on me. As it was with the guerrillas, family is the most important thing to me, and I have a big one. My grandparents on both sides were formative in ways I will never truly understand. Both sets of my grandparents—Bill and Aleene Rule, and Art and Josephine Beilein—worked to create lives for themselves that were different from the lives of their parents. In the process, the Rules and Beileins created family cultures that instilled love, accountability, work ethic, and independence into their children. My aunts and uncles and my thousands of cousins (it seems like that) have also been there to reinforce our family values. I feel grateful to have my brother-in-law, Nick Azar, and the entire Azar clan in my life. You are my family (whether you like it or not). My sister Jill is my best friend in the world and a pillar to lean on when things get heavy. Her children, my adorable nieces and nephews, are not only endlessly entertaining but also serve as a source of inspiration. Joe and Kathy Beilein are a great team and the best parents a guy could ask for: strict when they had to be, nurturing when they could be, and always supportive. I must also note that their support was quite active—reading different pieces of this book and making appearances at conferences—with both of them giving me very helpful feedback and generating ideas about the guerrillas that strengthened this volume. Finally, I need to thank Rachel, who might not have been there at the beginning but was there for the last push, and this book as well as its author are better for it. To everyone, I appreciate all of your love and support.

A Curiosity and Specimen

*Or, a Sincerely, Vengeful Man
and His Guerrilla War*

MORE THAN ANY OTHER MAN who fought in the Civil War, the Southern guerrilla was the most contradictory, contested, and arresting of them all. Sitting atop his horse in one of Missouri's dark timber bottoms, the guerrilla's hair dangled down to his shoulders like that of his sister's, while his beard dropped to his chest like that of an Old Testament patriarch. His face was hard to see, obscured in shadow by a large slouch hat that was bedecked with ribbons, metal stars, shiny crescent moons, squirrel tails, and feathers. On his chest he wore a beautifully embroidered shirt made for him by his sweetheart or his mother. Over his shoulders, he sported the blue jacket of his Union enemy. Darkening this colorful image were the scalps that dangled from the bridle of his thoroughbred horse, bloody reminders of his vanquished foes. In one hand he held the reins of his charger, and with the other he fingered the handle of his revolver. While the distinctive look of the guerrilla would suggest that the particular—even peculiar—form of manhood he embodied helped to shape his war, exactly what it meant to be a guerrilla has remained a mystery.[1]

"I am a guerrilla," proclaimed Bill Anderson in his July 7, 1864, open letter to Union officers, newspapermen, and the citizens of Missouri. Anderson used the language of manhood to define what such a title meant. The document was replete with references to honor, pride, nobility, truth, glory, principles, force, power, and violence. All of these characteristics came together in the form of vengeance, the driving impulse that seemed to be the

Perhaps no image better illustrates how the guerrilla looked during the war than the portrait of George Maddox. Here he was captured by the photographer's lens decked out in full guerrilla glory: plumed hat, long hair and beard, military overcoat left open to show his ruffled guerrilla shirt, a brace of dragoon pistols, and riding boots. We need only imagine a horse under him to see him as he was in the brush. (Courtesy of Wilson's Creek National Battlefield)

most definitive element in the identity Anderson laid bare for his readers. He claimed his right to avenge the attempts made on his life, the killing of his father, the destruction of his property, and the death of one sister and the maiming of two others, all of which he said were perpetrated by the Yankees. He explained, "I have chosen guerilla [*sic*] warfare to revenge myself for wrongs that I could not honorably avenge otherwise." Moreover, when he declared that he "never belonged to the Confederate Army," Anderson was stating that his war was not about service to a country or a state. Rather, while he was ideologically aligned with the South, his war was a way of being, a subjective experience, a personal contest grounded in his identity as a man. Although Anderson's letter provided important clues about the true nature of the guerrilla and his war, Union officers were confounded by the manifesto, calling it "a curiosity and specimen."[2]

Similarly, since the war Americans, both men and women, have struggled to understand the essence of the guerrilla. For some, the guerrilla was a veritable collage of different men—a mixing and matching of masculine forms—that allowed him to appear as nearly anything, depending on the perspectives of those who would write about him. This was especially true of the histories written in the immediate wake of the war, but it was a trend that continued through the mid-nineteenth century. To John Edwards, the guerrilla looked rather like a hero, a champion of the causes of the pro-slavery South and of Missouri. In his 1877 book, *Noted Guerrillas*, he actively tried to turn the likes of Anderson and William Clarke Quantrill into mythical figures complete with superhuman powers and impeccable virtue. This shameless attempt at Reconstruction-era propaganda was not seriously challenged until 1910, when William E. Connelley published his biography of Quantrill, *Quantrill and the Border Wars*. In this telling, Quantrill and his cohort were depraved demons, driven exclusively by selfish and evil desires. As these early histories suggest, the guerrilla has never been presented in moderate terms, instead appearing at the extremes of interpretation: he has been a demon and a hero; he has been imagined as an outlaw-in-training and as a social bandit; he was thought of as a valiant soldier of the Confederacy and as a bloody opportunist.[3]

Despite their best efforts at a balanced approach, most modern scholars continue this trend. To historians of the last few decades, these men appear as the very embodiment of anarchy and confusion. Studying the guerrilla and his war, these historians contend that the guerrilla war was an orgy of destruction, a dehumanizing carnival of blood in which even the men who survived lost their humanity. In his work *Inside War*, Michael Fellman revolutionized the field of guerrilla studies by portraying the war as utter chaos and destroying any notion of romance in the guerrilla war or in the Civil War more generally. For Fellman, the war represented a complete lapse into insane animalism. Or, to borrow from Thomas Hobbes: it was a war of all against all. In other words, the guerrillas turned their violence inward toward their own communities, attacking friend and foe alike. In the process, they destroyed their prewar, civilized selves and any connection they had to that world, whether it was to their antebellum institutions, to their neighbors, or even to their own kinfolk. In his ambitious and award-winning book, *A Savage Conflict*, Daniel Sutherland took Fellman's argument one step further—or broader, as the case may be—and applied it to the South as a whole. Here we see the guerrillas playing a decisive role in the Civil War as they undermined their own war effort and simultaneously brought the Union's hard war down on themselves, leading to the Confederacy's collapse.[4]

All of these historical images of the guerrilla have deep-running ramifications for our overall understanding of the war. For the older histories, the emphasis on one part of these central actors has created distorted pictures of the war. As a one-dimensional character—either good *or* bad—each guerrilla plays out a predictable narrative that does little to complicate or make real our understanding of war. Modern scholarship works to correct this simplicity in an attempt to move the guerrilla war from the "sideshow" of Civil War history into the limelight of that scholarship. However, in complicating the guerrilla, these studies have overcorrected and made him so complex, so fractured, that he is unknowable as a man; we cannot see ourselves in him; he is incomprehensible. Indeed, as compelling a picture of war as chaos is, the guerrilla remains inaccessible in these modern analyses, still partially obscured, and waiting in the wings for his moment at center stage.[5]

To bring the guerrilla into the spotlight, it is not enough to get inside the conflict in which he fought. We cannot begin the study of the guerrilla at the moment in which he began to kill. Instead, we must go back to his roots and observe his development into manhood. His origins must be retraced back into the antebellum South, where the men who became guerrillas shared some characteristics with white Southern men more generally. A long series of important works have constructed a general framework for understanding the identity of men in the South. Historian Stephen Berry asserts in his book *All That Makes a Man* that Southern white men were driven by the pursuits of both love and immortality, which were "each beholden to the other. The woman, once acquired, would sustain and bear witness to the male becoming; the male would in turn reconceive his becoming as a tribute to her love." As men, the guerrillas pursued both immortality and love in the manner described by Berry. The young men in this story shared a common belief with men across the South that violence was both an important component of masculine identity and a tool that allowed men to achieve their goals—or facilitate their becoming, as it were. John Hope Franklin's monumental work, *The Militant South*, demonstrated that the ability to be violent and bring to bear the tools of violence solidified a man's standing in the antebellum South. Hunting, dueling, fighting, and punishing others allowed a man to navigate through the masculine realms of the antebellum South.[6]

It is more than a bit ironic that these masculine virtues often undid men across the South during the antebellum period and especially during the war. Such firm, even unrealistic expectations were difficult for young men to achieve, in no small part because of the self-centered nature of their pursuits. Unable to empathize with anyone beyond male kin and close friends, Southern men often failed to secure a romantic relationship that fit their ideals of love and fell well short of achieving immortality. Furthermore, placing such incredible emphasis on their martial talents was a contributing factor in driving the white men in the South regardless of class to war with the North. During the war, men on both sides were wrecked by the dehumanizing quality of a war that did not match their starry-eyed visions of combat. Men in the South, though, were totally smashed by the gruesome realities of the conventional war because they were defeated by men they had imagined to be inferior in the arts of war.[7]

Hardly crushed by masculine expectations or the war, the young men who became guerrillas embraced their reality and evolved within the conflict. Rather than be pulled apart by conflicting pursuits, they folded all of the existing parts of their identity together into one, singular drive. The guerrillas remained at home to wage their war, holding fast to bonds with their families, relying upon their kin for support, and creating a dynamic in which the so-called homefront and the battlefield shared a location (as if there ever could be a true division between the two). Resulting from this household war, young men who had been focused on themselves and their own pursuits were forced to engage with others on a different level. Whether they were avenging some act against their women, imagined themselves defending their families, or were receiving support from kin and kith, the guerrillas were infused with a powerful sense of empathy that enabled them to grow in the face of tragedy and destruction. In so doing, they transcended the traditional and neatly contained forms of manhood as they were known as to nineteenth-century Americans and became something new.[8]

The guerrillas took on a different form than their counterparts in part because their war had evolved differently than that of the conventional war. With the passage of the Kansas-Nebraska Act in 1854, the subsequent violence between abolitionist settlers and their proslavery counterparts, and the full blown raiding war between abolitionists and Missourians over the border, the soil was made fertile for the guerrilla war that would follow. With the formal declaration of war, Union forces seized St. Louis and spent the second half of 1861 and the first few months of 1862 driving formal forces of the Confederacy out of the state. Simultaneously, the Union Department of the Missouri set about occupying the state. From the fall and winter of 1861 into the summer of 1865, warfare in the state would be characterized by relatively small engagements like the near daily raids, ambushes, and running fights between guerrillas and Union troopers. Beginning with John C. Fremont and then Henry Halleck, the early leadership of this department was both radical and iron fisted in its governance of the state. Fremont attempted to free the slaves of Southern sympathizers on August 30, 1861, but his order was rescinded by President Lincoln, who would also remove the ideologue from command. Halleck replaced Fremont and immediately recognized the threat posed by the guerrillas. In the spring of 1862, he declared that guerrillas would not be given quarter. Fighting actually intensified through 1862 and into '63 until that August, which was the most tumultuous month of the war, at least along the western border. On the twenty-first of that month, an army of guerrillas under the command of William Clarke Quantrill raided the abolitionist town of Lawrence, Kansas. In response, Union brigadier general Thomas Ewing proclaimed General Order 11, which banished all Southern sympathizers from three and a half counties along the western border of the state. The following year, the guerrillas returned. During Sterling Price's raid of the state in the fall of 1864, the guerrillas acted more violently than ever before. After all the bloodshed of '64, Unionists hoped that the guerrilla violence might have come to an end. However, the abolition of slavery in the state of Missouri on January 11, 1865, saw another uptick in the violence. The guerrilla war carried on until the summer of '65, with most of the guerrillas not surrendering until June, and many not surrendering at all.[9]

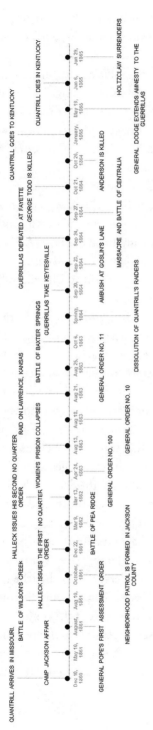

The guerrilla war followed a very different timeline than the narrative arc of the "regular" war we have come to know so well. (Courtesy of Andrew Fialka)

Within the context of this war, it is important to try and understand the guerrillas on their own terms. Guerrilla writings are at the center of this story. While the remainder of the book will place these men within the particular circumstances of their war, we must first try to gain a grasp on their mindset, as difficult as that may be. Once we have established the significant thoughts whirling around in the minds of the guerrillas, whether it was their beliefs, their motives, or their emotions, we can better understand how they saw their world. With their worldview fleshed out, then their wartime actions and reactions will make all the more sense.[10]

Guerrilla sources are buttressed by Union military records, census materials, and newspaper accounts. This book is not, however, a history of the guerrilla seen exclusively through the eyes of the Union, nor is it a history of the guerrilla blurred by the politics of the mythmaker's tales. Additionally, in using the sources, the book employs not only social and cultural analysis but also analysis that is in keeping with military history. The guerrilla, after all, was a military man, even if he was not considered so in a formal sense. This merger of military history and gender history will give us a history with an unprecedented depth of understanding when it comes to the conduct of the guerrilla war (read: logistics, strategy, and tactics). Such an intimate portrait of the guerrillas should also restore proportion and clarity to the guerrilla conflict. Indeed, it will destroy the existing paradigm through which we understand the guerrilla war in Missouri and replace it with one that is true to form. Furthermore, while the guerrilla movement varied from region to region across the South, it is the hope that this method of study—using the guerrilla's own words, reading sources through a gendered lens, and merging military and social history techniques in the deep analysis of local communities—will be applied to other guerrilla conflicts and benefit our overall understanding of the guerrilla and the Civil War.

In their writings, the guerrillas offered a picture of themselves that was consistent with Bill Anderson's manifesto. Hamp "Babe" Watts, who was just fourteen when he fought with Bill Anderson, said that the guerrilla was "impulsive, rash and reckless, [and] recognizing no middle course . . . rushed blindly into the hottest and the fiercest part of the conflict, his only thought, 'To conquer or to die.'" Watts saw in Anderson a hypermasculine warrior. He recalled that "a price had been offered and set upon his head; he was human; being put under ban and ostracism, he retaliated and was unforgiving. The brilliancy and splendor of his daring and fearlessness made him the idol of his following." As Watts remembered, "His presence here in

Map of Missouri, with counties. (Map by Andrew Fialka)

1864, was the equalizing force and safety valve 'twixt southern sympathizers and the enemy. He and a large majority of his band held the admiration and confidence of the first, the hatred and fear of the latter."[11]

To a man, the guerrillas agreed on the driving force behind their war. Samuel Hildebrand, a guerrilla who operated in southeast Missouri, recalled his reason for going to war: "The die was cast—for the sake of revenge, I pronounced myself a Rebel." In remembering what drew him out into the war, Cole Younger said that the "conflicts and troubles centered on our home . . . planted a bitterness in my young heart which cried out for revenge." Younger's cousin and fellow guerrilla, John McCorkle offered his explanation for bringing down brutal violence upon his enemies in the form of a rhetorical question: "People abuse us, but, my God, did we not have enough to make us desperate and thirst for revenge?" Over and over, the men who fought as guerrillas described themselves as avengers.[12]

For the guerrillas, there was no question that they should be the ones to respond to the troubles brought into their communities. The preexisting social structure gave these men the freedom to respond to attacks and occupation. Moreover, it required their response, not simply to protect others but to maintain their place atop a profitable but fragile system. William H. Gregg, who was William Clarke Quantrill's right-hand man, remembered his guerrilla cohort as "men and boys, from the very best families of Missouri." Andrew Walker, himself the son of one of the wealthiest men to settle along the western border of Missouri, repeated Gregg's claim recalling that the guerrillas were "young men of the best families of the district."[13]

Violence could not be random, nor could killing be anonymous; they were personal acts for the good of the community. The young men who became guerrillas had much more to lose from the anarchic destruction of society than they would ever stand to gain. For instance, from the perspective of Anderson, it was the Union's "petty hirelings" who had caused tumult in Missouri, and that tumult made room for "thieves and robbers" to prey upon the innocents. As Anderson believed, he was an agent of the proper order and the protector of the Southern community, or as he said, "My command can give them more protection than all the Federals in the State." When it came to dealing with these criminals—or, as Anderson probably thought of them, insurgents—he promised, "I will help the citizens rid the country of them. . . . I have used all that language can do to stop their thefts; I will not see what I can do by force." For the young men out in the brush, and really the vast majority of white men across the country, order and violence were not mutually exclusive. Instead, violence was subjective: it mattered who was wielding it and what they were hoping to accomplish with it. In Anderson's mind, he was fighting to return his community to peace: destroying the property of Unionists, executing unarmed men, and mutilating the dead were all done in a desperate effort to repair the cracks in the tumbling edifice that was once his world, the very same structure that had propped him and other white men up.[14]

As men, the guerrillas were expected to meet war with war. McCorkle recalled his reasons for going into the brush. He said, "I could not and I would no longer submit, and I then resolved that if die I must, I would die fighting for my own people and for their cause." Hildebrand put it a slightly different way. In a thinly veiled association between manhood and resistance, he proclaimed, "I pity the poor miserable, sniveling creature who would tamely have submitted to it all." Walker remembered the time before he became a guerrilla as a difficult one. For him, it was "hard to resist joining one's angry neighbors in visiting retribution on those meddlesome and blood-thirsty Yankees." As fanciful as the idea was that the guerrillas were left without any other options than to act violently, in their minds resistance was necessary for retaining their manhood.[15]

All of this culminated in the guerrillas becoming killers. After it was all over, the guerrillas who scribbled down their memories of the war were proud; they had become killers and were mostly honest and accountable for their bloody deeds. As if thumping his chest, Hildebrand boasted that he had personally killed over a hundred men as a measure of his value as a man and as a fighter. Fully acknowledging the blood on his hands, Gregg said of the guerrillas' mission when they raided Lawrence in the summer of 1863 that "we went there to burn and kill and we did it." Although he would die before the war was out, a story that survived him recounted that Anderson proudly claimed to have killed fourteen at Lawrence. In the minds of the guerrillas, these acts of killing were not things from which men should hide.[16]

While all guerrillas were killers, the intensity with which they applied their bloody medium varied from man to man. There were quite a few reasons for the range of violent behavior that could be found within the guerrilla ranks, but perhaps the greatest factor was the effect of the war on a man's household or his community. A threat—or perceived threat—to a household could be enough to send a man into the brush, and a direct assault on household or kin would almost certainly either drive him into the brush or, if he was already fighting as a guerrilla, to exact some kind of reprisal beyond the general aims of the guerrilla war. The destruction of a man's household, the killing of a family member, the execution of a comrade, the mutilation of a guerrilla or a guerrilla supporter, or the sexual assault of a kinswoman often led men to extraordinary acts of violence. This is not to say that every act of violence committed by the guerrillas was reactionary, only that the increase in violent behavior was a process, and that men in the brush simultaneously operated at different levels of violence.

To tackle the complex masculine identity of the guerrilla, we must approach him from multiple angles. This book is broken up into three sections. The first examines the structure and organization of the guerrilla war effort. It includes chapters on the household, kinship relations, and the importance of hired hands to the guerrilla movement. The second section looks at the guerrilla through the varied lens of material culture. These four chapters study the guerrilla through the food that sustained him, his clothing and appearance, his horse, and his firearms. The concluding section intertwines all of these different perspectives in one chapter that looks closely at the guerrilla in combat and in another that examines him in death. In tracing the guerrilla as he moved from his home into the brush, these different approaches occasionally overlap, adding bits of the wide-ranging perception that colors reality, memory, and history. Moreover, each chapter has its own chronology, all of which fall within or around 1861–1865. However, some chapters only cover a couple of years, while others may extend beyond the chronology of the conventional Civil War. The composite image generated by views of the guerrillas from these different perspectives will offer the first multi-dimensional portrait of the masculine identity of the guerrilla, creating much needed depth to what has only existed as a silhouette of manhood.[17]

Even with this multifaceted approach, it may still be impossible to ever fully know the guerrilla. Nonetheless, an effort to understand what lies in the hearts and minds of these men is a mission worth undertaking. In his novel, *The Glass Bead Game*, one of Herman Hesse's characters, Father Jacobus, describes the need for history as a futile but indispensable human pursuit, a leap of faith. He says, "Studying history, my friend, is no joke and no irresponsible game. To study history one must know in advance that one is attempting something fundamentally impossible, yet necessary and highly important. To study history means submitting to chaos and nevertheless retaining faith in order and meaning. It is a very serious task, young man, and possibly a tragic one." At first glance, the guerrilla's world may seem chaotic. With a touch of curiosity, a little bit of faith, and a dose of empathy, the anarchy swirling all around will slow down, the dust will settle, and the logic and organization of the guerrilla's realm will become clear.[18]

What follows, then, is an effort to take you deep into the dark woods of Civil War Missouri and see the deadly world of the guerrilla, the world he helped to create. Only when we hop into the saddle and grip the reins of his charger can we begin to feel and understand the forces that lived inside him. Only after we ride alongside the guerrilla through the timber bottoms and down the shaded roads of the rural landscape can we see just how it was that this man became a killer. Only then will we see the guerrilla as a man whose reasons for killing, no matter how detestable or illegitimate they appear to us, were congruent with the morality and expectations of his culture. Only then will our fears of this killer subside, allowing us to see him as something other than just a curiosity and specimen.

CHAPTER 1

Household War

IN FEBRUARY OF 1863, Union Colonel William Penick led a patrol of seventy-five men on a sixteen-mile trek through wintry weather from the town of Independence, Missouri, to a rebel neighborhood near Blue Springs. Decades after the war, William H. Gregg told the story of that day's events. At the home of Colonel John Saunders, the Union patrol split into two groups: one went into the house to get their dinner, and the other rode over to Jeptha Crawford's home to do the same. Gregg recounted that "Mrs. Saunders and her daughter prepared dinner for the half stopping there, the [Colonel] furnished feed for their horses, all went well until dinner was over . . . when [Colonel] Saunders was placed under guard[,] the house burned, the women not allowed a bonnet or shawl." The course of events was the same at the Crawford home. According to Gregg, when the Union patrol reunited "they dismounted Crawford and Saunders and shot them to death."[1]

In defense of these Union troops, this attack was neither random nor the culmination of pent-up rage unleashed on innocent victims. Instead, Penick's men were merely responding to what they knew to be true: as Southern sympathizers, the Crawford and Saunders families supported the guerrilla war effort. In August of 1863, Union brigadier general Thomas Ewing, who was the commander of the District of the Border, observed that "about two-thirds of the families on the occupied farms of that region are of kin to the guerrillas, and are actively and heartily engaged in feeding, clothing, and sustaining them. The presence of these families is the cause of the presence there of the guerrillas." Ewing concluded that "they will, therefore, continue guerrilla war as long as they remain, and will stay as long as possible if their families remain." Ewing was articulating the principal problem confronting all Union officers in Missouri. Though they would just as soon make war on other men in a "civilized" manner, their orderly battlefields were beset by the households of the enemy. More to the point, it was these households from which the guerrillas like Gregg and his cohort originated and from which they were supplied; it was from the guerrilla household that the entire war in Missouri emanated.[2]

Leaving home to make their war without *really* leaving gave young men like Gregg a decidedly unique vision of warfare. Though they received emotional farewells from their fathers and womenfolk at the thresholds of their houses, they did not go far. Unlike the millions of men in the North and South who marched hundreds of miles from home, most guerrillas began the war in their own neighborhoods. With the attacks on their homes, they were already aware that in this war their houses and their battlefields shared the same space. By staying out in the brush, close to their homes, families, and slaves, the guerrillas actively embraced this spatial dynamic, even helping to create it. Fighting within this uniquely structured system of war led

William H. Gregg was described by John Newman Edwards as a "grim Saul." This portrait would seem to confirm that description, as he seems serious and humorless compared to some of his more flamboyant counterparts. (William E. Connelley, *Quantrill and the Border Wars*)

the guerrillas to interpret warfare in an altogether different way than did a soldier, whose family and slaves were far from the battlefield on which they fought and died. The same forces that had informed guerrilla identity and outlook before the war remained in place. Explosions of powder, houses aflame, the charred ruins of barns, and the spilled blood of kin would only increase the intensity of these forces on the guerrillas' character. Over the course of the war, the guerrillas became ever more attached to their households, even working to create new households where their old ones had been destroyed. Within the context of their war, it was the household more than any other force that shaped the masculine identity of the guerrilla.

Indeed, the household offers the best perspective from which to study the men who actively engaged in this informal brand of warfare. The guerrilla war effort was not dictated by a centralized government or a bureaucratically organized and hierarchal army. Rather, the strategy, tactics, and logistics of guerrilla warfare came about as the result of the roles, relations, and identities that were established within the antebellum household. As the war raged on for years, the challenges brought against the rebel household required its structure to bend and flex into a configuration that best facilitated the war. However, the household was never broken as the primary framework through which the guerrillas and their supporters understood themselves and their war effort. For Gregg, his fellow guerrillas, and their supporters this was a war of the household and one that would ultimately be waged against enemy households.[3]

Before examining the household at war, we must first understand its antebellum structure. A great deal of work has been done on the Southern household during the antebellum period, with the majority of it looking at women, both white and black. Scholars of women and gender have reestablished the household as the center of the Southern world and the primary unit of production. The Southern household was ordered along lines of gender and race, explaining why white and black women were divided by the color line. The so-called "mistress" sided with her husband as they shared both class and race privilege; she operated as his lieutenant in the running of the household. Meanwhile, black women found themselves on the subjugated side of vertical gender, race, and class relations, residing at the mudsill of the household hierarchy and vulnerable to everyone in the household, especially, but not exclusively, the white men who sat at the top.[4]

Although they were typically smaller, the households that would support

Although Morgan Walker was wealthier than most of the men whose sons became guerrillas and whose households supported the guerrilla war effort, his house gives us an idea of what the physical representation of the Southern household looked like during the war. It was outward from homes like this that the guerrilla war emanated. (William E. Connelley, *Quantrill and the Border Wars*)

the men in the brush shared the same basic structure as the plantation households. The Gregg family was a representative example of a rebel household. Inside this household there were several white women, four slaves, and a few white men. Jacob Gregg, the head of household and William's father, was born in Tennessee and carried his proslavery beliefs with him to Missouri, where he relied upon enslaved men and women to accumulate nearly $15,000 in real and personal estate. He had two sons in addition to William, Christopher and Jacob. These young white men were positioned below their father in the household order, but as their father aged, he most likely gave them a larger amount of responsibility. In the hierarchy of the household these men were above all other members, with the possible exception of their mother.[5]

The social location of Gregg and his brothers within the household—dependent white men—offered a great deal of potential power that was realized when the war came to Jackson County. Within his household, young men like William Gregg and his brothers had a vested interest in holding together both the household and the hierarchy of society. At twenty-two years of age in 1860, Gregg was on the cusp of owning his own land and slaves. He and the other men who went out into the brush stood to lose the most from the destruction of this system and the most to gain from its successful defense.[6]

Long before they would leave home to wage their war, William Gregg and the hundreds of other guerrillas understood their manhood not simply as an outgrowth of their position in the household but as a product of their labor. Gregg, a farmer, shared the most common profession among the young men who would become guerrillas. More than four-fifths of the guerrillas were farmers. These men understood agriculture in a way that allowed them to bring along a successful crop and manage a farm, infusing them with a sense of self-worth. The actual labor necessary to farm had other benefits that many professions did not. Most notably, working outdoors helped to create solid bodies for these men; it was the best peacetime training for nineteenth-century combat. Men like Gregg worked outdoors by themselves and alongside their white kin and slaves from sunup to sundown. They often worked consecutive days in the field for weeks and even months at a time. They knew how to use their bodies to move the earth and handle animals; they thought of themselves as masters of their environment. Furthermore, their knowledge of the environment became intuitive, especially their familiarity with their immediate surroundings: the fields, woods, prairies, hills, bluffs, creeks, and rivers around their homes. When they eventually traded their oxen for horses, plow straps for reins, and shovels for revolvers, they did so knowing that they had the physical and mental strength to handle the rigors of war.[7]

Social position and labor were important pieces of manhood, but a sense of mastery was perhaps the greatest source of power for nineteenth-century men. Although men like William Gregg hoped to be masters of many things—land, tools, animals, women, children, and, most important, themselves—their relationship with slaves offered the most tangible example of mastery for Southern white men. As Gregg worked in his fields, he would have been toiling alongside slaves, most likely the two young black men, owned by his father, who were fourteen and nineteen in 1860. Two black women, who were fifty years old and thirty years old in 1860, would have spent their time in the house or close to it. It would not have been uncommon for women, especially black women, to join the men in the fields during the planting and harvesting seasons. Gregg's character as a slaveholder is unknown, but there were two expectations of white male slave owners that can help us understand the relationship between the guerrillas and slavery as well as their understanding of race. In the first place, whites expected that the enslaved persons behave as the subjected persons (or property) that the white community thought of them as. Second, should any of the four African Americans in bondage on the Gregg farm resist their position, it was the expectation that white men nudge, push, whip, beat, or use whatever means necessary to restore them to their "proper" place within the order of the household.[8]

Slavery came under siege even before the war. Though the labor system on which the slaveholding section of the country was built had been in existence for nearly two hundred years, it was a fragile thing, and the rickety institution became unstable when a third party entered the mix. This happened along the western border of Missouri in the form of the abolitionist presence in the Kansas territory on the other side of the border. African Americans often saw freedom in the form of the jayhawkers, who rode onto slaveholding farms and pulled slaves up onto wagons that took them to Kansas. James Lane, James Montgomery, John Brown, and Charles Jennison led bands of politically and morally compelled men who were willing to fight to the hilt until the institution of slavery bled out.[9]

This war against the Southern household was also waged from within by those who were actively trying to break from its control and begin their own households. Whether jayhawkers assisted them or not, it took action on the part of African Americans to push against the forces at play in their subjugation. When they ran away, or hopped on the back of a stolen wagon, they were actively reversing the same currents of power that held them in slavery. Though the firsthand sources on this flight to freedom are limited, the presence of black men and women in Kansas at this time illustrated the phenomenon. Furthermore, freemen and -women would fight for their new free households against their old ones. A great number of black men from Jackson County and the surrounding environs who now saw themselves as heads of households would form the First Kansas Colored Infantry, the very first black unit raised in the war. The First Kansas would go on to fight against the armies of slavery for the remainder of the war.[10]

Even though slavery was indeed at the base of their motives, white men in both the North and South collapsed slavery into highly gendered motivations. Men were fighting to protect their respective gender systems. One system of gender was framed by slavery, while the other was not. So, while white men from Southern places like Little Dixie set out to hold on to their property in slaves (or the property of their friends and family), they also interpreted the destruction of slavery as the destruction of much more. Pulling out the slaves from the foundation of their households would disrupt the entire structure of the unit and alter their relationships with others in the household forever, especially relationships with their women.[11]

The Southern community on Missouri's western border was threatened in immediate, direct, and tangible ways. Jayhawkers not only liberated enslaved people but robbed their victims of other goods and they murdered slaveholders. Even when a distinction between jayhawkers and Union troopers could no longer be drawn, similar events continued to take place. The Northern war agenda, which was relatively moderate elsewhere in the early stages of the war, was radicalized by the direct influence of Kansas abolitionists. As a result, Union troopers in Jackson County were not only trying to identify and pacify rebels, they tended to act much as the jayhawkers had before the war. One observation of the effects of this increasingly radical occupation early on in the war came from William Gregg, who remembered, "I counted thirteen houses burning at one time on the 28th day of January 1862. This burning was done by [the jayhawker] Jennison's men, although government officials said Jennison was not a U.S. officer and had no authority, yet he carried the U.S. flag."[12]

With such devastation in mind, it is easy to see why guerrillas, as well as their supporters, conflated these attacks on the peculiar institution with assaults on other members of the household. Lizzie Hook recalled some years after the war that "[she] had never known a sorrow or a care until one day a company of Federal soldiers came to our home with wagons in which they loaded the negroes and their belongings. . . . We children were broken hearted and cried ourselves nearly to death." While this was a rather romantic view of slavery, it was evident that the liberation of enslaved black men and women resonated with every member of the white family. In the same recollection, Hook also remembered an especially terrifying violation felt deeply by her own family, her future husband, and her in-laws. She recalled that "Captain Gregg's mother wore her watch and jewelry concealed in the breast of her clothing, but alas, they finally discovered the watch chain around her neck. They tore her dress open, robbed her, almost choking her to death in trying to release the chain."[13]

Young men left home to answer what they interpreted as challenges to their collective manhood: outsiders coming into their homes, taking family property, and assaulting their women. William Gregg recalled the day when he left his mother, father, sisters, and brothers to join a band of other young men who were out in the brush doing what men should do: protecting their families and their property. Whether or not Gregg wished to acknowledge it, his cohort was also out there fighting to protect their place at the top of society. He remembered fondly that on Christmas Day 1861 "James A. Hendricks, John W. Koger and myself joined Quantrill's command then consisting, all told, of eight men, we three swelling his force to eleven. We found Quantrill at Mrs. Samuel Crumps place, on Independence and Blue Springs road, and this was the nucleus to the greatest guerrilla band the world ever produced."[14]

Youth was one of defining features of "the greatest guerrilla band the world ever produced." By and large they were sons, brothers, and husbands; they were not fathers. In an 1862 report to Union major general Samuel Curtis, Brigadier General Ben Loan observed of the Southern sympathizers in his District of Central Missouri that "they have sons and other relatives in the bush." This relational description of the guerrillas was common among Union officers. One guerrilla who rode with Quantrill estimated that nine-tenths of the guerrillas were young men. He knew of only one guerrilla over the age of forty, a man appropriately named "Daddy" Estes, who was anomalous at nearly sixty years old. Eighty percent of the guerrillas held a dependent position in their households, and the average age of the guerrillas in 1860 was under twenty-two years of age, the majority of these being twenty years old or younger. A few guerrillas, typically the leaders of the bands, were a bit older.[15]

As young white men began to embrace their new, prominent roles as guerrilla fighters, the oldest male members of the household saw their power decline. Just as the jayhawkers had in the days before the war, Union officers targeted the head of the rebel household. The provost marshals, magistrates placed across the occupied South by the Union army to deal with rebellious citizens, required that men considered to be Southern sympathizers take an oath of allegiance to the United States. To secure that oath and their future loyalty, these men were also required to put up a bond, which could range from $1,000 to $5,000. Breaking the oath meant arrest and the forfeiture of the bond. Judges, mayors, and other municipal office holders with Southern sympathies were also required to take oaths, which most of them could not in good conscience take. They were removed from office to reduce their public influence.[16]

When these oaths and bonds did not end guerrilla violence, a direct economic counterinsurgency policy was employed by Union authorities to target these heads of household. This policy took the form of an assessment system that tried to focus more narrowly on those households or neighborhoods that were involved in aiding and abetting guerrillas. When Union troops were attacked or a pro-Union citizen was assaulted, the Union army could assess a fine of up to $5,000 to the rebel neighborhood in which the attack took place. They could also assess a single family up to $5,000 if it was thought that the attack originated from their specific household. The average Missouri household was worth less than $4,000, making an assessment of $5,000 or losing a bond worth the same amount fatal for the average farm household. While the guerrillas' households were typically valued at more than the average household, losing a bond would at least result in the loss of one's slaves, the root cause of the war in the first place.[17]

Union efforts to stall the engine of guerrilla war would only truly affect the actions of older white men. A few just laid low, hanging up a loyal façade and limiting the visible participation of their households in the war while continuing to aid their friends and family in the bush through their back doors. Other men were caught, or simply found guilty of going back on their oath. They not only lost their estates but were banished from the Missouri and sent south of Union lines, not to come back. A few were arrested and imprisoned. Perhaps the most noted punishment, though maybe not the most common fate of older men, was their execution at the hands of Union troopers. This form of household decapitation had begun long before the war, continued through the war, and would last until its conclusion.[18]

Attacks on their fathers' estates may have even encouraged young men to engage in guerrilla warfare. At least one scholar has pointed to the seizure of property as the reason for an increase in the intensity of guerrilla violence at particular places and times during the war. The process through which elite white men found themselves vulnerable was actually of their own making. At the beginning of the war, patriarchs from the state's first families funded the Missouri State Guard by taking out a series of risky and perhaps even fraudulent loans that were eventually called in by the lending institutions, many of which had fallen into the hands of Unionists. When the men could not repay the loans, their lands were seized. In his award-winning book, *Financial Fraud and Guerrilla Violence in Missouri's Civil War, 1861–1865*, Mark Geiger contends that it was this seizure of property that explains the increase in the intensity of guerrilla violence in the later years of the war across wide swaths of Little Dixie. This type of relative deprivation would certainly contribute to the motivation of young men to fight for what they thought would be theirs someday.[19]

Although that type of financial loss would have encouraged individual men to fight as guerrillas, it was not the primary reason for their violence. Instead, land seizure was understood in the same vein as the assessment program or the bond program that attached a monetary penalty to their fathers' loyalty. These were important, but they were indirect assaults on the household. They were not understood in the same way as the direct, physical attacks on their households such as the theft (or liberation) of slaves, assaults on the bodies of their women, the murder of their fathers, or the torching of their childhood homes, all of which were felt as attacks on their own persons. The financial loss cited by Geiger was more of a factor in the reduction of the power of older men that allowed young men to become the focus of their households.[20]

Without much assistance from the old patriarchs, women supported their men and the larger guerrilla war in which they were involved. It was obvious to men on both sides. John Edwards, the postwar, pro-guerrilla propagandist remarked that "it is probable that the nature of the work performed by the Southern women during the war will never be understood fully nor to its most important extent. Without their aid, guerrilla warfare would have been heavily handicapped." Edwards's sentiments were confirmed by a man who fought for the Union and who was not an admirer of the guerrillas. Wiley Britton said that "the women of southwest Missouri surely deserve mention for their noble conduct in sticking to their homesteads and maintaining themselves and their children in the absence of their husbands and fathers and brothers in the war." More specifically, he said that "they raise their own foodstuffs, and in many instances spin and weave and manufacture most of their own clothing."[21]

All of the energies of women were focused toward the bush. Lizzie Hook suggested that her household supported the guerrillas "by furnishing horses, clothing, provision and money." She remembered that a "Southern soldier always got something to eat at our house, and if practical, a place to sleep." John McCorkle recalled an instance when the Hook household provided him and two fellow guerrillas with much-needed clothing. McCorkle explained that the "three of us were barefooted. At Mr. Hook's house, there were three young ladies, his two daughters and Miss Wayman." According to McCorkle, "Miss Wayman laughingly asked us what size boots we wore and told us to come back there the next night . . . the next night we returned to Joe Hook's where the young ladies presented us with a nice pair of boots and yarn socks each."[22]

The ability to continue to support their men out in the brush was grounded in women's ability to lead their households. The mantle of leadership that was thought to be a quality that was innate to men was easily taken up by women. When we consider the prevalence of widows in the antebellum South and the significance of their position, it was obvious that the ability to lead a household came as naturally to women as it did men. Take for instance the Spencer household of Post-Oak Township, Johnson County. With the men of the household gone, Eliza Spencer, who was fifty-three years old at the outset of the war, led a household that was comprised of three adult daughters and two boys. Eliza ran the household with such efficiency that the four women were able to feed thirty guerrillas at one time during the conflict. Another time, the Spencer women raised enough money to outfit seven men with hats and boots.[23]

The expansion of female roles during the war also broadened the scope of the household. One of the more noted ways in which rebel women widened their roles and expanded the household's viability as a fundamental institution of warfare was to include military-oriented tasks, especially the acquisition and delivery of information to their men. Early in the war, rebel women used the nineteenth-century notion that women were passive and subordinate to men as a cover for spying. After some success, Union officers realized the trick. Union Captain Joseph Peak reported to his commander that he knew the Spencer women "to be spies for guerrillas and [had] known that they have been aiding them in various ways such as feeding and giving them information." Once illicit information was acquired it was communicated to the necessary parties. Louis Benecke, one of the more successful guerrilla fighters in northern Missouri, discovered a complex mail system set up in Chariton County by rebel women. Benecke said that the system, created to convey letters to the guerrillas "was almost equal to the U.S. Post Office service in the Western States." The officer observed that "the mail was carried almost exclusively by ladies." Men, moving about the countryside, could stay connected to their families and informed of their enemies as if they still resided comfortably inside their homes.[24]

The guerrilla war was conducted as a partnership between these women and young men out in the brush. War in Missouri initiated a revolution within the household that had the effect of flattening its hierarchy. Things did not change immediately; rather, a slow rotation was catalyzed by the shift of young men from their antebellum place as dependents in the home to their new station as fighters in the bush. This move was accompanied by older white men either being pushed from their position of power or simply receding back into the home from their position as the outward representative of the household. Although some African Americans would remain a part of these households, most notably black women, they could no longer be held firmly in place at the bottom of the household, nor could their labor be counted on as it had been before the war. With the members of the household who had dwelled at the top and bottom of the structure gone, the men and women who lived in the middle of the household structure—dependent white men and white women—were left to wage the guerrilla war. Not to argue that prewar concepts of gender were forgotten, but relations that had been vertical were now more horizontal, if only slightly so. Being closer to the same level, young white men and white women saw nearer eye to eye, viewing their relationship as one of reciprocity.[25]

Products of the household, the guerrillas were formidable fighters. The solid logistical foundation of their antebellum unit of production gave these young men the freedom and stability to fight a war that fit the rough outlines of the most traditional form of warfare on the American continent: *petite guerre*. Literally "small war," petite guerre featured small, informal bands of men fighting in fluid, unconventional, and opportunistic ways. This brand of warfare, which had been used by both Native Americans and later their European enemies, was characterized by ambush, lighting raids, hit-and-run assaults against soft targets, and running fights. The guerrillas made war a challenging prospect for their enemies. Britton, writing in 1863, gauged just how deadly the guerrillas were to the conventional Union forces trying to contend with them: "Our losses in this State by this mode of warfare, during the past year, would probably foot up, if we could get correct figures, several hundred soldiers killed, besides as many Union citizens." Fighting on the guerrillas' terms proved costly and perhaps wholly untenable for the Union army who sought to contain or destroy them.[26]

Instead of continuing to let the guerrilla dictate the engagement, the Union army turned its attention toward their source of supply. In April of 1863, the Union government declared General Order No. 100, known as the Lieber Code. This new set of policies marked a shift in focus by Union forces toward the homes and bodies of people imagined to be outside the bounds of civilized warfare. Although they were often covered by vague terminology, these so-called civilians were typically women. The Lieber Code originated a year earlier in Missouri, where Henry Halleck was faced with the challenge of fighting a counterinsurgency, something new to him. He wrote to his friend and fellow scholar of international and military law—Francis Lieber—and his response outlined what would become the foundational policies of the Union army's hard war strategy. In its final maturation as General Order No. 100, the Lieber Code directed Union forces on the ground to take warfare into the innermost reaches of Southern resistance—attacking the homes of Southerners, arresting and banishing women, procuring and destroying property, and of course liberating slaves.[27]

In other words, the Union made war against the household its official policy. Missouri would see General Order No. 100 applied in some of the most direct and comprehensive ways by General Ewing. He made the interior of the rebel community a priority in his new strategy for combating the guerrilla war. He documented his strategy in what was called General Order No. 10, which went into effect on August 18, 1863. Although it would be one of the shortest-lived orders of the war, being superseded by General Order No. 11 just a few days later, General Order No. 10 stated that "the wives and children of known guerrillas, and also women who are heads of families and willfully engaged in aiding guerrillas, will be notified . . . to remove out of the district and out of the State."[28]

It was in this context—an official war on their households—that the guerrillas understood the severity of the circumstances facing them in the summer of 1863. All of the smoking ruins, the blood drained from old men like Crawford and Saunders, and the vulnerable women and children pushed out into the cold cast a long, dark shadow over the future of the guerrilla war. This violence prompted the guerrillas' collective desire to reach out and touch their enemies' households with the flames of war. In describing the mindset of the guerrillas, Andrew Walker put it best when he said, "You glanced toward your gun while a picture took shape in your mind's eye of houses in flames, violent deaths, fleeing herds, pillaged smokehouses, and driven slaves." When they rode through the darkness to Lawrence, Kansas, the guerrillas carried with them these nightmares of household war.[29]

On August 21, 1863, the worst atrocity of the Civil War took place at Lawrence. The numbers were staggering—180 unarmed men and boys gunned down, 80 women made widows, 250 children orphaned, and more than 100 buildings burned to the ground—but the details of the individual acts of violence were all the more horrifying. In one instance, two wounded men were bound and thrown into a burning building, experiencing an excruciating death. In another, a father who held his daughter in his arms was executed—shot in the head, as so many were. His body crumpled and his daughter tumbled from his lifeless arms. From the perspective of the Reverend Richard Cordley, one of the few men to survive the raid, it "was the most perfect realization of . . . 'Hell let loose,' that could ever be imagined." Two years after the event, Cordley was still trying to understand and articulate the scope of the massacre and the men who perpetrated it. He said, "History gives us no parallel, where an equal number of such desperate men . . . were let perfectly loose in an unsuspecting community." Of the men who were responsible for this destruction, Cordley could never get beyond the images that were still alive in his mind, remembering that they "had the look of wild beasts they dressed roughly and swore terribly," and "the citizens could not believe that men could be such fiends."[30]

Despite the horrible violence undertaken by the guerrillas, their allies saw them in a positive light. In the wake of the bloodshed at Lawrence, the Richmond (VA) *Examiner* described the guerrillas as "gallant," while the Charleston (SC) *Mercury* called the massacre "a perfect success." On November 2, 1863, E. Kirby Smith, lieutenant general of the Confederate army, described the guerrillas under Quantrill as "bold, fearless men . . . under very fair discipline." Moreover, Smith claimed that "they are composed . . . of the very best class of Missourians." Similarly, Southern-sympathizing Missourians had a hard time seeing the guerrillas as fiends. Mrs. R. T. Bass, who was just a little girl during the war, remembered seeing for the first time William Clarke Quantrill. In 1912 she recalled that "he looked as little like the horrible bloodthirsty bandit he is usually described as it is possible to imagine. Instead of this, he was a modest, quiet, good-looking man, with

"The War in Kansas—Fearful Massacre at Lawrence by Quantrill's Guerrillas." (*Frank Leslie's Illustrated Newspaper*, September 12, 1863)

blue eyes, light hair, gentle of manner and courteous as well." This is a pretty picture of the architect of the mayhem at Lawrence.[31]

Neither fiends nor gallant heroes, the guerrillas who went to Lawrence were simply household warriors. When William Gregg looked on men and boys old enough to carry a rifle, he saw fighters; it was the role of men in the household system of war, in his system of war, to fight. Even if they were ripped from the arms of loved ones, they were shot down. Black men were shot down next to the white men who had helped to free them. The guerrillas saw these newly freed men as inherently dangerous to the white men and women who had once enslaved them. Next, the guerrillas' gaze fixed on whatever household goods there were in these homes. The guerrillas attempted to carry as much as they could from the abolitionist households of Lawrence back to the other side of the border. Finally, the guerrillas understood each house to be a location of support, a source of war. Each home was put to the torch.[32]

One Yankee artist provided a very different perspective on the attack. On the front page of the September 12, 1863 edition of *Frank Leslie's Illustrated Newspaper* ran an image with the caption, "The War in Kansas—Fearful Massacre at Lawrence by Quantrill's Guerrillas." In the foreground of this image we can see that there are five women, all in various stages of victimhood. One is kneeling to pray for the dead man at her feet, another is shaking her fist at the hoard of guerrillas sacking the town, a mother runs barefoot with a baby in her arms, and a fourth woman is trying to ward off a fist-clenched guerrilla who is trying to take her possessions. In the very middle of the fray, we are shown the depths of guerrilla brutality as imagined by Yankee artists: a girl is being grabbed around her waist from behind, her dress torn from her shoulders, making her fate a foregone conclusion: the girl will experience "a fate worse than death"; she will be raped. Here the guerrillas were merely bullies, savages, and rapists, the crushers of domesticity and the household, destroyers of the very core of civilization. Here the guerrillas were not hypermasculine householders, farmers, and masterful men; their target in this household war was women.[33]

This rendering is flawed, though, stemming from some deeper anxiety regarding gender. There were no women in the streets of Lawrence at dawn, nor were women the targets of the guerrillas. The gruesome nature of what the guerrillas had done at Lawrence needed no exaggeration, and yet the *Frank Leslie's* image is pure embellishment. By catching their enemies unaware, in bed, unarmed, and undressed, the guerrillas had unmanned

"The Destruction of the City of Lawrence, Kansas and the Massacre of Its Inhabitants by the Rebel Guerrillas." (*Harper's Weekly,* September 5, 1863)

the male residents of Lawrence. This picture becomes much more accurate when we imagine men in the place of women. Although the streets were quiet when the guerrillas first arrived, at various points in the massacre individual men attempted to make their escape from the killing zone in their nightshirts. Senator James Lane was the most famous of these men to turn tail and run for safety in his nightgown. While Lane would escape the clutches of the killers, the majority of the men who attempted to flee were eventually caught from behind by a bullet, knife, or fist while their women and children looked on helplessly from the thresholds of their homes until those too were razed by the bushwhackers.[34]

Not all the images of Lawrence sketched by Northerners were inaccurate. Another artist cut a picture that was grounded in the realistic gore of Lawrence, depicting the guerrillas in a more truthful turn as killers of men. In the September 5, 1863, edition of *Harper's Weekly*, a picture appears that is entitled "The Destruction of the City of Lawrence, Kansas and the Massacre of Its Inhabitants by the Rebel Guerrillas." It shows the town in flames, but there are no women running through the streets. Instead the street, sandwiched by rows of burning buildings, is filled with men being shot down by guerrillas on horseback and on foot. In the right foreground is a prominent, mustached man on horseback, presumably Quantrill, about to fire his revolver into the head of a man with his arms in the air. Though this death scene is provocative enough, it is the scene on the left side of the picture that is even more evoking. A guerrilla stands at the porch of a residence, firing his revolver into the face of a man while the house behind him burns. The man's children and wife simultaneously hold onto him while trying to restrain the killer on their doorstep.[35]

The *Harper's Weekly* illustration is able to capture an impression of household war that was congruent with the guerrilla's own vision of war. While they tried to live a romantic vision of war, defending their kin and holding their own households together, the guerrillas exacted brutal violence against their enemies. What comes through from the *Harper's Weekly* image is something of an inverse of what the war had wrought in Missouri's Southern community. On both sides of the Kansas-Missouri border structures were razed, but the attacks by jayhawkers and Union troopers in Missouri were scattered and took place over years. In contrast, the guerrillas made one attack against the greatest concentration of abolitionist households in Kansas, were able to catch the men of Lawrence napping, and killed them while putting their homes to the torch.[36]

Following the raid on Lawrence, General Ewing enacted General Order No. 11, which not only drove individual rebel households from the border but uprooted entire kinship networks. This effectively destroyed the logistical side of the guerrilla war on the western border. Order No. 11 was successful in its systematic and widespread removal of those people labeled by Ewing as the "families" and "kin" of the guerrillas. Of course, what he meant to say was the "women of the guerrillas." Mrs. Frances Fristoe Twyman, an aunt of John McCorkle and Cole Younger, recalled that "the road from Independence to Lexington was crowded with women and children, women walking with their babies in their arms, packs on their backs, and four or five children following after them—some crying for bread, some crying to be taken back to their homes." Mrs. Twyman concluded, "Alas! They knew not that their once happy homes were gone. The torch had been applied—nothing left to tell the tale of carnage but the chimneys." Lizzie Hook recalled the aftermath of General Order No. 11 in much the same way. She remembered, "O, the misery! Old men, women and children plodding the dusty roads barefooted, with nothing to eat save what was furnished by friendly citizens." [37]

After rebel women were removed from the border and their houses put to the torch, the guerrilla warfare in that region never fully recovered. Now that their families had moved from the border, guerrillas no longer needed to protect the households or communities in that area. Of course, their departure also meant that the support system for guerrillas no longer existed on the border. If the guerrillas remained, they would be starved, naked, unarmed, and exposed in nearly every way. As a consequence, there were no more raids into Kansas, like the one that ravaged Lawrence, or that much guerrilla activity in Jackson, Cass, Bates, or Vernon Counties for the remainder of the war. [38]

Amid the Union attempts to obliterate the household, young men and women created new ones. Both before and after General Order No. 11, young men and women in the guerrilla movement who were otherwise cut loose from the stability of a household attempted to form new connections with one another. In some ways this trend was simply an extension of the courting rituals that characterized male-female relations during the antebellum period. In the early years of the war, it was not uncommon for a farmer to host a dance when a band of guerrillas visited his neighborhood. Harrison Trow remembered that a dance was held at Press Webb's home and was attended by neighborhood girls when he and Webb visited. A mixer like this

Map of the border region. (Map by Andrew Fialka)

gave the young men who had been out in the brush and the girls who had remained in their homes a social outlet through which they could meet and dance and flirt and do all of the things that young men and young women do, regardless of the historical period. The war was never far off, however. At this particular dance, Union troopers ambushed the merrymakers. Despite the girls' attempt to help him escape discovery by dressing him up in female attire, Trow was arrested. Attending the dance might very well have been worth the risk, however, because after he escaped imprisonment, Trow was off to visit an unnamed lady friend.[39]

A few guerrillas carried on a regular courtship with young women throughout the war. McCorkle remembered that, sometime in the summer of 1863, "Cole Younger decided that he just must see his sweetheart, a Miss Lizzie Brown who lived about two miles northwest of Harrisonville." Such a visit was risky business, though, so Younger "persuaded Tom Tally [sic], Will Hulse, George Wigginton and George Jackson and myself to go with him and act as his bodyguard and to protect him while he talked to his sweetheart." Younger and crew had enough to occupy themselves that they stayed in the "neighborhood for about a week, Cole going to see his girl every day and every night." While the Eros that was so evident in Younger's daily visits to the Brown household was typical of teenagers and young adults, whether they were in peace or at war, armed conflict made what little time they spent together all the more precious and the passion all the more intense.[40]

Some guerrillas took advantage of the circumstances of the war to begin informal relations with women. The diary of one such guerrilla lothario was made famous by the publishers of *Harper's Weekly*. Although only part of it was released, the excerpts of Joe Hart's daily record of his time in the war were informative. There was some mention of friends being shot down by Union troopers and similarly cold accounts of his killing of Union men. Interspersed between these were the confessions of a cad. The diary included a poem written to Hart by a Miss M. Lou Claybrook that read, "Frank I can not forget, You I love you to well [sic], Your smiles is endearment [sic], Your whispers a spell . . ." Later, Hart admitted that his true sweetheart was Miss A. V. "Virdie" Kinnison, with whom he spent a day that he called "the happiest so far of my life." On another visit, he offered more intimate details of their love: "All the world is wrapped in dream and sleep; but I am still sitting by my Virdie's side, my arm is softly stolen around her slender waist—softly I press her to my beating Heart, and one, two, three, yes, half a dozen sweet kisses I steal from her pouting lips. . . ." After his evening with Virdie, Hart was off to raise hell again, and after fighting he met a new young lady, a Miss Kate Rupe, who he described as "a lovely girl, with whom I passed the entire day very pleasantly." Then while in Atchison, presumably Kansas, just on the western side of the Missouri River, he was "visited by Miss R., Miss E., Miss B., and Dr. B . . . I think Miss R. was particularly pleased with me. She is a lovely girl with true Southern principles." And on it went. Equally a lover and a killer until the end, Hart was shot dead in 1863. We don't know if any of Hart's sweethearts shed tears for the fallen warrior, as he most certainly imagined they would. It seems likely, though, that someone cried for the philandering bushwhacker.[41]

Men were not the only people forming connections with multiple partners throughout the guerrilla war. Women also took advantage of the changing nature of intimacy created by the war. One witness against a woman and guerrilla supporter named Isabella Fox claimed that "there is no one in all the county, who has a worse reputation." Two other persons questioned by the provost marshals' office in regards to Fox asserted that she kept "a house of ill-fame." The same term, "ill-fame," was used to describe each of the Cull girls, a group of sisters living together in Johnson County. Also, witnesses brought forth against the Culls had "good reason to believe [they] cohabited with the bushwhackers." Although none of these people explicitly claimed to have seen or taken part in these acts, there were so many testimonies that corroborated these claims that it was hard to discount them.[42]

If one chooses to read the evidence as such, these interactions can be seen as nothing other than sexual activity. In fact, these relationships were more revealing of the critical nature of the male-female bond than just a romantic tryst. For the guerrillas, love and material support went hand in hand. For their female supporters, connections with men could provide an immediate sense of security, even if it did mean that their household could become a target for the Union army down the line. Men and women needed one another, and one without the other was in a precarious position. For the unattached guerrilla—the Joe Harts of the war—the footloose quality of the lothario could be made to fit with the strategy of the guerrilla war. The more supporters one had, the more support one got. Also, by having supporters spread over a number of different counties these unattached guerrillas were allowed to maximize space and mobility to avoid Union troopers and still remain supplied. Women like Isabella Fox who provided hospitality for multiple bands of guerrillas could expect that much more in terms of protection. For the participants in the guerrilla movement, regardless of how formal or informal their ties, without love there could be no war.

The Union army did what they could to prevent new connections between men and women from being made. While so many of the steps taken by Union officers to neutralize and even root out the guerrilla households that were already in existence, there was a policy aimed at preventing them from ever being created. In Missouri, ordained ministers had to take an oath of allegiance like any other men suspected of Southern loyalty. Beyond the stipulations that they could be forced to lose bonds held as security for their oaths, there were penalties contingent on their specific duties in the community. For instance, a disloyal minister was not allowed to preach to his congregation, but of much more interest here was that until he swore his allegiance to the United States, he could not solemnize a marriage. Obviously, the Union was very much concerned with the dispersal of ideas—especially traitorous ones—but they were also very concerned with the creation of rebel households that would increase the logistical support of the guerrillas.[43]

Often this urge to create a permanent connection led to wartime marriages despite any Union policy or the risk of bullets and bloodshed. On the evening of Saturday July 9, 1864, a patrol of 150 Union troopers under the leadership of Major T. W. Houts left Warrensburg, Missouri, and headed north toward the Missouri River with orders to "scout the country thoroughly." By early Sunday morning the patrol was deep in Lafayette County and very near the river, where "they discovered abundant signs of the presence of the guerrillas." A runaway slave informed Major Houts that the guerrillas were at nearby Warder's Church, "where a Hardshell was in the habit of preaching to the 'Brushers' the unsearchable riches for good whiskey and guerrilla warfare." Houts detached 50 men under Captain Henslee and sent them ahead to the church. As Henslee and his men rushed the church, "The cry of 'Feds!' thundered from the audience." The 7 or 8 guerrillas in the congregation were caught off guard, especially the "one, who was to be married—perhaps that very day—to the pastor's daughter." They caught him, presumably in an adjacent building, "standing at the window, making love to his inamorata." The wedding crashers announced themselves with a volley of gunfire. The small group of guerrillas fired back over the heads of the women and children who were running from the church. When the dust settled, the Union troopers had picked off 5 guerrillas, including the infamous guerrilla Jefferson Wilhite, who was shot twenty-eight times.[44]

The disaster at Warder's Church would seem to suggest that there was no romance in this war. Brutality like the destruction of Wilhite's bullet-ridden body served as evidence that an idealistic vision of what war entails—honor, glory, a noble and pretty death—was mythical. Also, the bloody interruption of the wedding demonstrated that war literally destroyed love. However, the congregation at Warder's Church knew the possible outcome of such a public ceremony and participated anyway. They believed that love and war coexisted; regardless of the threat posed by war, they were happy to come together as a community and pass the loving cup. Whether it was risking one's own life or taking another life, in war love gave value to death. Reverend Warder's daughter and her guerrilla beau believed in this vision of the war so much that they worked to create it.[45]

William H. Gregg and Lizzie Hook shared this vision, too. On November 3, 1864, John McCorkle bore witness to what he dubbed later in his memoir as "a strange scene." Colorfully dressed in their best clothes and adorned with their polished pistols and spurs, McCorkle, Gregg and eleven other guerrillas rode through the night to the Hook household in Lafayette County, Missouri. Gregg was to be wed to his longtime sweetheart, Miss Hook. McCorkle described Hook as "a beautiful, black-eyed, black-haired Southern girl," who stood next to Gregg "with her little hand placed on the arm of a stalwart soldier with four Navy revolvers buckled around his waist and with twelve long-haired, heavily-armed soldiers standing as witnesses." Because the battlefield of the guerrilla war was all encompassing, it was necessary for the guerrillas to remain armed during the ceremony. In addition to the warrior-groomsmen "only the members of the family ... [were] present." After the ceremony, the wedding party feasted, celebrating the marriage and that night the groomsmen returned to their role as guerrillas and "stood as guards for the bride and groom."[46]

The wartime wedding had come about when Gregg thought it was necessary to remove his fiancée from the possibility of arrest and banishment. According to Hook, on a day in late October or early November of 1864, Gregg had ridden over to her home and "persuaded me to marry him and go to Texas." Gregg was not the only guerrilla with the idea of removing the woman he loved from the battlefield. His brother-in-law, James A. Hendricks, and another guerrilla named Dick Mattox both wished to take their wives to Texas. Following the marriage of Gregg and Hook, the three married couples, with an escort of fifty guerrillas, left for Confederate lines. After several armed engagements with Union militia, Indians, and "Negroes," the wedding tour ended in Sherman, Texas. Gregg returned to his command with General Jo Shelby's cavalry unit in the formal Confederate army, with whom he would fight as a regular soldier far from Missouri, and Lizzie Gregg spent the remainder of the war in Waxahachie, Texas. For the Greggs and some of their kin, the guerrilla war was over. For the fifty or so guerrillas escorting them, however, the spring of 1865 called them back to Missouri, where the presence of their extended kinship networks gave them both a reason to fight and a means to do it. Where rebellious households remained, there would be guerrilla warfare. Indeed, for the guerrillas, for their women, and even for their Union enemies, the household was the war.[47]

CHAPTER 2

Rebel Kin

THROUGHOUT THE SUMMER OF 1863, Clifton Holtzclaw and his band of guerrillas rode across central Missouri, raiding towns and harassing members of the pro-Union militia, who were sprinkled throughout the population. On July 8 Holtzclaw and thirty men rode to the home of W. H. Sidner, a Unionist living in Linn County. Upon arriving within sight of Sidner's house, Holtzclaw left the bulk of his party in an adjacent field and approached the home with seven of his men. Knowing the answer to the question, the guerrilla captain asked Sidner if he was a member of the Union militia. When Sidner responded in the affirmative, the guerrillas demanded his guns and horse. Taking his guns as contraband of war, they left Sidner with his horse because "he was not good enough." Then, just before the guerrillas left, Holtzclaw uttered a few words of warning to Sidner. According to Sidner, the chieftain said to him that the Union militia had "choked some of his friends not long ago," and if this practice was not stopped "he would return with his *whole family* and retaliate."[1]

Holtzclaw, as a family man, understood that kin was critically important to the guerrilla war effort. Family helped to shape masculine identity among the guerrillas, and kinship networks served as a dynamic force in the lives of young men. In short, kinship served as an extension of the household. If the household provided young men with their general shape as a man, then kinship provided a secondary layer of growth through which manhood was refined by relations with grandparents, aunts and uncles, and, most of all cousins. In antebellum Missouri, cousins grew up alongside one another, worked together, and competed against each other. There was an ever-present desire within boys to discover who among their male kin was the fastest and the toughest, the most skilled rider, and the best shot. Competition between cousins served as the first testing ground for those particular skills that were attributed to masculine prowess. A man without a family would find his growth stunted and his potential untapped, a reality that remained true during the war.[2]

Whether it was Holtzclaw's band in central Missouri or the more famous bands that originated in western Missouri, kinship—*real* and *imagined*—was an important organizing principle for guerrilla warfare. In some cases, guerrilla warfare was an effort of interconnected clans that formed links in a chain stretched across portions of the state. This was especially true along the western border of the state, where a distinct system of guerrilla warfare was created and sustained by a web of households connected through kinship ties. However, in the central part of the state, guerrilla warfare did not spring forth from a single web of households held together by blood relations. Rather, men like Holtzclaw worked to bring clusters of rebel households together, essentially creating an extended guerrilla family. Unlike the conventional system of warfare that was governed by a formal bureaucracy, hierarchy, and logistics, guerrilla warfare was a family enterprise that relied upon organic principles like hospitality and deference to form a complex system of local, popular defense.[3]

Historians of the guerrilla conflict argue that guerrilla warfare was a force of division. In fact, historians would interpret the interaction between Holtzclaw and Sidner as evidence that guerrilla warfare only served to divide communities. One such historian argues that "regions, of which Missouri was the most extreme example, were . . . bitterly divided internally." Historians have gone on to argue that these guerrilla-driven internal divisions led to Confederate defeat in a decisive way. The actions of rebel guerrillas led to the formation of rival Unionist paramilitary organizations and a local conflict between these groups. Rebel guerrillas also forced the Union army into a "hard war" against Southern civilians. The rebel guerrillas, who were "increasingly independent and ungovernable," could not defend their communities against the destruction brought on by either Unionist guerrillas or the Union army, and the Southern populace was forced to submit to Northern conquest.[4]

Given their understanding of the term "community," historians of the guerrilla war make a compelling argument for the divisive power of guerrilla warfare. In making their argument that guerrilla warfare divided communities, historians define community in broad geographic and political terms. However, the war's participants defined their community differently. Given the socioeconomic nature of antebellum Missouri, a rural agricultural society with the household at its center, interpersonal relationships defined their community. The social world of a person was as big as the people he or she knew firsthand, and of these relationships, familial relationships were primary to any other type of bond. Friendships were secondary only to those of family. Beyond these two types of relationships were acquaintances, people who had been heard of but were not known personally, and then outsiders, or people who were totally unknown. Instead of defining a community as all the people in a geographic area, such as a county or state, the guerrilla community must be defined as a group of individuals who shared reciprocal, interpersonal relationships grounded primarily in kin and extending to friends as well as those reputed to have Southern sympathies.[5]

Defining community as one's family and friends is hardly a modern reinterpretation of the past. John Edwards knew that guerrilla warfare thrived because of the close, often familial ties shared by the war's participants. In his much maligned work, *Noted Guerrillas*, he seemed to accurately describe the interpersonal character of guerrilla warfare. Edwards asserted that among other unique features, "the Guerrilla also had a dialect. In challenging an advancing enemy the cry of the regular was: '*Who goes there?*' That of the Guerrilla: '*Who are you?*'" The guerrillas knew their fellow guerrillas and supporters on a personal level from the very outset of the war. As the guerrillas did not share uniform dress and did not draw a front line of battle on a map, familiarity was the standard by which pickets judged advancing persons.[6]

The guerrillas' firsthand knowledge of the other members of their community was evident by John McCorkle's account of his entrance into the guerrilla war. In August of 1862 McCorkle decided to leave home and join the guerrillas. When George Wigginton, McCorkle's cousin, heard that he was leaving, he said, "'John, I'm going with you.'" In order to find the guerrillas, McCorkle and Wigginton relied on other members of the community who knew and supported the men out in the brush. The two men went to Daniel Talley, McCorkle's neighbor and a second cousin to both men, for help. He led the young men to a place in the woods where Cole and Jim Younger, Jabez McCorkle, Dick and Tom Talley, Jim Morris, and Tom Rice were gathered. The Youngers, Talleys, McCorkles, and Wiggintons were all related, while Jim Morris and Tom Rice were neighbors and friends. Because their mothers were all sisters or first cousins who had lived in close proximity to each other, the young men had grown up together. This family of guerrillas made their way to the home of Wigginton's parents, where the Wigginton women fed their sons, brothers, nephews, and cousins before their first battle together.[7]

As McCorkle's account illustrates, the participants of the guerrilla conflict on the border relied heavily on kinship to maintain strong interhousehold relationships. Both men and women used kinship as a means of connecting with each other, but they did so in different ways. Young men used kinship as a means of constructing their guerrilla bands, and as Edwards suggested, a way of differentiating between friend and foe. Kinship was also used by men to create a harmonious order within the band itself. Women used kinship to construct and maintain the rebel supply line. Operators of the logistical branch of the guerrilla war system, women tied together autonomous households by using familial bonds. They coordinated their efforts and created a dynamic system of support for the guerrilla bands comprised of their men.[8]

Guerrilla warfare on the border was constructed with a single, albeit prominent family at its core. The Fristoe family, of which McCorkle and his cousins were a part, dominated the system in both its membership and through the conspicuous action of its members. The Fristoe system of guerrilla warfare consisted of 82 households that were home to 586 white people. The households could be found in ten counties, but the vast majority of households were located in Jackson County. Out of the white population, 71 guerrillas have been positively identified. While the Fristoe family was at the core of this system, there were other households that were not kin to any others in the network. In addition to the Fristoe family, other kinship groups were represented.[9]

The Fristoe kinship group was representative of other families that produced guerrilla warfare. In 1817, Richard Fristoe, his wife, Polly, one infant and six slaves migrated to Missouri from Tennessee. Richard and Polly eventually had five girls and one boy live to adulthood. Daniel, Richard's brother, settled in the area as well. He and his wife, Barbara, had nine children. Just as their fathers had done, most of Richard and Daniel's sons moved away in search of greater opportunity in the West. Richard's girls were married off to up-and-coming young men like Henry Younger, Reuben Harris, Daniel Talley, and Dr. L. W. Twyman. Daniel's daughters married Alexander McCorkle, Jabez McCorkle, and John Wigginton. By 1860 the second generation of Fristoes occupied more than ten households in and around Jackson County. Furthermore, the third generation of Fristoes, numbering more than forty, was coming into adulthood. Just as Cole Younger's sister,

John McCorkle and Tom Harris were not just brothers in arms, they were kin. In addition to being second cousins, Tom's sister Nancy (or Nanny, as she was known) married John's brother, Jabez. Quite representative of the bonds between guerrilla fighters, the lives of these men were deeply intertwined in ways that reached far beyond their common experience in the war. (John McCorkle, *Three Years with Quantrill*)

Josephine "Josie" Younger, married John Jarrette, the girls of that group were beginning to marry promising young men, increasing the reach of the family ever further.[10]

As the development of the Fristoe clan indicates, women played an important role in the growth of the group. Women like Polly Fristoe were bearing and raising children that as adults would begin their own households and repeat the process. As was the case with Beersheba, Laura, Nancy, Mary Ann, and Frances Fristoe, the female children of these settlers often created households in the same locale as their parents because they were limited by social norms and legal restrictions to land. Marriages like those between Fristoe girls and prominent local men merged notable families and provided a strong foundation for social and political alliances. The marriages of one generation of daughters could expand the size of a kinship group exponentially. Three generations of Fristoes on the border had multiplied from four members in 1817 to over one hundred members by 1860.[11]

In addition to the growth of the size of the Fristoe family, their wealth grew as well. One example of this increase was the household of John L. Fristoe, son of Daniel Fristoe and uncle to John and Jabez McCorkle. He, like most of the other men of the Fristoe family, was a farmer, farming being the most common profession among white men residing in Missouri. He was successful at his trade despite the fact that his agriculture was not focused on the production of cash crops. His land was worth $7,000, with his largest crop being corn, of which he produced nearly two thousand bushels annually. Even though Fristoe was a bit wealthier than some of his siblings and cousins, he was not nearly the wealthiest of his generation. Just like his peers, John Fristoe was assisted in the production of his crops by slaves. He owned four slaves, three adult males and one adult female. With the exception of his land, his slaves were his most valuable property.[12]

During the 1850s, the households of the Fristoe system were rich in dependents, both slave and free, making the sectional unrest along the border especially threatening. Households banded together to defend themselves. A legacy of community defense had existed among these households since the earliest days of settlement, and it remained throughout the development of their communities. The original threat had been Native Americans. The next major threat was potential slave uprisings. Outsiders such as the Mormons who had settled in the area were a danger only briefly, until they were thrown out of the state. While the threat of a slave uprising remained, jayhawkers became the most immediate threat during the 1850s and well into the early years of the Civil War. Just as they had to guard against Native American raids and keep an eye out for runaway and rebellious slaves, young men who were often cousins rode about the countryside together in search of jayhawkers. Their goal was to protect the collective lives and the property held by their families.[13]

Like McCorkle and Wigginton, who went off to join the guerrillas together early in the Civil War, other men departed for the brush with a male relative of their generation. Two of McCorkle and Wigginton's kin, Cole Younger and his brother-in-law, John Jarrette, joined together. Brothers Jim and John Little had become two of the original eight members of Quantrill's band even before the beginning of the war. Andrew Walker often rode by the side of his brother-in-law, William Cox, and his cousin, Al Ketchum. In late December of 1861, William Gregg and his brother-in-law, James Hendricks, along with another man, joined Quantrill. These men were part of the original eleven members of the band and would remain at its core.[14]

The trend of men going to war with a male family member reveals something about the nature of recruiting in guerrilla war. George Wigginton could not let cousin John McCorkle go off to war alone, nor could Hendricks let Gregg join Quantrill by himself. In these cases, it was clear that instead of gaining one man, the guerrilla war effort got two. Moreover, these new recruits were familiar with the band because they had a family member already in the brush. It was likely that Jabez McCorkle had told John and George about the band, and he may have even tried to persuade them to join. Riley Crawford, the son of the slain Uncle Jeptha Crawford, who was known as "the youngest Quantrill recruit," may not have been sent to join the guerrillas by his mother had she not known that many of Riley's kinsmen were already members of the gang. The Crawfords were tied into the Fristoe clan through marriage.[15]

It was not unusual for large groups, indeed guerrilla bands in their own right, to go to war together. One such group was the Fristoe boys, and another was the Hudspeths. The Hudspeths would go on to be supporters of the James brothers during their outlaw days after the war, but they clearly established a strong relationship with the brothers during their shared time together as guerrillas along the border. Rufus, Babe, and Robert Hudspeth, along with their cousins, Ben and George Morrow, rode with Quantrill. In addition, two hired hands living in their households—Harrison Trow and Frank Shepherd—joined the Hudspeth clan with Quantrill. The Hudspeths lived in a neighborhood along the Six Mile Road in eastern Jackson County and formed a crucial part of the Fristoe system.[16]

The large percentage of the guerrillas who were related to at least one other guerrilla in the group was a contributing factor to the success of the band. Of the seventy-one guerrillas that came out of the Fristoe system, twenty-six men were related to at least one other man in the group. That was a little more than 37 percent of the entire group. Elsewhere in the Civil War, in the formal Confederate and Union armies, kin was critical to unit cohesion. Most of the volunteer units were raised out of the same local communities, including men from the same nuclear families as well as extended kinship units. Here the original participation of the Holtzclaw clan in the

Southern war effort is instructive: five boys all joined the same unit for the formal army going off to war. Adding credence to this observation, some scholars assert that bonds between comrades trumped all other factors for battlefield success, whether it was the cause for which they were fighting, their morale level, or leadership.[17]

In addition to bringing men together and giving them an immediate motivation to fight, kinship allowed the band to function in a harmonious way. Without a state-generated hierarchy, family ties provided the basis for an organic hierarchy among the guerrillas. While some men, such as Quantrill, received an officer's commission to lead a partisan band, leadership was determined based on organic standards. Within the matrix of kinship, organic ordering principles of society like age and family order were the primary standards for status in the band. At the outset, older brothers and cousins led their younger counterparts. However, once in the band, merit and experience came into play as a measurement of one's rank. For instance, men who performed well in battle gained the respect of their comrades and were voted into higher positions in the band. Experience also affected "rank." Novices started at the bottom of the ladder, while more experienced men elevated themselves with every battle. Conveniently, experience often reinforced age and birth order, as older brothers and cousins were the first to leave home for the brush and therefore proved themselves before their younger siblings and cousins.[18]

A close look at the band of Fristoe men who rendezvoused in the woods in August 1862 serves as an example of how kinship provided order among the guerrillas. On that August day, Cole Younger gathered around him his less experienced brothers and cousins. Younger had joined the guerrillas earlier in 1862 after his father was killed by jayhawkers in the fall of 1861. Within the little band, Younger was the de facto leader. Even though he was about the same age as the other men, he was the most experienced in battle. Also, he came from perhaps the most prominent family within the Fristoe clan. His mother Beersheba, the oldest of Richard Fristoe's children, married H. W. Younger, who was a wealthy man and a politician. When Younger's band joined Quantrill's larger guerrilla band however, he fell under the command of his brother-in-law, Jarrette. By the time of the Lawrence Raid, Jarrette was one of Quantrill's captains and Younger was Jarrette's first lieutenant, with his brother, the McCorkles, the Talleys, and Wigginton serving under him.[19]

Just as the guerrillas of the Fristoe system worked well together, so too did their women. Fluidly moving from peace to war required women on the border to maintain their kinship ties with other households, transforming these relationships into the links in a supply line. The guerrilla supply line was as important to the success of the guerrillas as the supply line of any formal army in the field. Unlike the supply line of regular armies—made up of moving trains, boats, wagons, and pack animals carrying ammunition, food, clothing, and other materials—the rebel supply line was more or less stationary. The physical representations of the household, the actual houses and outbuildings did not move. In order for the supply line to continue to function, the links between households, which were more or less invisible to an outsider, had to be maintained. They were the product of the relationships between the women who lived in the households and could only be cut by removing the women.[20]

Functioning along lines of kinship, the support provided by the rebel supply line for the guerrillas in the brush took the traditional form of exchange: the gift. Missouri's Southern sympathizers, although exposed to the marketplace, still took part in the ancient but no less systematic ritual of gifting. Gifts were not voluntary, as we often think of them being today; rather, with gifts came certain obligations. In what the sociologist, anthropologist, and philosopher Marcel Mauss calls a "system of total services," it was often obligatory to give a gift, accept a gift, and reciprocate the gift. According to Mauss, this was absolutely the case when it came to kin relations: "For a clan, a household, a group of people, a guest, have no option but to ask for hospitality, to receive presents, to enter into trading, to contract alliances, through wives or blood kinship." As long as these obligations were adhered to, relations would be harmonious. However, "to refuse to give, to fail to invite, just as to refuse to accept, is tantamount to declaring war; it is to reject the bond of alliance and commonality."[21]

Exchange in the form of the gift best explains the interaction between the guerrillas and their supporters. It has been presumed that this interface between combatants and unconventional participants of war somehow lacked legitimacy or was proof of the chaotic nature of guerrilla war. Even if the interaction ended in violence, however, these moments of contact were read and understood through the powerful lens of cultural logic. Hospitality bound rebel women and the guerrillas together, especially when these men and women were not of the same household. As a rule, rebel women provided for guerrillas. Guerrillas were obligated to receive that support, and in exchange they reciprocated by defending the household that had fed, clothed, armed, and informed them.[22]

To the contrary, hospitable relations did not exist between rebel women and Union troops. At times, hospitality was denied to men in blue—a domestic

declaration of war. This often ended in some manner of assault on the bodies
or the homes of the women in question. Sometimes, to mollify them, hospitality was offered to Union soldiers, who at times would reciprocate by leaving
the family alone. Other times, however, they did not reciprocate but burned
down the home in which they had just dined, a formal declaration of war that
guaranteed that family's support of the other side.[23]

The memoirs of guerrillas in the Fristoe system are filled with stories of
receiving hospitality from female kin living in a multitude of households.
Andrew Walker mentioned visiting family members' and friends' houses.
In one such case, Walker visited the house of a friend, Green Baden, where
Baden's sister-in-law stole a horse for Walker. After the war, Walker's wife
died and he married the young lady who had provided him with the horse.
McCorkle's account of his participation in the war was more or less a litany
of his visits to the households of friends and family. A representative moment
came when McCorkle and Wigginton arrived at the Wigginton household
late one night in January of 1863. Not only was Wigginton's mother there,
but the two men were surprised to find that McCorkle's mother was there
as well. Here kinswomen came together to support one another and provide
for their sons.[24]

The rebel supply line for the Fristoe system was not only large enough
to keep the guerrillas well supplied, but the close ties between a large percentage of the households suggests that coordination between supporters
from multiple households occurred often. Twenty-seven of the eighty-two
households in the Fristoe system were related to a guerrilla or to another
household, or one-third of the households on the supply line. Also, sixty-
four of the eighty-two households, or four-fifths of the households in the
Fristoe system, were directly related to at least one guerrilla.[25]

The white members of the Fristoe system had black kin as well. The
well-known irony that slaveholders and their slaves were related in the
slaveholding South affected guerrilla warfare. The mulatto men and women
who were the product of sexual encounters between white male slaveholders
and their black female slaves can readily be seen in the slave schedule that
accompanied the federal census. The 1860 slave schedule reveals that this
phenomenon among the enslaved population of a few prominent members
of the Fristoe system of guerrilla warfare. McCorkle's uncle, named John
Fristoe, owned four slaves in 1860, and two of them had an *M* by their names,
signifying they were mulatto. William Fristoe, another uncle of McCorkle,
had six slaves, and three were mulatto. Of Morgan Walker's twenty-five
slaves, six were mulattos, including three who were under the age of six. As

the offspring of white and black sexual encounters were born into slavery, most were treated as slaves and nothing more. They were subjugated for that indistinguishable portion of their blood that was "black," even when most of their blood was "white." Just as with any other enslaved person, when the opportunity came to gain their freedom, family ties to whites rarely held these mixed-race men and women back from running.[26]

Kinship drew some mixed-race men into the war in ways that divert from the traditional historical narrative of black men in the Civil War. The best example of a peculiar involvement in the war came in the form of John Noland. Noland was a black man who was born in or around 1844 and was raised on a farm in Jackson County that was owned by Asbury Noland. While we do not know for sure, it is likely that Asbury or one of his white male relatives was the father of Noland. In fact, the 1860 census lists Asbury as having two mulatto slaves, and Noland was probably one of them. While all of this was common enough, when war broke out Noland would not run away to Kansas, even though he had the chance. Instead, he joined up with Quantrill and assisted the guerrilla war effort.[27]

Noland understood his participation in the guerrilla war effort as a test of manhood that was facilitated by kinship. Up until now, Noland's experience in the war has been misunderstood and misappropriated. Although neo-Confederates would have Noland be a symbol for the states' rights argument—or even worse, that slavery was a positive good—they would be mistaken. Within the proper context, however, it is easy to see that Noland's actions resulted from kinship ties to members of the white community who participated in guerrilla warfare. There is evidence that Asbury treated Noland differently from a slave and that he freed him before the war began. This bond, something closer than a slave-slaveholder relationship and perhaps even familial, may have been something worth fighting for rather than against. Other bonds, especially those between Noland and his white cousins who fought with Quantrill, also gave Noland a reason to help the guerrillas. The war would give Noland a chance to prove himself as a man, perhaps validate his freedom, and defend his white cousins while impressing upon them his stature as an equal. It is also important to consider that no one knew how the war would play out, and local, familial, and personal relationships often held sway over the broad national political motives that historians often use to frame every experience of the war, regardless of how well they fit with the immediate perspective of the war's participants.[28]

Though Noland seems to have been quite active working on behalf of the guerrillas, the most notable of his missions as a spy for Quantrill came

The black man who appears quite conspicuously in this photograph, taken at the 1906 reunion of Quantrill's men, is John Noland. He attended several of these reunions where the men who fought under Quantrill gathered to celebrate their service in one of the more exclusive and unique fighting units of the war. As bizarre as it seems now (and must have seemed to many people at the time), Noland actively joined in these annual meetings that not only commemorated the war that they waged but also celebrated the cause that these men fought for, most notably slavery and the effort to defend an institution that kept black men like Noland in chains. It is important to remember that Noland's presence did not signal his complicity in the cause of slavery. Instead he fought for his kin—of which there were likely a few who were present in this photo—and to affirm his manhood amid prejudice on all sides. (Courtesy of the State Historical Society of Missouri)

in his reconnaissance of Lawrence before the raid on that town. Because Noland was a black man, his race and the assumptions held by white abolitionists regarding his race served to cloak his true loyalties. He could travel in Kansas and white Unionists or Kansans would think that he was a runaway or a freeman (which of course he might have been) and let him pass without questioning him. In mid-August Noland did just this, crossing over into Kansas to inspect the situation in Lawrence. He was supposed to count the troops there and study their movements so that guerrillas could arrive at a time when there were the fewest number of troops stationed in the town. According to Noland, he was able to reach Lawrence and do his duty, but he claimed that he was not able to make it all the way back to his rendezvous point to meet with Quantrill and share his information because he was captured by Union troopers and held in Kansas City until after the guerrillas had left for the raid.[29]

Despite the fact that Noland was unable to share his discoveries with Quantrill, there was evidence that he proved himself as a man and was relatively accepted by his white kin and the guerrillas more generally. More than a few of the guerrillas kept up with Noland, and through what evidence we have of their interactions, it seems that there was a general respect for Noland. Even stronger evidence can be seen in the reunions held by Quantrill's men around and after the turn of the century. Not only do the guerrillas record the presence of Noland, but he appears in the group photographs of Quantrill's men each year that he was present. A lasting memory of their time together, these photographs were sacred objects that these men kept, passed down to their relatives, and published in the newspapers for all to see who the men were that comprised Quantrill's storied band. This is not to say that these old men did not carry with them the racial prejudice of their time, or the bitterness that most Southern whites held following the destruction of slavery. Rather, it simply shows that while they no doubt saw Noland for his race, they also saw him as a member of their guerrilla family and, most important, as a man.[30]

Following the raid on Lawrence in which Noland had tried to assist, General Ewing enacted General Order No. 11, which not only drove individual rebel households from the border but uprooted the entire rebel supply line of the Fristoe system, effectively destroying the system's logistical side. The strength of the system was also partly responsible for its destruction. Close proximity between so many interrelated households in Jackson and surrounding counties allowed them to quickly create a system of guerrilla warfare to defend themselves while maintaining that system with relative ease. But it also meant they could easily be uprooted if the relatively small geographic area in which they were located was targeted for banishment.[31]

The locus of the guerrilla war in Missouri moved geographically from the border to the central part of the state, where the guerrillas relied more than ever upon hospitality for their support. This shift was partly a product of the migration of many border residents, including guerrillas, to the central part of the state, where some joined relatives. This migration also destroyed many of the tight-knit kinship networks on the border, meaning that guerrillas from the border had to reconstruct a supply line. As individuals and

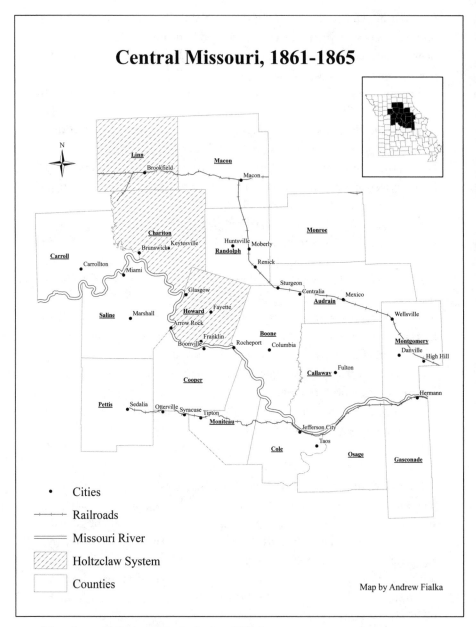

Map of central Missouri. (Map by Andrew Fialka)

as bands, guerrillas from the border allied themselves with guerrillas in the areas into which they had moved. As a result, they were able to develop new supply lines.[32]

In addition to the geographic move, the emphasis on family also shifted. To understand this shift, it is critical to return to Holtzclaw and his "family." For Holtzclaw, kinship was as imagined as it was real. Holtzclaw had few blood relatives by the time he became a guerrilla in 1863. At the outset of the war, he and his brothers James, William, Benjamin, and John organized a Confederate company that left the state and fought in the South. All of the Holtzclaw boys, with the exception of Clifton and perhaps one other brother, were killed at places like Corinth and Vicksburg. In addition to these losses, one of Clifton's sisters was killed in an explosion that occurred while she was attempting to dry gun powder with fire and accidentally blew herself up. According to John Edwards, Clifton's father, James Holtzclaw, sixty years old in 1860, was executed in the summer of 1863. Edwards said, "Lieutenant Jo Strett of Guitar's regiment, a cruel militia officer who tied southern men to trees and sabred or shot them, went to Capt. Holtzclaw's house, took the aged father from the arms of his aged wife and remorselessly killed him." While they disagree on a couple of details, *The History of Linn County* confirms Edwards's story. According to the county history, "In 1862 the militia under Lieutenant Street killed [Holtzclaw's] father, in the latter's barnyard, and left the body for the hogs to devour. It was recovered by his daughters before it had been *much* mutilated."[33]

None of the leaders in the middle part of the state were as dominant as Quantrill had been in the West, but it appears that more than any other guerrilla captain, Holtzclaw was the architect of the guerrilla war system in central Missouri. In a report to his commanders in May of 1865, the Union detective and scout Harry Truman said, "I can have all of the guerrillas that is in Mo surrender if you will agree to pardon them . . . [and I will] then kill the last one of them." Truman then listed the top five guerrilla captains who he believed he could trick into surrendering and then execute. They were listed in order of importance, and at the top of the list was Quantrill. After only Quantrill was "Holsclaw," the second on Truman's list. Given that at the end of the war Quantrill was in Kentucky, Holtzclaw was the most important guerrilla captain in Missouri. Beyond this endorsement, Holtzclaw is mentioned as much as, or more than, any other guerrilla in the central part of the state in the compiled and published Union reports.[34]

When Holtzclaw returned to his home, he went about building a family to replace the one he had lost. Unlike families of blood, this family was one that came together by choice. Holtzclaw, like other guerrilla captains in the central part of the state, returned home from the Confederate army with the express goal of recruiting a band of fighting men and waging a guerrilla war against Union troopers in the area. This drive to create what he would later call his "family" was what separated Holtzclaw and the other guerrilla leaders in central Missouri from those on the border. Whereas in the war on the border the guerrillas and their leaders were the products of family, Holtzclaw's family was a product of the war.[35]

As the story of the Holtzclaw family suggests, the circumstances of war in the central part of the state originally worked to loosen familial bonds. Not threatened by raids from jayhawkers, there was little immediate threat to the central part of the state at the outset of the conflict. As a result, young men like Holtzclaw and his brothers believed they could best defend their households by joining companies and regiments that would fight on behalf of Missouri and the Confederacy wherever they might be needed. After some time, the absence of these young men exposed their households to the antagonisms of pro-Union men and the Union army. Despite the circumstances, some women were able to hold tightly to their kin, while others were cut off from their families and isolated, just as the Holtzclaw family appeared to be.[36]

Orphans did not make good guerrillas, and broken families did not provide a very strong foundation for warfare. Aware of this reality, Holtzclaw saw family as an inspiration in creating his guerrilla band and its network of support. The guerrilla chief was aware that although they did not share blood, there was a common experience among Southern sympathizers throughout central Missouri. The war had played out in other households in similar ways as it had in the Holtzclaw household, creating common ground over which an imagined guerrilla family could be bound together. Once united, this manmade guerrilla family could operate on the strengths of family while minimizing its weaknesses. The guerrillas were more or less hand picked by Holtzclaw, and many were veterans of the conventional war, giving them some experience with warfare. Also, the infrastructure of this guerrilla system of war was different from that of the Fristoe system. While there were clusters of rebel households, these clusters were separated by dozens of miles, making it difficult to capture or kill Holtzlcaw and nearly impossible to root out all of his supporters. In adopting these wayward rebels, Holtzclaw not only gave them a family but redeemed the destruction of his real family and theirs.

Holtzclaw's recruiting was facilitated by the inhospitable actions of Union troops and pro-Union militia. One illustration of the effects of Union antagonism can be seen in a speech given by Edwin Price, Confederate general Sterling Price's son, during the summer of 1864 to a large gathering of guerrillas. Edwin Price was a brigadier general in the Missouri State Guard but had since taken the oath of allegiance to the Union. At least nominally working on behalf of the Union army, Price was sent as a go-between to confer with several guerrilla chieftains who had brought their troops together in Chariton County. The chieftains—Anderson, Jim Jackson, and Holtzclaw—welcomed Price into their camp near the town of Brunswick. According to E. A. Holcomb, who reported the events to Union General Fisk, instead of trying to dissuade the men from fighting as guerrillas as the Union had hoped, Price "made a speech . . . where he said that he three years ago enlisted Holtzclaw into the Confederate service." The guerrillas cheered loudly in reaction to hearing this. Price went on to say "that he recognized many of his old neighbors and friends" in the crowd and that many "were Confederate soldiers [who] had been driven into the bush by Stanley's and the Brookfield Company." The *History of Linn County* offers another example in which Holtzclaw recognized the assault of Union troopers on Southerners as a source of unity among otherwise isolated families. It says that upon "learning that a number of men in Jackson and Clay townships were anxious to join the Confederate service in order to escape and avenge the persecutions of the Grundy and Sullivan militia, [Holtzclaw] came in to afford them an opportunity."[37]

Holtzclaw united his band of guerrilla-brothers by folding their shared experience into a sanctioned war effort. Holtzclaw had an official commission from the Confederate government. Just before he raided the Linn County house of Sidner in July of 1863, Holtzclaw and his band confronted James Callaway, also of Linn County, in much the same way. Callaway recounted that Holtzclaw said "he had recruited lots of my neighbors boys and that this was his business to recruit for the CSA." Frank Stewart, a member of Holtzclaw's band who lived not far from either Callaway or Sidner confirmed the chieftain's claim and told his wife that "Capt [Holtzclaw] was recruiting for the Confederate service." A year later, at the time of Price's speech, Union Captain Joseph Stanley claimed that Holtzclaw's band had swelled to three hundred. Stanley reported that Holtzclaw had "recruited many in [the] forks of Chariton," on his "instructions from [the] Confederate Government."[38]

As the testimony suggests, Holtzclaw recruited a band of men from a few neighborhoods across the north-central part of the state. Of the twenty-two guerrillas who have been positively identified as members of Holtzclaw's band, the majority come from one of three neighborhoods. Seven guerrillas were residents of Prairie Township in Chariton County. Five guerrillas lived in Linn County, in the area surrounding the town of Linneaus. Six guerrillas lived in Howard County, more or less near the home of Holtzclaw. A few of the other men came from counties some distance from the area in which Holtzclaw's group operated, while one or two were not even from the state of Missouri and only ended up there as a result of the war. Each of the three neighborhoods from which the bulk of the guerrillas came were quite a distance from one another but not so far as to be unmanageable for men on horseback.[39]

Within the groups of men recruited from these different areas, there was a familiarity with other rebels in that area. This knowledge enabled Holtzclaw to better recruit a band of worthy men. In Linn County, Holtzclaw recruited young men from the Gooch family, all of whom had been soldiers for the Confederacy. Holtzclaw first recruited Joseph Gooch, who facilitated the recruitment of other men he knew. For instance, Holtzclaw also recruited Joseph Gooch's younger brother, Jenkins Gooch, as well as their brother-in-law, Howard Bragg. While it is unclear just how he attained his rank, Joseph Gooch became one of Holtzclaw's lieutenants. He may have been appointed by Holtzclaw or elected by the men of the band. Eventually, Joseph Gooch branched out and led his own band. Bragg then filled the void left by Joseph Gooch and become Holtzclaw's lieutenant. Following the pattern, Bragg also led his own band from time to time.[40]

Even though Holtzclaw's band was not the direct product of kinship, familial ties were instrumental in its construction. As the Gooches' recruitment suggests, just as on the border, young men from the same family wanted to fight together. This fact allowed Holtzclaw to recruit in a quicker way than he would otherwise have been able to do if he was recruiting one man at a time. For instance, in recruiting one man, Joseph Gooch, Holtzclaw had actually gained three. Around the same time as he recruited the Gooch men, Holtzclaw recruited Frank Stewart to join the band. When Stewart joined Holtzclaw, he brought with him his brother-in-law, Reuben Jackson.[41]

The knowledge of the local population allowed the band to identify households in each neighborhood that would offer hospitality to the guerrillas. When Holtzclaw was spending time in Chariton County during the summer months of 1864, he amassed a group of men from that area who were in touch with local residents. For example, Holtzclaw was able to recruit men like Benjamin Boydston and James Plunkett from the Prairie Township area of Chariton County around Keytesville. These young men knew which of their neighbors were willing and able to give aid to their guerrilla band, and they may have been the men who introduced Holtzclaw to Nathaniel Butler, a wealthy neighbor of theirs who was more than willing to help the cause. Or perhaps they led Holtzclaw to the household of James Starks, another neighbor and a man of relative wealth, who was willing to offer his assistance.[42]

Of course, familial connections were also important in developing the rebel supply line for the Holtzclaw system. In Linn County the Gooch brothers tapped into their kinship network for support. In one instance, two men visited the home of Henry Gooch while on their way to Howard County during the summer of 1863. Henry was younger than his cousins, Joseph and Jenkins. It seems that he spent the war at home, assisting his widowed mother with their farm and overseeing the slave labor they had been able to retain at least into the summer of 1863. To the assistant provost marshal at Brookfield, E. J. Crandall, Henry Gooch said, "I knew one of these men. He was my cousin Joseph Gooch." Henry continued, "My cousin gave me an introduction to the [man] with him and I think his name was Holtzclaw." Joseph and Jenkins Gooch, as well as Holtzclaw, ate and stayed with Henry Gooch several times in the days after this first meeting. At one time, the three men avoided a Union patrol led by a Captain Buckman, who was clearly looking for the guerrillas. This was around the same time that Holtzclaw's band was visiting the local members of the Union militia in Linn County.[43]

The latent influence of kinship was true in Chariton County as well. In 1864 Holtzclaw began receiving assistance from the Fox household. This was the same household that had been raided by the Union officer Truman, who executed the head of household, Peter Fox, making his wife a widow. On numerous occasions the widow, Isabella Fox, aided Holtzclaw's band as well as the band of one of Holtzclaw's lieutenants, Jim Jackson. She and her daughters capably fed and clothed the guerrillas who came to their house. Further, they enlisted the assistance of their extended family, namely Amanda Huckshorn, Fox's sister, who was a seamstress. As Isabella's daughter was seen riding to and from the house of Mrs. Huckshorn with guerrillas, it was likely that she took active part in sewing shirts and pants for the men, or at least assisted her niece in doing so.[44]

Military theory suggests that Holtzclaw's system of guerrilla warfare was a near perfect application of military principles. By constructing his supply line over such a large area, Holtzclaw used space and mobility to his advantage.

It is important to understand that the area in which guerrilla warfare was waged was only as large as the distance between the households that were the farthest from one another on the supply line. On the border, there were a large number of supporters, but they existed in a relatively confined area. Guerrillas stayed within the boundaries of one county for the majority of the war on the border. Holtzclaw's supply line was embedded in three different counties, with quite a bit of distance between each cluster. This prevented the Union army from locking on one neighborhood. Instead, the Union army was given a wider area over which to pursue Holtzclaw's band.[45]

Within this wide area of activity, Holtzclaw could maximize the mobility of his mounted force. Not only could the guerrilla band outrun Union troopers and lose them in the thick underbrush of the timber bottoms, but they could use their speed to attack exposed areas of the Union command. Attempting to cover a wide area, the Union control of the countryside was strained, making some areas more vulnerable than others. Even when they were not exposed, the Union outposts in this vast area were unable to predict the direction from which an attack might come. The outpost at Keytesville in Chariton County might send out a scout to the southeast toward Howard County, and Holtzclaw and his men might enter the county from Linn County to the north. To understand the strategic and tactical implications of Holtzclaw's family-style warfare, one only needs to skim the reports published in the *Official Records of the War of the Rebellion* during August, September, and October 1864. Holtzclaw appeared in any one of a handful of counties—Linn, Howard, Chariton, Boone, Randolph—only to attack and disappear once chase was given, no doubt sprinting to the farthest cluster of rebel supporters in his guerrilla family. He then reappeared just as quickly in another one of the above mentioned counties, and the pattern continued.[46]

The adopted sisters and cousins of Holtzclaw's guerrilla family allowed him and his guerrillas to wage their war and avoid capture or death until he surrendered. Having been promised amnesty along with the other guerrillas, Holtzclaw rode into the town of Glasgow, Missouri, at the end of the war and surrendered to the provost marshal there, Captain W. A. Lyle. At this point, the Union army actually had a form letter with blank spaces for the particulars of the service for each man who surrendered. Holtzclaw obligingly answered the queries in the document: he was thirty-six years old, he was a captain of rangers, and now that he was no longer at war with the Union, he would go back to being a farmer. With that, the one-time guerrilla chief rode without incident from Glasgow toward home.[47]

The bonds that held Holtzclaw's family together were invisible to Captain Lyle. The Union army assumed that Holtzclaw's system was as impersonal, bureaucratic, and hierarchal as their system of war. Lyle walked Holtzclaw through the sanitized, formalized, and virtually anonymous ritual of submission with the intent of recording something of the guerrilla and his war for posterity. However, there was no place on this inflexible document to list the connections between the guerrilla captain, his men, and all those women who supported them, let alone articulate the origins and nature of these bonds. Despite the fact that Holtzclaw's family does not appear anywhere on the document, one fact that was jotted down in a blank space serves as a reminder of the viability of family warfare. In the space where Lyle was to jot down the date of his surrender, the provost marshal recorded "June 29, 1865," months after most of the formal armies had laid down their arms and their soldiers had filled in the blank spaces on the submission questionnaires. The guerrillas of middle Missouri were still at large because their war flowed along bloodlines that were too dynamic to be captured in the cold, inhospitable lines of ink that marked the Union's predrafted document.[48]

The strength of kinship bonds like those that held together the communities along the border produced a system of guerrilla warfare that could not be easily contained. Instead, the Union army was forced to enact one of the hardest, most radical war policies of the conflict, General Order No. 11, which uprooted the rebel families in four counties. Tearing asunder the fabric of kinship along the border only created a more complicated system of warfare in the interior of the state. Holtzclaw and others created a more heterogeneous family enterprise by tapping into the kinship networks that remained strong and adopting households that had been orphaned by the destruction of war. In these guerrilla families, we can see that this was not the "war of brother against brother." Rather, it was a war effort that was inclusive, not only bringing families together but also adopting men and women who were unrelated. Indeed, the guerrilla conflict in Missouri was a war fought *by the family, for the family*.[49]

Chapter 3

The Hired Hand

William Clarke Quantrill wandered into the history books on December 10, 1860. Andrew Walker, who was shucking corn in the middle of his father's field, looked up to see his brother John walking toward him with a suspicious-looking young stranger. The border war that had been waged in an informal, off-and-on manner over the past half-decade kept white Missourians like Walker on guard, always on the lookout for jayhawkers. Andrew Walker took the outsider to his father, Morgan. To Morgan, Quantrill revealed that he had come into Jackson County from Kansas with three so-called jayhawkers who planned to rob Walker of his slaves, his livestock, and his money and then kill the old man and his family. Although he may have been skeptical of the warning or the motives behind it, the elder Walker did not take any chances: he gathered his sons and a few neighborhood men at his home to wait for the would-be thieves and murderers. When Quantrill and his cohort returned later that night, the trap was sprung. The Missourians, armed with shotguns and rifles, killed one jayhawker outright, but the other two men ran off into the darkness, one wounded and the other untouched. Transplanted into this Missouri soil, Quantrill would grow into the most powerful guerrilla leader west of the Mississippi, at least until he was overtaken by his subordinates.[1]

Although navigating the history of Quantrill is a treacherous venture full of pitfalls, to fully understand the household system of war, it is necessary to examine his role within it. A poor, landless, homeless, outsider,

Quantrill's elevation through the ranks of the Southern community was exceptional, although his life in Missouri began as something much more commonplace. Like so many other landless white men who were in search of the opportunities available in the expanding country, Quantrill was constantly in pursuit of work and therefore dependent upon other men. He would serve the Walkers and their neighbors as a hired hand in exchange for money, while also receiving the protection and support that came with being a dependent (white) member of a Southern household. As the war came on, Quantrill's roles as a guerrilla fighter and then captain of a guerrilla band were direct outgrowths of his antebellum position at the bottom of the white household. Doing the bidding of the wealthy classes, the hired hand became a hired gun who began to define himself as a warrior, earning respect and even deference from the men to whom he once deferred.[2]

To read Quantrill's role in the war in a systematic way is to deviate sharply from the persistent historiographical debate that has engulfed the history of the guerrilla chief since the war ended. The major arguments of this debate were outlined more than a hundred years ago by men with obvious political agendas. In his 1877 book *Noted Guerrillas*, John Edwards thrust upon the public a grand narrative of the guerrilla war in which the guerrillas were reluctant killers, driven to their extreme violence as a last resort by the even more vicious jayhawkers. Like other Lost Cause writers, Edwards minimized the role of slavery as a cause of the war and created a canon of heroes for the guerrilla war, among whom Quantrill reigned as the greatest. On the other side of this debate is a picture of Quantrill, as a demon. Beginning with William E. Connelley and his book *Quantrill and the Border Wars* which came out in 1910, historians have used the narrative of Quantrill's life as an opportunity to moralize. The sketchy and perhaps criminal antebellum career of Quantrill and his bloody wartime deeds offer plenty of opportunities to expound upon his possible personality flaws and psychological shortcomings, the evils of slavery, and the illegitimacy of guerrilla warfare as a way of fighting. As admirable as the politics of Connelley might be, just like his counterpart on the other side of the aisle his personal views played too heavily on their analyses of the guerrilla chief. Resulting from their opposed positions of the subject, these two sides and their equally ahistorical takes on Quantrill are at loggerheads regarding their subject.[3]

Rather than join the disagreement that has dominated the historical discussion, it is more useful to understand Quantrill's actions within the context of his world. Like the immediate family members of the white head

Here is the most reliable portrait of William Clarke Quantrill. While there are quite a few published pictures of the man, this was the same image his men had framed and brought to each of the reunions for his men. It stands to reason that Quantrill's raiders knew well what he looked like. Sometimes this image appears with a graffiti mustache on his face, most likely added because he was rarely clean shaven, opting for the mustachioed look that was becoming so popular in the West. (William E. Connelley, *Quantrill and the Border Wars*)

of household, there was a place in the antebellum Southern household in Missouri for unrelated white men and women. They ate at the same table and lived under the same roof. As these households transitioned from peace to war, the nonrelated white members were not jettisoned. Instead, they made the changeover to war with the rest of the white community. In fact, given their precarious position at the bottom of the white hierarchy (but above the enslaved population), they were all the more driven to act in concert with the goals of the slaveholding community of which they were an adopted member and through which they were able to maintain racial superiority over black men and women. Also, studying Quantrill as a part of the household war will provide a remedy to the major flaws of previous biographies. For instance, Quantrill has been given too much credit for his influence over events, while too little credit has been given to the people whom he served and fought alongside. These two conclusions will be recalibrated so that Quantrill's role will be presented in a more humble light and the slaveholders will be restored to their dominant positions as leaders of the movement with great influence over the men in the brush. None of this is to say that Quantrill was not violent, or that he did not help to create the strategy and tactics that facilitated so much bloodletting during the guerrilla war; there is no doubt he was the chief of the killers. But it would be wrong to imagine that the guerrilla war was *his* war; instead, he was an agent of the household war.[4]

Deference played an important role in the way that hired men like Quantrill related to their social betters in the antebellum South. Although there were exceptions, within local communities poor whites and their wealthier neighbors often maintained reciprocal relations throughout the antebellum period. Although class differences could potentially create divisions, commonalities of race, politics, proximity, and kin provided bridges over which the upper and lower classes of whites could relate to one another. This same quality characterized relations in Missouri and facilitated the guerrilla movement that sprang out of the white community in such an organic manner.[5]

Quantrill was representative of a small group of men who were outsiders or bottom dwellers in the white community that nevertheless became a part of the guerrilla system of war and even became some of its most infamous leaders. Unlike the typical guerrilla, Quantrill was born outside Missouri in the North to parents who may have been antislavery. Twenty-five years old when the war began, he was older that the average guerrilla and had no family among the guerrillas or their supporters. As atypical as he was, however, there were other noteworthy men on the scene. A Canadian-born mason who had moved to Kansas City with his Scottish father, George Todd nevertheless rose through the ranks to become one of the guerrilla movement's most dominant personalities. He was a capable fighter who was both ferocious and ambitious and had the necessary charisma to become a successful partisan leader. Another man whose story began like Quantrill's was Harrison Trow, a hired hand for "Uncle" George Hudspeth in the Six Mile neighborhood of Jackson County. He had been born in Pennsylvania and moved to Illinois before ending up in Missouri, to where he had run away in search of a better life. Trow would join up early with the other Hudspeth boys and became an important member of the guerrilla community during the war and after. The Little brothers—Jim and John—were insiders to the Jackson County community, but they were poor boys who had to sell their labor. They would help to make up the core of Quantrill's band early in the war and fought with him for the duration. In central Missouri, Jim Jackson was the most infamous outsider to become a guerrilla captain. Jackson was born in Kentucky, then lived in Texas and began the war as a soldier from that state. He fought under Clifton Holtzclaw but proved himself to be a

George Todd

This portrait of George Todd shows him in a Union cavalry jacket. He is the only guerrilla to sit for a portrait in their well-known disguise. While other guerrillas took off their enemies' clothes before having their pictures made, Todd's personality would seemingly require him to turn his likeness into an opportunity to taunt his Union enemies for eternity. (Edwards, *Noted Guerrillas*)

capable commander worthy of his own band and would become known for leading a raid into southern Iowa.[6]

Before he ended up in Missouri, Quantrill spent years wandering. He was among the crowd of young men who migrated to the West to make their way in the decade or so before the war. Quantrill's shadowy backstory, a mixture of lies, truths, myth, and conjecture, has served as fertile ground for the seeds of the ahistorical portrayals of his life that have weighed down our overall understanding of the war. Skirting the sinkholes of legend, there were parts of Quantrill's past that form a solid foundation for understanding his wartime experience. We know that after the Walker affair, Quantrill told two lies about his past. First, he said that he was originally from the slave state of Maryland, even though he was from the free state of Ohio. Second, he claimed that he had a brother who was killed in Kansas by the same men he had just betrayed, although no such event ever took place. These were obvious attempts to ingratiate himself into a skeptical community of slaveholders and avoid the lynch mob's noose. It should be noted that once Quantrill had made his way into the Southern community, he did eventually tell Andrew Walker the truth about his Northern origins, a revelation that Walker did not hold against him. What else we know of Quantrill's past is this: he had a falling out over a plot of land with his traveling companions from Canal Dover, Ohio; he worked as a teacher; and he likely served as a teamster during the Mormon War in the Utah Territory. We know that his political allegiances changed over time from being an abolitionist to becoming a believer in the proslavery cause, but it is unclear exactly what sparked this change. There is some speculation that he was also known as Charley Hart, and that he may have been a jayhawker, border ruffian, or both.[7]

Evidence of Quantrill's antebellum exploits is sparse. To his credit, the early biographer Connelley exposed Quantrill's lies. His evidence came directly from the source. Quantrill's boyhood playmate and a shameless opportunist, W. W. Scott, enlisted Quantrill's mother to dispel the lies told by her son. After Scott died, his notes were acquired by Connelley and used to write an extensive backstory of Quantrill's life before the war in *Quantrill and the Border Wars*. When we begin to look at other parts of the record, however, evidence of Quantrill's dastardly character becomes harder to find. Again, most of the evidence for this period was rounded up by Connelley, who has been continually cited by professional historians and amateurs alike. However, an investigation of his published work against his own notes and other primary source materials has revealed that the pro-Kansas, pro-Union writer quoted selectively and intentionally tried to mislead his readers. One of the best examples comes from his treatment of the Morgan Walker affair, in which he used the testimony of sources who were not present at the event. At the same time, he discarded legitimate sources whose presence was doubtless, all in an effort to write a particular version of the story that played to his values and beliefs.[8]

Some of the speculation regarding Quantrill's antebellum experience in the West comes from the words of the man himself. In often cited letters to his mother, sister, brother, and W. W. Scott, the young Quantrill describes his life in Illinois, Indiana, Kansas, and his journey across the Rockies and back. Historians have read these letters through the thick distortion of hindsight. They speculate that the man who switched sides just before the war and planned the bloody raid on Lawrence must have been a hustler and a murderer before the war. When the blood-smeared lenses of retrospection are discarded, however, these assertions fade away.[9]

More troubling than the faulty speculation regarding his actions is the psychoanalysis of Quantrill's state of mind. Certainly, the recorded

thoughts of our subject should allow us some window into his consciousness, but these conclusions should not be blown out of proportion. In a
famous May 25, 1860, letter to his mother and one of his last before crossing
over from anonymity to infamy, Quantrill wrote, "I think every thing and
every body around me is happy and I alone am miserable, it seems man is
doomed to aspire after happiness; but never in reality to obtain it; for God
intended that this earth should be earth and not heaven for mortal man."
This quote was written in the wake of an awful tragedy that Quantrill had
lived through the previous winter. More than half of his party crossing the
Rockies starved or froze to death, while Quantrill and a few others lived.
If the letters are read as the true feelings of a young man on his own in a
rough and dangerous world, they hardly reveal the seeds of some deep, dark
force inside him. Had Quantrill turned out to be anything other than the
guerrilla chieftain—perhaps, for instance, an abolitionist who was later
killed by another guerrilla chieftain's men at Lawrence—his letters would
be read by scholars as evidence of his struggle to become a man. And in the
history of manhood there is no more common theme.[10]

Between May and December of 1860, we lose clear sight of Quantrill.
Historians assert that he began to move about under the alias of Charley
Hart and slipped from legitimacy into criminality; this was the point when
he completely lost himself. Teetering on the brink of the moral high ground
of abolitionism in the spring of 1860 and then completely stepping off the
edge of the cliff, this period witnessed his fall from grace. This plunge into
darkness would seem to confirm Quantrill's break with humanity. A man
with no family to speak of, living far from his birthplace, caught between
the great forces spurring men to war on the border, whose own internal
structure had been weakened by the great strain of tragedy *should* break
into pieces. However, this reading of Quantrill could be more about the
scholars who have studied him—their morals, frailties, and insecurities. As
is so often the case with projections like this, it leads to a flawed historical
vision of the past. Certainly, it is easier to have history's villains appear weak.
Although scholars might not like the man he became, it is just as possible
that during this period Quantrill did not fall apart but instead rediscovered
the confidence that had pushed him westward in the first place. Regardless
of its mysteries, Quantrill's time in the wilderness was the crucible in which
the man was cast.[11]

Whatever his temperament when he strode onto the Walker farm, the
manner in which Quantrill related to the Walker family resembled the way

in which a hired hand related to his employer. The very night of the ambush, Quantrill slept in Morgan Walker's house with all the other men who took part in the fight. The next afternoon Sheriff Major Burris came out to the Walker farm, performed an inquest on the body of the dead jayhawker, and then according to Walker, Burris said he was arresting Quantrill "for his own safety." Andrew Walker followed them to the town of Independence and bailed Quantrill out of prison almost immediately. The next morning, mobs gathered in the streets of Independence with the intent of hanging Quantrill, but Walker stood between the mobs and their target. He later said, "I couldn't understand why, among Southern people, they should be feeling against Quantrill. They evidently knew only half the facts." After the confrontation, Morgan Walker arrived in town and rode away in his buggy with Quantrill sitting beside him.[12]

It was not long before Quantrill was assisting the Walker men with their most pressing needs. While Quantrill and the Walkers were in Independence, a slave owned by Jim Liggett found the two remaining jayhawkers hiding out in the brush near the Liggett home. The slave immediately went and told his owner, who brought the news to the Walker farm. With Liggett's slave piloting them through the brush, the Walkers—Morgan, Andrew, and Zach—Jim Liggett, and Quantrill all rode quickly to the spot where the jayhawkers were camping. Andrew Walker recalled that the posse came within fifty yards of the two men before the brief exchange of fire took place. He claimed that both he and his father shot the man who had escaped the initial ambush untouched, with a round from Morgan Walker's rifle landing in the center of the man's forehead. The other men fired on and killed the jayhawker who had been wounded a few nights before. Based on Andrew Walker's recollection, it is unclear who Quantrill fired upon, or if he fired at all.[13]

Following the skirmish in the brush, Quantrill gained recognition as a member of the Southern community in Jackson County. For a few weeks, the hired hand assisted around the Walker farm. The type of work performed by a man like Quantrill was the product of firm social constructions as well as factors such as the changes of the seasons. Quantrill would mostly have labored with the other white men in the household. Because he was positioned below the men of the Walker family, someone like Quantrill could be asked to perform tasks that the men of the white family did not want to do. A variable factor that also contributed to the type of work done by a laborer was the time of year. In the planting and harvesting seasons, he worked in the fields. During the wintertime, which was the time in which

Quantrill had come to the Walker farm, field work was not as necessary. Instead, he would be asked to work a wide variety of jobs to earn his keep. If there were no tasks to be done, then a hand had to move on to the next farm. Whatever work he did for them, the Walkers gave Quantrill a horse, along with a bridle and a saddle, $100, and a much-needed new suit of clothes for his trouble.[14]

Eventually, Quantrill looked to pick up work elsewhere. As a result of his affiliation with the Walkers, Marcus Gill asked Quantrill to help him move his slaves and livestock to Texas. According to Andrew Walker, "Gill was a well-to-do farmer, a particular friend of my father's, and, living only two miles from the Kansas line, he thought it the part of prudence to take his stock and slaves to a friendlier location." Quantrill, who was an experienced teamster, may have been asked to handle one of the wagon teams, or perhaps he served as something of an overseer. Poor white men in the South comprised the class of men who were often tasked with the brutal work affiliated with enforcing the subject position of enslaved men and women. Regardless of his exact job on the trek to Texas, when Quantrill left Andrew Walker said of his family's feelings toward the hired hand that "we had learned to like him, and rather hated to see him go."[15]

In addition to the social dynamics of the household and the seasonal nature of agriculture, the role of this laboring class was determined by conflict. While Quantrill was away in Texas, the formal Civil War began. Like many other able-bodied white men in the slaveholding states, Quantrill joined the fight against the Union. Although men from all segments of society volunteered, historically the rank and file of the military came from the bottom ranks. Of course, in the slaveholding South the lowest class could not fight on behalf of the system because they would not fight for it—with the rare exception of someone such as John Noland, whose own participation is still a contentious subject; the idea of slaves or black men fighting to protect slavery in large numbers was as equally far-fetched as is the idea that slavery was not the root cause of the war. After he helped Gill move his slaves to Texas, Quantrill was heading back to the Walker farm when the first shots of the war were fired on April 12, 1861. By his own account, he joined up with a pro-Confederate company led by a Cherokee named Joel Mayes and took part in the Battle of Wilson's Creek in August of that year. It has been suggested by at least one scholar that Quantrill learned some of the nuances of guerrilla warfare from Mayes, whose perspective on waging war would have been grounded in the Native American way of fighting.

At Wilson's Creek he may have received a wound that led to his return to Jackson County around September 1861. Andrew Walker, who briefly served in the Missouri State Guard and fought at the Battle of Lexington, returned home around the same time.[16]

After each returned to the Walker household in the fall of 1861, both Quantrill and Andrew Walker found that while their time in the formal armies of the Confederacy had ended, their war had just begun. With the coming of the Civil War, the same jayhawkers that had pillaged from and killed slaveholders along the border in the years leading up to the conflict continued to do so. Now, however, they did so in the name of the Union. It was not long before the presence of these antagonistic Union soldiers threatened the neighborhood around the Walker farm. Eleven men, including Andrew Walker, his brother Zach, Quantrill, and Jim Little, who was acting as a hired hand in the Liggett household, set about patrolling the area. This patrol was a hybrid. It was a combination of the structures of the slave patrols intended to protect the community from the interior threat of slave rebellion and the local militias, which were intended to deal with threats from outside the community.[17]

While the first action taken by this neighborhood patrol foreshadowed some aspects of Quantrill's guerrilla band, its command structure was very different. Instead, it was more reflective of the social hierarchy of the community from which it came. The patrol picked up the trail of some unruly Union soldiers at the DeWitt farm, only two miles from where the Walkers lived. The patrol tracked the soldiers to the Stone household, where Mrs. Stone told them that "the soldiers had ransacked her house … [and] struck her on the forehead with [a] pistol." She told the patrollers that the soldiers were now at the Thompson house, only a quarter mile away. According to Walker, as they rode away Mrs. Stone yelled to him, "Kill 'em all, Andy." When they neared the Thompson house, it became clear that they had caught the Union troopers unaware. They ambushed them, killing one soldier and wounding two more without a loss to their own ranks. While the speed and effectiveness can be likened to the attacks of Quantrill's band during the war, according the Andrew Walker, during this time Quantrill "was content to be one of the privates." Walker was the captain of the patrol.[18]

Following the ambush of Union troopers at the Thompson household, the transition of Quantrill from a hired hand to a hired gun began. Men like Andrew and Zach Walker left the patrol, entrusting the task almost exclusively to hired men like Quantrill and Little. They left for a couple of reasons. Walker said that the patrol's "members found employment ... recovering stolen property, and earned the thanks of many southern sympathizers in this way." The patrol became a permanent service in exchange for money, which was viewed as an appropriate occupation for hired men but a job that was below the sons of wealthy members of society. Also, a father and head of household like Morgan Walker may have simply preferred to pay a man like Quantrill to fight instead of exposing his own sons to the danger of combat. In recalling his reasons for leaving the band, Andrew Walker said that he had "in obedience to the advice of [his] father, returned to the farm and given up bushwhacking." He would not stay away very long, however.[19]

Quantrill displayed martial prowess that established him as the leader of the small neighborhood patrol and drew in new recruits. Around the same time that Walker left the patrol, Bill Thompson and Strawder Stone were arrested and charged with complicity in the death of the Union soldier who was killed at Thompson's place. They were both sentenced to be shot. To get these men off the hook, Quantrill sent an affidavit to the authorities in Jackson County that said that he and he alone was responsible for the ambush of the Union soldiers at the Thompson place. Walker later remembered that when he warned Quantrill against this tact, Quantrill coolly said of the Union soldiers, "They can't catch me." It was not long before the Union army had sent a squad out to kill Quantrill. His act was perceived as one of self-sacrifice, which garnered respect from the other men in the band; they subsequently rallied around him as their leader. When the Federals did come after him, Quantrill "began dodging among the fastnesses of the vicinity and young men of the neighborhood began joining him."[20]

Now in a position of leadership, Quantrill shaped the way in which the guerrillas fought. Andrew Walker described the situation for Southern sympathizers in Jackson County as potentially dire during the winter of 1861–1862. Walker recalled that the county was "overrun, almost from the first, by an overpowering Union force." Nevertheless, the patrol that had protected them before the war proved a suitable defense even as the county was engulfed. Quantrill's band, which was comprised of men on horseback who were familiar with the area, quickly adjusted to deal with the changing circumstances and the odds against them. Of the successful transformation by the antebellum patrol into a wartime guerrilla band, Walker said that "the only effective resistance possible, to the domineering of the troops and the villainies of the Red Legs, was by an agency of the irregular, dashing, vanishing pattern that Quantrill's band conformed to."[21]

Quantrill's small band, while initially successful, could only continue to survive with the approval and support of the community. The band won a series of victories against the Union occupying forces. These victories and disaffection for Union policies resulted in the growth of Quantrill's force. Even the sons of the wealthiest families in the area joined or rejoined him, and when they did, they did not supplant Quantrill as leader. Rather, they accepted Quantrill's leadership because of his clear talent for guerrilla warfare and a general trust in this man who had not long before been considered an outsider. As members of the same household, they were accountable to the same people and shared the same interest in the successful defense of that institution. It is also possible that the wealthier men thought it just as well that a hired man be accountable in case the war turned nasty—as it did—but this seems unlikely. There was no way of knowing how the war would turn out, but it seems that the trust placed in Quantrill was genuine. The flow of deference from the hired hands to their patrons within the peacetime household was changing direction in the brush. Now the sons of the wealthy slaveholders deferred to the hired guns.[22]

By spring 1862 Quantrill had won the approval of the Southern men in the community and secured his position as captain of the guerrillas in Jackson County. He never forgot his role, however. Quantrill made the number one priority of the guerrillas the protection of Southern men and women and their property. Although enslaved men and women were the most valuable property that needed protecting, he was well aware of the value of all property. Quantrill was also very conscious of the guerrillas' public perception. If, for instance, there was even a rumor that his men had participated in the theft of anything of value, it would turn public favor against them immediately. As such, Quantrill put a great deal of emphasis on catching any and all perpetrators, regardless of their political affiliation. The best example of this comes from his interaction with a man named Searcy, who had been a Confederate soldier but deserted the war and became a horse thief, stealing from the people of Jackson County and the surrounding environs. Walker recalled that it was "a difficult matter to locate his corral, but they finally discovered it on the bank of the Missouri River." Searcy had twenty-two fine horses in his enclosure. Quantrill, knowing that it was the guerrillas' job to protect the rebel community, decided that they had to hang the man. And, Walker said, it was "to our chieftain's credit that he returned every stolen thing to its owner." This action by Quantrill further endeared him to his constituents.[23]

Quantrill also had to keep other fighters in line. Before he was brought under Quantrill's sway, Bill Anderson and his followers, of which there were only a few, stole horses from Missourians in the spring of 1862. It is unclear if this was intentional or not because they were operating along the Kansas-Missouri border, but Quantrill nevertheless felt the need to act. Rather than string them up as he had with the deserter Searcy, he disarmed Anderson and his men and ordered them not to steal anymore. According to Gregg, "It seems that Anderson did not heed this warning, for late the following fall he was still stealing." Gregg was instructed to go out and retrieve Anderson and his gang, which had grown a bit since the spring. Gregg remembered that he and his men met Anderson's band on a country road. Their horses walked up until they "were opposite and parallel to those of Anderson, then he halted them—halted both columns. He explained his mission and said that he obeyed orders—that for the purpose of those orders and their origin Anderson and his men would have to look to Quantrill." Anderson's men handed over their revolvers and were brought before the guerrilla chief, where they also had their horses taken from them. During that meeting, Gregg recalled that "Quantrill told Anderson in short and sharp words that if he ever stole again and he could get hands on him he would hang him and his men to the first tree he came to that would bear their weight. And he sent them afoot and unarmed from camp." Other guerrillas, even if they were not directly under his command, would be held accountable for the same rules as his men.[24]

During this period of transformation, Quantrill took another step toward becoming a part of the Southern community. In what was quite typical for a hired hand, Quantrill married the daughter of a farmer in the neighborhood. Much has been made of this marriage to Kate King—who was thirteen years old when the war began. Most of the historical interpretations paint the marriage as a farce and use it as an example of Quantrill's depravity. Even a century and a half ago, the twelve-year difference between the bride and groom stretched the limits of propriety, leading Kate's parents to discourage and ultimately forbid the union. This did not stop it from happening: the two lovers ran away and were married in secret. There was little criticism from Quantrill's male peers regarding the relationship. While a few guerrillas did hold negative views of their chief or were at least critical of some of his decisions, they did not fault him for his love of the young Kate. In any other circumstances, for a hired hand with money in his pocket to woo an eligible neighborhood girl would be normal.[25]

For men from the outside who lacked kin, it was necessary to establish a relationship with a woman within the community. Here the experience of another outsider, Jim Jackson, is illustrative. Despite the inherently undocumented nature of the guerrilla war, when Jackson appeared in the record of the provost marshal and the *Official Records*, it was revealing of his relations with women. For instance, Jackson was known to frequent the home of the widowed Isabella Fox, who one witness testified was "a strong rebel, and aider, abettor, and harborer of bushwhackers, of keeping a house of ill fame, of giving dances to bushwhackers," and so on. On another occasion, the bloody evidence that the wounded Jackson had been sleeping in Mahala Drew's bed was discovered. As an outsider, he had to form bonds with the rebel women in the area who would provide logistical support for his band. Somewhere down the line these relations with women who were otherwise without a man—widowed, uncertain of their man's whereabouts, or the unmarried daughter of a farmer—became intimate, or at least the evidence suggests that they were.[26]

Whatever he knew of loving, Quantrill was a savvy fighter. Very early in the war, he won a reputation as an "infamous scoundrel" from his enemies for his successful use of guerrilla tactics. In a February 3, 1862, report from Captain W. S. Oliver of the Union army, he described Quantrill's activities in the first winter of the war. According to Oliver, the situation was becoming somewhat unwieldy: "Quantrill will not leave this section unless he is chastised and driven from it. I hear of him to-night 15 miles from here, with new recruits, committing outrages on Union men, a large body of whom have come in to-night, driven out by him. Families of Union men are coming into the city to-night asking of me escorts to bring in their goods and chattels, which I duly furnished." Oliver continued, "I have seen this infamous scoundrel rob mails, steal the coaches and horses, and commit other similar outrages upon society even within sight of this city. Mounted on the best horses of the country, he has defied pursuit." While on patrol, Oliver reported that "the first night there myself, with 5 men, were ambushed by him and fired upon." Oliver claims to have gotten the best of Quantrill time and again, but the guerrilla chieftain's operating style and prowess were certainly clear to the Union officers tasked with hunting him down.[27]

It was not always enough to hide out in the woods and ambush the Union army patrols in the area. Quantrill knew that sometimes a calculated risk had to be taken, not just to keep the enemy on their heels but to demonstrate through his assertiveness that he led with the interests of his men in mind. One example of this was the February 22, 1862, raid on the town of Independence that was currently in Union hands but had been temporarily vacated by the garrison stationed there. According to William H. Gregg, "Quantrill with fifteen men went to Independence not knowing the enemy was there, on our arrival we were met by an Ohio cavalry regiment ... while we lost two men and the enemy held the town, we had the better of the fight, their losses being much greater than ours." Some men would be lost in such a venture, but to kill more of the enemy was viewed as a positive result. A counterstrike like this, even if it did not achieve its explicit goal, served to raise morale among the bushwhacking rank and file.[28]

As a man, Quantrill projected quiet confidence. He won over his men without the need for chest-thumping braggadocio. His style was more of a balance between the hypermasculine horseman and shootist on the one hand and the thoughtful strategist and empathetic leader of men on the other. In fact, one gets the sense that he distanced himself from the brutality of the war and even planned his strategy to avoid unnecessary bloodshed, at least among his own men. Even before the war, Andrew Walker's testimony regarding the shootouts at his father's home and a few days later in the brush are silent on Quantrill's participation. The implication being that the future guerrilla chief never fired his gun. Just as his plan to raid Independence was based on the (incorrect) reconnaissance that there were no Union troopers in the town, the overall evidence shows that Quantrill was also very thoughtful about where he sent his men, knowing that they had entrusted their lives to him. According to Gregg, Quantrill was unique among the infamous guerrilla leaders in that he "had the greatest care for the lives of his men." This stands in contrast to the fierce and bloody men like Bill Anderson and Todd, who earned respect by demonstrating brutality through their own personal acts of violence. Additionally, they often endangered their men by dragging them into devil-may-care frontal assaults.[29]

The guerrillas used manhood to gauge the quality of their leaders. Early in the war, Quantrill's moderate brand of leadership allowed him to pull together under his command a number of smaller guerrilla bands. As Gregg remembered, "During the year 1862 the men were kept close together and all under the watchful eye of Quantrill." In fact, with the approval of the men, Quantrill established a hierarchy of leadership within his band. Gregg recalled that "Quantrill and his men were sworn into the Confederate service and, reorganized by electing Quantrill Capt. Wm Haller first Lieutenant, Geo. Todd second Lieut, and Wm H. Gregg third Lieut." At the time around 150 men had swelled the guerrilla ranks. While there was always quite a bit more autonomy in the guerrilla war, Quantrill's officer corps followed orders when the men were altogether. In one instance, when an officer from the formal Confederate army joined the men and asked to lead an attack, Quantrill replied, "'No, I do not know you, I do not know if you would carry out my instructions, here are my Lieuts. Gregg and Todd, I know that either of them will do just as I tell them.'"[30]

Men of the same social standing tended to size one another up. During the spring of 1862, Quantrill and Todd seem to have developed a close friendship. Perhaps it was their common standing as outsiders or their shared love of combat, but they saw eye to eye in those early days. In May 1862 Quantrill and Todd donned Union uniforms and undertook a covert mission from western Missouri to Hannibal in the eastern part of the state to acquire percussion caps for the cap-and-ball pistols used by the guerrillas. Cole Younger claimed to have been along as well. According to Younger, "Todd passed as a major in the Sixth Missouri Cavalry, Quantrill a major in the Ninth, and I a captain in an Illinois regiment." They successfully passed through Union lines and purchased 50,000 caps. On their return, however, they began to worry that two majors traveling together was a suspicious sight that might lead to their discovery. Younger recalled that Todd said, "Too many majors traveling together are like too many roses in a bouquet . . . the other flowers have no show." He willingly reduced himself to a captain and downgraded Younger to a lieutenant. Such an awareness of rank among men, even in a playful masquerade like this, planted a seed that had the potential to grow into a thorny bush that could drive the guerrillas apart.[31]

Throughout 1862 and 1863, Quantrill continued to be the overall leader of the movement in western Missouri. More and more during this period, however, the captains under him began to operate with increased autonomy. According to Gregg, while everyone worked directly under Quantrill during 1862, it was "not so in 1863, there was Todd, Pool, Blunt, Younger, Anderson, and others each had companies [that were] widely separated, and only called together on special occasions, all of whom, however recognized Quantrill as Commander in Chief, with Lieut Gregg as adjutant." The spring and summer of 1863 were the most intense of the guerrilla war along the border. With so many small bands operating in concert, the Union army simply could not keep up. Gregg gave the warfare during this time a fitting description: "thick and fast." He remembered how "Todd would annihilate a party of the enemy in western Jackson County Blunt another in the Eastern portion, Anderson somewhere in Kas, or Cass Co. Mo. Pool in Lafayette or Saline, Younger on the high Blue." Gregg gives the impression that there was a perfect balance between competition and cooperation between these leaders. They would physically unite their bands if they had to, but while operating on their own, each commander wanted to win a bigger victory than his comrade, kill more Union soldiers, and pull off the more amazing battlefield feats. Unless they did something to change their policies in the District of the Border, the Union stood little chance of ever getting a handle on these men striving to outdo one another.[32]

Attacks on the Southern households along the border would inspire retribution by the guerrillas, who sought to strike at the households of their enemy in the infamous assault on Lawrence. Offering an explanation for the brutality in Kansas, Gregg said, "Why we made the raid to Lawrence, Jennison, Lane, Burrus . . . had visited various Missouri border counties, and never left the state without murdering, plundering and devastating the houses . . . of our citizens." And according to Gregg, "To kill, it was only necessary to know that a man sympathized with the South, but, as to robbing, they robbed everybody without distinction." As far as what the enemy stole, "These parties until early in sixty three did not haul away much [but] household plunder, contenting themselves with such as blankets, quilts, wearing apparel and jewelry." In terms of who they killed, Gregg remembered that "the enemy had been more savage, if possible, than ever before, they had killed numerous old men and boys, one boy, son of Henry Morris, only eleven years old. There could have been no better argument for the people to flock to Quantrill." As Gregg would claim forty years later, it was this brutality that served as the primary motivation for going to Lawrence.[33]

While his officers were ripping up the enemy across the countryside, Quantrill began to formulate a plan for reaching out to the households of the guerrillas' enemies. Certainly, the plan was Quantrill's, but the debate about whether or not to go to Lawrence was understood by the guerrillas in the context of household war. Gregg, who was Quantrill's right hand man in those days, recalled that on "about the 10th of August 1863 Quantrill called his various captains together for a council of war," to propose going to Lawrence. The guerrilla chieftain did not call such a meeting in a vacuum but was influenced by the changing circumstances of the war in the summer of 1863. Quantrill was not only prompted by the increased onslaught against rebel households, but he seems to have articulated the wishes of the dozens and perhaps hundreds of recruits who had "flocked" to the guerrilla chief in recent months as a result of these attacks. Gregg remembered that, after the raid was suggested, "in support of this proposition [Quantrill] said, 'Lawrence is the great hotbed of abolitionism in Kansas, and all the plunder, (or the bulk of it) stolen from [Missouri] will be found stored away in Lawrence.'" The raid would be a reaction to the strain being felt by the household system of war in Jackson County and the surrounding counties.[34]

Whatever his motives or the bloodshed that resulted, Quantrill has since become the scapegoat of Lawrence for Kansans, Unionists, and many historians who lay blame for the raid squarely on the guerrilla chieftain. According to Connelley, "Quantrill had reserved his strongest argument to the last of the debate. Revenge and money." Indeed, "revenge was well enough for the others of the band. For [Quantrill], money, money." Moreover, Connelley claimed that the raid was merely an excursion to sate Quantrill's bloodlust and that the men who followed him were dupes. He said, "Quantrill cared nothing for Missouri. He cared only for Quantrill," continuing, "That is why he sought authority in Richmond to raise a regiment of outlaws. For then he could shed blood like water in Kansas."[35]

Without apologizing for Quantrill or the guerrillas, it was the system of warfare of which they were a part that drove these men to kill and destroy with such brutality in Lawrence. Quantrill would unleash the collective rage of his men on Lawrence. Gregg remembered that there was a consensus regarding the trip to Lawrence. He recalled that "the men were then informed of the contemplated raid[.] Quantrill, telling them of the great hazard of the trip, that the entire command stood a chance of being annihilated, and all who felt that they were not equal to the herculean task not to undertake it, and, that any man who refused to go, would not be censured." Not a single man stepped out of line. According to John McCorkle, right before they were about to ride into Lawrence, the guerrilla chieftain turned and said to his men, "Boys, this is the home of Jim Lane and Jennison; remember that in hunting us they gave no quarter. Shoot every soldier you see, but in no way harm a woman or child." There is no doubt that to the guerrillas "soldier" meant military age man. Gregg remembered, "Quantrill's order was to kill, kill, and you will make no mistake, Lawrence is the hotbed, and should be thourougly cleansed, and the only way to cleanse it, is to kill." As the orders filtered down the ranks, there was no confusion; they all knew what to do and who to do it to.[36]

Seeing the war through Quantrill's eyes, the raid was an effort to shore up the household system of war. According to Gregg, Quantrill never intended to keep the "plunder" found at Lawrence for himself or even for his men. Rather, Gregg remembered that Quantrill "told me in support of his argument for the raid that there was a great deal of money there, 'and' said he, 'I want to compensate the people who have and, still will divide their last biscuit with us.'" Gregg continued: "'Now,' said Quantrill, 'my plan is that whatever money that may be gotten at Lawrence will be divided among the men with instructions to give to those people very liberally.'" But the repayment for all of those broken biscuits could only occur if the guerrillas did in fact find all that household plunder that Quantrill claimed was at Lawrence. In one corner of Lawrence, Gregg "found about forty shanties, built, three sides boards, the fourth a hay stack and covered with hay, all of these shacks were filled with household effects, stolen from Missouri." He knew the goods that filled these shanties were from Missouri because plenty of it he "recognized, many of these had feather beds, quilts, blankets [etc.] stacked in them higher than I could reach, [and] fine bedstands, bureaus, sideboards, bookcases and pianos that cost thousands of dollars." This loot was under the care of some black women, Gregg said, "many of whom we recognized." One woman he remembered "distinctly, was the property of Col Steel who lived near Sibley Jackson County, Missouri." The bulk of whatever wealth, at least in the form of money, that was recovered from Lawrence never made it back to its intended recipients. Gregg recalled that the money was given by Quantrill to George Todd's men who would redistribute it, but a guerrilla named Charlie Higbie got hold of the largest portion of it and ran off with the money. Gregg said that Higbie was "in the eyes of the survivors of Quantrill's band and, the people of Missouri, a 'traitor.'"[37]

Although they had touched the households of their enemies deep within the jayhawking hotbed of Lawrence, the attack had unintended consequences. General Thomas Ewing's response to the raid—General Order No. 11—shattered Quantrill's attempt to take pressure off the domestic supply line along the border. After Order No. 11, a huge column of guerrillas made their way south earlier in the fall than usual. This would be the last time Quantrill would serve as the overall leader of the united guerrilla bands of western Missouri.

The first cracks in the unity of Quantrill's command began to appear early in the trip, at a place called Baxter Springs. On October 6, 1863, the guerrillas came across Fort Blair, an isolated fortress housing a relatively small Union garrison in southeastern Kansas. At first, only the lead portions of the guerrilla army came across the fortress, which was well defended for

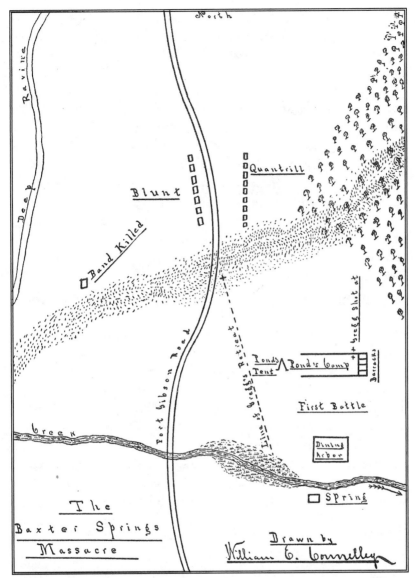

Although this map appeared in *Quantrill and the Border Wars*, with Connelley crediting himself for drawing it, it was based on a conversation with William H. Gregg. It is even possible that Gregg's consultation included his own sketch of the battle that Connelley then co-opted. The area marked "Pond's Camp" was actually Fort Blair, an instillation that Union Lieutenant James Pond commanded during the fight. (William E. Connelley, *Quantrill and the Border Wars*)

its size. Before all of the guerrillas could come up behind them to assist, Gregg and Dave Pool decided to attack the fort. They were able to get close to the fort because of their disguises—Union uniforms and a Union flag, supposedly Jim Lane's taken from Lawrence—but the fortification proved too strong for a frontal assault. Once Quantrill arrived on the scene with the body of the column, he decided that a full frontal assault on the fort might be successful, but it would be too costly to warrant another attempt. He knew that behind the works of this fort riflemen could fire aimed shots at a distance and maintain a high enough rate of fire to kill many of his men.[38]

Meanwhile, another fight broke out nearby. The body of the guerrilla column, somewhere between 100 and 200 men in all, came across the escort of Union General James Blunt by accident and took the opportunity to undertake one of the most one-sided victories of the war. Like the men who attacked the fort, the guerrillas owed much to their blue federal jackets, which disguised them and allowed them to get very close to Blunt's column—well within pistol range. In the close-quarter fighting that ensued, the guerrillas shot down men all around them. In just a few moments, somewhere between 84 and 95 of the 125 Union troopers were killed, Blunt being one of the lucky few who escaped.[39]

The attention of the guerrillas immediately returned to the fortress. According to Gregg, "Todd and Anderson both insisted that we should storm and take the fort," which was in keeping with the aggressive nature of both of their personalities. Todd was seemingly always one of the more belligerent commanders, and Anderson's fiery brand of leadership has been well documented as well. However, the success of the guerrillas up to this point owed much to the calculations of Quantrill. It had been the balance between bloody rage and a thoughtful application of petite guerre tactics that had allowed the guerrillas to fight without too much sacrifice. So, in response to Todd and Anderson's demands, "Quantrill said, 'no, there is nothing to be gained by taking it, beside' he said, 'we would probably loose fifteen or twenty men, and, I would not give the life of one of my men for the whole business.'" This response was not what his subordinates wanted to hear. Rather than take this as the order of a commander, they took it as a snub.[40]

In Texas, not long after Baxter Springs, the company unraveled. Some men left for themselves, notably Gregg and Younger, who joined the formal Confederate war effort in one fashion or another. There is some speculation that things had gotten too bloody for these men, or that the factions popping up around the different guerrilla officers had worked to drive their rivals out of camp. These departures were a trickle until Bill Anderson led his men out of camp after a violent dispute with Quantrill and Todd over the arrest of a few of his men. Later, after the remaining members of the company began their march home, Todd would take command of most of the men. He had been caught trying to cheat at cards by Quantrill, but Todd had drawn his revolver first and forced his chief to back down. Quantrill's time atop the guerrilla movement in western Missouri was over.[41]

The very same dynamic that led Quantrill to the front of the guerrilla column also led to his demise. There is some truth to the notion that violence was the capital that guerrilla leaders traded in, and therefore Todd's overtaking of command and, to a lesser extent, Anderson's secession from the company, resulted from these two men having demonstrated superior martial skills that outshined Quantrill's. Certainly it was important for a guerrilla captain to be a capable fighter. After all, captains were determined by their men through either an explicit election or a de facto deference granted by the bushwhacking constituency. To earn such a position, it never hurt to be the baddest of the bad, but being capable of brutal violence was not always the great indicator of leadership. For instance, many guerrilla leaders were determined by their position in their antebellum communities. They were wealthy, at the top of society, and their standing in the brush was a direct reflection of this antebellum status. However, if a man had used his martial prowess to advance himself to the top rank of his men, as Quantrill and his fellow hired hands had, then it was the only social capital available to him. When read this way, the interaction between Todd and Quantrill makes more sense; the two hired guns were playing a game within a game. This was the hired gun's duel: there were no formal invitations, acceptances, or seconds, only the daring, speed, and accuracy required to kill and the courage to be killed. Like the formal duel, however, the only way you could bring shame onto yourself was by declining the fight. Neither had a family name to fall back on or prewar fame that would earn them the respect of their men or maintain deference through times of struggle. Instead, they were there at the top because they had proven themselves as expert fighters of the brush. For his part, Quantrill had held sway with the men and had been able to keep Todd, the other hired guns, and the various wild men under his thumb. However, when Todd gained leverage on him by turning a game of cards into a violent defense of honor that was not met by the chieftain, who kept his gun holstered, he usurped power from his rival hired gun.[42]

A break like this was bound to happen, however. Less to do with the need to maintain a violent chokehold on the position of leadership, these breaks in the bands were actually the norm in guerrilla warfare. Although it is impossible to know the average size of a guerrilla band, it seems that the default size, when the group was not joined with other bands for an attack, was around ten. A band of forty or fifty was not uncommon, but it typically broke apart to resupply itself. A company of several hundred like the one led by Quantrill was anomalous—an extreme outlier. Moreover, the cohesion of so many bands was only ever intended to be temporary, a means of maximizing the carnage at Lawrence. Perhaps in the wake of the raid Quantrill lost sight of the limited intentions of this large band and began to hold on too tight. That its dissolution happened in such an ugly way was probably not what any of the guerrillas had desired, but it was bound to happen in Texas or upon the return to Missouri.[43]

Quantrill went into exile. Rather than accept a position under Todd, he went into a sort of self-imposed hiding, where he most likely reunited with Kate. In a way this was a return to the wilderness for the man who had become the most powerful and infamous guerrilla leader west of the Mississippi. Again, Quantrill came out of his time away a different man than he went into it. How much of a role Kate may have played in his remaking is not known to us, but certainly her presence restored something of his sense of self. Little is known about this time, other than that few men saw him until the end of the summer of 1864, when he reappeared to participate in the guerrilla campaigns being undertaken in conjunction with Price's invasion of the state. He did not demand a return to a position of power with the guerrillas in the brush but instead made it clear that he would fight and follow orders like the other men. Despite his humility, he was occasionally asked for his opinion, placing him into the netherworld that leaders who are forced into early retirement sometimes find themselves. He became a consultant of sorts, a nod to his accomplishments without any recognition of authority.[44]

Quantrill would outlive the men who had usurped his leadership. Todd was killed by a sniper while reconnoitering for Price's army, and Anderson was killed while charging straight into a line of Union troops. Quantrill's more moderate style of leadership seemed to improve his chances of survival and the survival of the men under his command. Following the death of Todd, many of his followers rejoined Quantrill. Anderson's gang mostly fell

in with Archie Clements and Jim Anderson. Despite his time away, by the
end of the war many of the same men he had led at the outset were again
following Quantrill.[45]

Quantrill had formulated a plan to take his band eastward. The reason
for Quantrill's expedition across the Mississippi River into Kentucky in early
1865 is still disputed. Some suppose that he wished to fight and surrender
with General Lee, so that neither he nor his command would be exposed to
the almost certain executions that would come their way at the end of this
war of no quarter. Others claim he was off to assassinate Lincoln. There is
another group that supposes that he simply wanted to mix it up in Kentucky
with the guerrillas who were fighting there in what he may have presumed
to be a less bloody or more forgiving environment where a guerrilla could
still be a guerrilla. It seems most likely that he desired to join up with one
of the more legitimate Confederate enterprises and surrender under their
official banner, but he would never make it close to Lee's Army of Northern
Virginia. Instead, he brought Missouri-style guerrilla warfare to Kentucky,
waging a fairly successful campaign against Union troopers and Unionists
in the western part of the state for a couple of months.[46]

Quantrill's life came to an end at the hands of another hired man. Edwin
Terrill was the man chosen to bring the infamous guerrilla chieftain low;
it was his only chore, and for it he was well paid. Terrill was a Kentuckian
and had embraced both extremes of the political spectrum in that state at
one time or another. Although it had moved in a different direction than
Quantrill's, Terrill's loyalty was also a shifting thing, moving from diehard
Confederate to Union sympathizer. There is no doubt that killing his
commanding officer in the Confederate army had something to do with
his switching sides, but nevertheless by 1865 he was an agent for Northern
war aims. He formed a band of like-minded killers familiar with the art of
bushwhacking, and on May 10 Terrill's guerrillas sprang upon Quantrill's
band and accomplished their task. One of them issued the mortal wound
to the most wanted man in the western theater. Quantrill would die nearly
a month later, on June 6, 1865, in Louisville, Kentucky.[47]

With that, the last rose in the bushwhacker bouquet withered and died,
or nearly the last. In addition to Todd, some other hired men had since
passed on: John Little was killed early in the war; his brother, Jim, who was
with Quantrill on the very first patrol, followed his old captain to Kentucky,
where he was killed. Jim Jackson, who surrendered a week after Quantrill

died, received amnesty but was arrested and killed by a vigilante mob trying
to right some wartime wrong. Trow lived through the war, became a permanent member of the Six Mile neighborhood of Jackson County, stayed
close with ex-guerrillas, including the James brothers, and was one of the
men brought in to identify the body of Jesse in 1882. Most of the rare ones,
the ones who stood out from the rest—whose very identities required that
they stand out—were bound to be cut down. More than any of the others,
these men had to be rooted out of the fertile ground of rebellion.[48]

Although these men were stamped out, the land from which they had
grown still remained. Early in 1860, Quantrill wrote to his mother and said,
"And now that I have sown wild oats so long, I think it is time to begin harvesting; which will only be accomplished by putting in a different crop in a
different soil." There was no prophecy in these words, only the well-observed
wisdom of the day. Quantrill would pick up and move, plant himself in new
soil where he could reap the benefits of his labors. He could not have known
that the war would come or that he would come to lead it. However, as the
whips, plows, and scythes were exchanged for the reins of a fast horse and
a Colt Navy revolver, hired hands became hired guns. With his pistols, his
horse, and his instincts, Quantrill represented the slaveholders' interests in
the brush, where he was as much an extension of his household as any other
man. At some point he must have imagined that he would die—not as a
fatalist, but as a realist. Any hired hand on any farm in antebellum America
knew that everything that lives must die.[49]

❦ CHAPTER 4 ❦

Rebel Foodways

ON A COLD OCTOBER NIGHT in 1861, Sam Hildebrand crept up to his home in St. Francois County, located in the southeastern part of Missouri. He was being hunted by the local pro-Union militia. Hildebrand, who had been hiding in the woods for three weeks, was cold and hungry. When he got close enough to his home, he whispered, "Margaret," through a gap in the planks of the shoddily constructed wall of his house. Hildebrand's wife recognized his voice, let him into their home, and quickly made supper for her famished husband. Then, as Hildebrand would recall some years later, "Just as I was going to eat, I heard the top rail fall off my yard fence." He got up from the table and with his "gun in one hand, [and] a loaf of cornbread in the other . . . instantly stepped out into the yard by a back door." With the militia closing in on the house and firing at him, Hildebrand ran to cover and ultimately made his escape back into the woods. When he remarked on the event in his memoir, he concluded that "though I had not made my condition much better by my visit, I gnawed away, at intervals, upon my loaf of cornbread."[1]

Guerrillas like Hildebrand went home when they got hungry. Just as it had been in the years leading up to the conflict, the hearth remained the primary source of nourishment for the young men who fought as guerrillas. As a result, the guerrilla movement's structure for feeding its fighters was very different from that of the regular army of the day. Whereas the formal armies of the Union and Confederacy would face a number of challenges in feeding their soldiers as they marched farther and farther from home, the guerrilla war effort did not experience the same difficulties. In fact, the armies of the North and South moved radically away from antebellum practices of food production and consumption. However, the guerrillas waged a war only their agrarian, locally oriented, slaveholding society could support.[2]

Since the Civil War, military scholarship has not acknowledged that the guerrillas were fed by their friends and families. Francis Lieber, a Civil War era military scholar, said in 1862 that the guerrilla band was an irregular military unit because "it consists in its disconnection with the army as to its pay, *provision*, and movements." It was not a great leap, then, to "associate the idea of pillage with the guerrilla band, because, not being connected with the regular army, the men cannot provide for themselves, except by pillage." This frame of thought, nearly 150 years old, is still being applied by historians to the guerrilla war. In their histories, they contend that the guerrillas were resigned to stealing food. Historians paint a picture of the rebel guerrilla as a malnourished wretch who used the circumstances of war to glut himself on the food made by and for other people. This rendering of the guerrilla suggests that his desperation for food led him to commit acts of violence against noncombatants to get a meal, regardless of whether they were a friend or a foe.[3]

Lieber's understanding of guerrilla logistics clearly influenced his under-standing of the character of guerrilla warfare more broadly. Because Lieber's knowledge of guerrilla warfare was framed by what he knew of the relation-ship between regular army soldiers and civilians, he used words like "pillage" to describe an interaction between guerrillas and the so-called "civilians" from whom the guerrillas received food. Through the eyes of the nineteenth-century scholar, women like Margaret Hildebrand were not active participants in the war, so the guerrilla took what he wanted without consent. Pillage, something more associated with the actions of pirates than soldiers, marked the guerrillas as dishonorable men. Men who pillaged could not be fighting for a cause, noble or otherwise; they fought only for themselves.[4]

Rather than the site of pillage by unscrupulous and violent brigands, the supper table was the crucible of community harmony. It was at both fine and roughhewn tables in dining rooms and kitchens where antebel-lum social exchanges played out over wartime meals. The members of the community—young men in from the brush and women bearing food-laden platters—came to the table to assert their self-worth and to be recognized by other members of their communities for fulfilling their respective duties. It was at these tables that the values and goals of the rebel community were affirmed and reinforced.[5]

When people like the Hildebrand family originally settled in Missouri, they either brought with them Southern ways of food cultivation or they adapted to the Southern ways being used by those who had already settled in the region. One of the more distinctive aspects of antebellum food production in the South was the practice of letting animals range freely for food. This was especially true with hogs. Rather than sequester their hogs in a pen and be responsible for feeding them, they let their hogs roam their unimproved acreage and the parts of the landscape that could not be farmed. The Hildebrands, upon settling in St. Francois County, let their hogs loose. According to Hildebrand, "The range was always good, and as the uplands and hills constituted an endless forest of oaks, the inexhaustible supply of acorns afforded all the food that our hogs required." The Hildebrands left their hogs in the wild until "they were fat enough for pork." Then the men would go up into the hills and kill as many hogs as they wanted. Different ear marks, like the distinctive marks branded into the hides of cattle, allowed farmers to distinguish their pigs from the pigs of a neighbor.[6]

Toward the end of the antebellum period and adjacent to the Hildebrands, some people settled who had a very different view on farming. Hildebrand remembered that "a colony of Pennsylvania Dutch . . . established themselves in our neighborhood." It was not long before these Germans, called "Dutch" in the failed attempt of the Missouri tongue to pronounce *Deutsch*, made up two-thirds of the local population in the township. The Germans, perhaps because of their strength in numbers or the relative newness of the southern community already there, felt no need to assimilate to the local traditions of the area. They brought with them the belief that animals—hogs, cattle, horses—should be fenced in.[7]

The existence of these two different types of farming within such close proximity led to the first of several disputes that would end with Hildebrand being chased, in the brush, by the pro-Union militia. In his memoir, Hildebrand suggested that the Germans did not understand the concept of free-ranging hogs and/or tried to take advantage of the situation for their own gain. He said that the Germans "soon set up 'wild hog claims,' declaring that some of their hogs had also run wild," which "led to disputes and quarrels, and to some 'fist and skull fighting.'" Hildebrand and his brothers seemed to win these tussles most of the time. Because they could not defeat the Hildebrand brothers in backwoods brawling, the Germans took the fight to the courtroom. According to Hildebrand, he and his family faced lots of "little law suits" in which the Germans "out swore" them, meaning the Germans brought more people to testify on their behalf. Whether or not it was the case, Hildebrand remembered that he and his family members were "branded by [the Germans] with the very unjust and unpleasant epithet of 'hog thieves.'"[8]

Hogs were not only important to the Hildebrand clan in the southeastern part of the state. The cultural affinity for raising hogs had a particular material importance for all Missourians. Some evidence of this material importance can be seen in the number of hogs owned by the rebel households being studied here. The households that comprised the Fristoe system of guerrilla war in the western part of the state owned, on average, forty-four hogs apiece. In the central part of the state, the average household on the Holtzclaw system of guerrilla war owned forty-eight hogs. Forty-plus pigs could provide meat for even a sizable household, and with a sow being able to give birth twice a year to a litter of fifteen piglets, the hog population could easily replace itself and grow from year to year.[9]

Hog ownership allowed Missourians of all ranks to profit in the market. Profits made from selling hogs and hog meat could be used to pay off mortgages and any debts acquired while a man made his way in the world. While hogs grazed freely to acquire the majority of their sustenance, some farmers supplemented their hogs' diets with corn. Corn, as fodder for fattening hogs, could be converted into a much more valuable product at market than simply being sold as is. Furthermore, strategic locations of these households, on or near rivers like the Missouri and its tributaries, allowed them to pack their pork and send it to other parts of Missouri and even other parts of the country and the world, by way of the Mississippi River and the international port of New Orleans.[10]

While it played a major role in disputes between Hildebrand and the nearby German community, methods of hog raising were just a small part of the incongruity between German beliefs and Southern farming methods. Many of the people of German descent who settled in Missouri during the 1850s had been participants in the radical revolutions of 1848 in Europe. They brought with them to the New World their radical views, including a strong antislavery belief. Besides St. Francois County, there were many of these self-contained German communities spread across the state, even in areas where slaveholding was extremely popular and the Germans were greatly outnumbered. These Germans looked out from their communities at the countryside surrounding them with disdain.[11]

Slavery was pervasive in Missouri, especially in Little Dixie, where people relied upon farming to make a profit. In 1860 there were 114,931 slaves in the state. This was roughly 10 percent of the total population at that time. Little Dixie, a largely rural area in which white property holders were reliant upon agriculture to make profits, had the highest populations of enslaved peoples. Howard County had 5,886 slaves, or 37 pecent of the population, with about half of the households owning at least one slave. The Holtzclaw household, which was located in Howard County, had 11 slaves before the war. While it was slightly smaller than the number of slaves in the Holtzclaw household, the average number of slaves owned by households on the Holtzclaw system was still relatively high. When the Slave Schedule for the 1860 US Federal Manuscript Census is consulted, it becomes evident that the households in the Holtzclaw system owned around 5 slaves apiece. Even if the white people in a household did not possess any slaves, it was likely that they were related to the members of at least one household who did.[12]

The crops that benefited the most from the addition of slave labor to a household were cash crops. In Missouri the major cash crops were tobacco and hemp, two labor-intensive crops that required quite a bit of work even after they were harvested. Tobacco had its roots in colonial Virginia. Sharing roughly the same latitude and having similar climates, it was logical for the settlers of the state who came from Virginia, or Virginia by way of Kentucky, to bring with them the same crops that had been successful back East. Also, tobacco was an appealing crop for farmers to grow because it had retained a high enough demand in the market to continue to make it a profitable crop. Hemp was a cash crop that was particular to Missouri. It was grown elsewhere, but not in the same quantity or quality. Hemp was used to make the rope used by the United States Navy before the war. Hemp rope was also used by antebellum cotton planters to bind their cotton bails.[13]

With the coming of the war, the Germans' hatred for slavery led them to join the Union forces. For instance, while St. Francois County was not a very prominent slaveholding county, the activity of Germans there followed the same pattern as elsewhere in the state where slaveholding was more popular. The Germans who fought Hildebrand over the wild hogs became members of the pro-Union militia. Similarly, the vast majority of unionists in Little Dixie were Germans. Louis Benecke, a Union captain and himself a German, recounted that with the outbreak of the war, the people who remained loyal to the Union in Chariton County were almost exclusively German. He said that on July 4, 1861, the community of Germans in Brunswick met at Martin Filzer's farm "where about one hundred men and women gathered, hoisted 'Old Glory,' and were addressed in the German language by several of our young patriots; and, according to German custom, drank enough lager beer to become fearless and more than ordinarily patriotic." It seems that in Little Dixie the only true loyalists to the United States government spoke German and drank lager beer, very different from the English-speaking and whiskey-drinking rebels. The names of the men who fought under Benecke, as well as the names of the pro-Union families they fought to protect, were names like Schlapp, Munson, Schoetker, Heiman, and Schmitt, all ethnic German names.[14]

In part due to the assistance of the Germans, the institution of slavery was gradually destroyed over the course of the war, leaving Southern farm households without the assistance of their black labor force. The Union army, applying, in Missouri, the concept of contraband to slaves, a tactic originally employed by Union General Benjamin Butler in Virginia, protected runaway slaves and found a use for them in camp or sent them out of the state as soldiers. In 1862 the United States Congress passed laws that allowed for the slaves of "disloyal" slaveholders to be emancipated, and in 1863 Union recruiting officers actively recruited male slaves off the farms in Missouri to serve in the Union Army. Eventually the state elections of 1864 would put in power a radical state government that would end slavery as an institution in Missouri in January of 1865. Whether they were voting into office the radical ticket in '64 or protecting the slaves who ran to German communities for succor, the Germans were the people on the ground expected to carry out the liberation of the slaves. One historian has observed that Germans were "generally considered the worst 'nigger lovers,'" by rebels in Missouri.[15]

Stripping away slavery was a political victory for the Germans. They forced Southerners to adapt their social and farming practices to be congruent with those practiced in the North, but ending slavery did little to injure the ability of the rebels in Missouri to make war. While slaves were important to the production of cash crops, as well as the crops being grown for sustenance, their labor was not so crucial that white members of the household could not survive without it. White dependents, notably white women, had the skill and the strength to perform many of the necessary tasks on the farm to produce all of the essential, edible crops. Acquiring and producing milk, eggs, and butter fell under the traditional domain of white women's work. Other jobs, like plowing fields and harvesting crops like corn and wheat, were typically in the purview of men. However, women were capable of performing these tasks in the absence of men, and during wartime they did. Herding and slaughtering animals was also traditional men's work, but in a pinch women could work together to bring in an animal and slaughter it. Cooking and preparing all of the meals was typical women's work. Therefore, without men and slaves, women could still feed themselves and their men when they came in from the brush.[16]

Men stayed home to fight because they were already engaged in a war over the source of food, a war for their household and the particular form of agriculture on which it was built. It so happens that such a cause guaranteed that the logistical infrastructure was already in place to feed them. In central and western Missouri, the rebel households of the Holtzclaw and Fristoe systems produced around 98 and 62 bushels of wheat respectively in the year before the war. Households of the Holtzclaw group also grew around 1,300 bushels of corn, while the typical household in the Fristoe group grew around 1,600 bushels. Wheat and corn were turned into flour and cornmeal from which bread was made. The average household in both groups grew around 30 bushels of Irish potatoes. There were 7 milch cows, or milking cows, in the typical Holtzclaw group household and 5 in the average Fristoe group household. From the milk produced by these cows, rebel women in the average Holtzclaw household churned around 200 pounds of butter while their counterparts in the Fristoe group produced around 230 pounds per household. In addition to these staples, the farms produced notable amounts of oats, rye, orchard products, and sweet potatoes.[17]

The alternative to leaving home and fighting in the regular Confederate army did not seem as attractive for the young men who chose to become guerrillas. It must have seemed counterintuitive to fight far from their homes and have the food that was grown on their farms shipped to them over great distances. In fact, many guerrillas experienced the results of this flawed equation firsthand. In the western part of the state, men like Quantrill, Andrew Walker, and John McCorkle began the war in the ranks of the regular army and soon after returned to the fertile lands of Jackson County. In central Missouri, Clifton Holtzclaw and much of his band were veterans of the regular service before returning to their homes. Hamp "Babe" Watts, a man who fought first as a guerrilla with Bill Anderson and then fought in the regular Confederate service, described the difference between the two types of service succinctly. He said going from being a guerrilla to being a regular soldier was like going "from fine uniform and 'the fatted calf,' to a baptism of fire and blood, starvation, vermin and rags."[18]

Indeed, elsewhere in the South farmers left their homes to fight in the regular Confederate armies and faired no better than the guerrillas and what they experienced and tried to avoid. Bell Wiley argues that "food was undoubtedly the first concern of Johnny Reb," even more of a concern than the Yankees or combat. This was the case because Confederate soldiers were so often hungry. While the Confederate government tried to maintain the same standard for feeding their soldiers as the antebellum United States Army, they quickly realized they could not, despite the agrarian nature of their society. Wiley says that one "cause of scarcity in the midst of plenty, particularly of meat, was the dearth of salt." However, "far and away the most serious difficulty was the inadequacy of transportation facilities." For these reasons, food rotted long before it could reach the mouths of hungry soldiers. These men resorted in many cases to eating mules and dogs to stay alive. In the end, "the long continuing and gradually increasing shortage of food, particularly of meat, was depressing" and was the primary cause of declining morale, aside from defeat on the battlefield. Of course, the two were very much tied together.[19]

While rebellious Missourians decided to stay on and around their farms, which produced plenty of food, the Union army was faced with the difficult task of feeding their soldiers. These logistical challenges were well documented even by the time the Civil War broke out. The Mexican-American War had illustrated to Americans how problematic feeding an army far from home could be. Given the total number of men enlisted in the Union army, and the size of the area they set out to conquer, the United States government and Quartermaster General Montgomery Meigs could only assume any previous logistical issues would increase exponentially. Over the course of the war, the government would have to feed two million soldiers stationed as far north as Minnesota, as far west as California, as far south as Florida, and as far east as the Sea Islands of the Carolinas. Within this context Missouri was not the most extreme place that the United States government had to get food to, but it was certainly west of where the majority of its soldiers were stationed.[20]

The burgeoning industrial capitalism in the North put it in a unique position to take on the supply challenges of this war. A system of supply on such an unprecedented scale required the Union Quartermaster Department to manage logistics in a new way. The men in the quartermaster corps managed the formal supply line as they would a business. The key to the success of the Quartermaster Department was dependent upon its members having previous experience in and knowledge of business to successfully navigate the supply channels of the Union army. This required having personnel with business experience and mercantile acumen, and the North just happened to have a large population of men with just those talents. In the decades before the war, the job of clerk had become popular for managing the everyday needs of business. Whether it was basic accounting skills, paperwork, or manipulation of the communication and transportation infrastructure of the army, business-savvy quartermasters succeeded.[21]

As a result of the logistical skills of these clerks, it seems that the diet of Union soldiers, generally speaking, was as good as it could be. The Union army actually increased the size of the rations for its soldiers at the outset of the war from what they had been before the conflict. According to Wiley, during the Civil War the average Union soldier was probably the best-fed soldier of any regular army in the world at the time. Still, the Union soldier found much about which to complain. Wiley points to two particular instances when Union soldiers experienced a shortage of food. It seems that soldiers in the western theater were the most likely to go hungry for extended periods of time. Also, during times of great activity, like the constant scouting troops in Missouri were expected to do, the chances of Union soldiers lacking adequate provisions increased. Wiley concluded, however, that a Union soldier "thought less and less about the quality of his rations and more and more about their quantity."[22]

Despite the claims made by Wiley about the difficulties faced by the Union Army in supplying their soldiers in the western theater, the business-oriented quartermasters did enough, at least according to one Union soldier. According to Wiley Britton, "The army ration is good, substantial food, and is all any man, not a glutton, needs to keep himself in excellent condition. And our men are in excellent condition, and I think it probable, that since they have become inured to the service, they had never enjoyed better health at any time before their enlistments." While this statement says as much about the diets of these men before the war as it does their time in the army, it seems clear that they were not starving in the Union army. In fact, Britton asserted that just the opposite was true. He said, "Each company accumulates quite a surplus of rations every month." The only shortages were of fresh meat and pork, which were important, especially for the morale of the soldiers, but not critical to their survival. In the end, Britton claimed that "perhaps no government has ever had a better system of providing for the comforts of its soldiers than ours, during the present war."[23]

While the Union army soldiers stationed in Missouri were kept in "excellent condition" by their government, they were not as well cared for as the rebel guerrillas. The guerrillas, unlike the Union soldiers, had the benefit of home cooking. One Union general pointed out the frustrating nature of this advantage. He said, "When a squad of [Union] soldiers who have, through storm and mud, day and night, week in and out, been on the hunt after the villains happen to come upon them camped snugly and comfortably in the dwelling or barn of a first family," no doubt enjoying a warm meal, the Union soldiers were obviously disheartened. Because they had access to their kitchens, the guerrillas' "rations" were not reduced to the hardtack on which Union troopers out on a scout had to subsist. Rather, the guerrillas' diets remained very much the same as they had been before the war. Although the men's dining schedule may have been a bit more inconsistent, they had access to fresh meat, soft, freshly baked bread, and luxuries like butter, fresh milk, and fresh fruit, as well as jams. These foods were not only important parts of a person's diet but they kept morale up among the guerrillas.[24]

Rebel women in Missouri kept their men well fed. In central Missouri, Holtzclaw and Jim Jackson were both fed by the rebel woman Isabella Fox. Fox, who was arrested by the provost marshal for her actions, stated in her testimony that "three of [the guerrillas] came in September of 1864 to my house and called for their breakfasts," which she provided. Fox had the assistance of three other women, her two daughters and a third "widow" women. The four women had no problem feeding the three guerrillas and were capable of feeding many more. Again, in the same month "seven other bushwhackers of Holtzclaw's band came to [the Fox household] in the evening and called for their suppers." One morning about a month later, Fox commented that "'Jim Jackson' came into my house with nine of his men," and likely got a meal from the Fox women.[25]

Support from an individual family like that from the Fox family was not isolated, but rather it was a small part of a larger system for feeding guerrillas. To get a more complete picture of how the guerrillas were fed in a systematic manner, it is important to look at the whole of the Holtzclaw system. Holtzclaw and his lieutenants were supplied by 32 households that have been identified in this study. Many of the households were like that of the Fox household above, a yeoman and female-headed household, but there were also many slaveholding households that were still headed by old men. Out of these 32 households 21 guerrillas have been identified. There were a total of 166 white adult supporters on the supply line, which was mostly spread over Chariton, Howard, and Linn counties in north-central Missouri. This was a ratio of 8 supporters for every guerrilla in the field. On a house-to-house basis, there was an average of 5 supporters per household, making their ability to feed a band of 10 or so guerrillas a relatively easy undertaking.[26]

The total amount of edible material available throughout the network made keeping the guerrillas as well as their supporters well fed a possibility. For instance, over the entire Holtzclaw system his supporters owned 1,395 hogs and over 400 head of cattle. These supporters combined to produce 39,324 bushels of corn in the year before the war and almost nine 900 bushels of "Irish" potatoes. The women in these households churned a total of 5,785 pounds of butter in 1860. To put this amount of food in context, there were 238 white people on the Holtzclaw supply line if we count the 21 guerrillas, their supporters, and the white children, or just over two companies of soldiers in a regular army. For each participant in these two companies of rebels, they had the equivalent of 6 hogs, nearly 2 head of cattle, 165 bushels of corn, and almost 25 pounds of butter per year.[27]

Despite their ability to periodically feed the guerrillas, there was a limit on how many men these rebel women could feed at any one time. The guerrillas were aware of these limitations, and in the hopes of receiving larger portions of food but not placing a heavy strain on any one household, remained in relatively small bands. However, large groups of guerrillas sometimes camped together or sought refuge and support together. One such occasion occurred at the Potter household, where a portion of Quantrill's company stopped on their way to Lawrence. At the Potter household "it was not unusual to prepare meals for squads of men. Sometimes neighbors were asked by a larger force to prepare food and bring it to the Potter place for consumption." More specifically, during this particular time "forty came, asking each of four families to cook for ten men, all to be served at Potter's." The evidence put forth in this paragraph as well as the testimony from the Fox case suggests that most households could host around ten men at any one time.[28]

In addition to having access to the cooking skills of their women throughout the war, the physical landscape of the agrarian society that they constructed in the antebellum years was perfect for sustaining the guerrillas in the brush. For instance, hogs shared the same brush as the guerrillas. Hildebrand recalled that once, while being actively hunted by the Federal troops, he "killed a pig with [his] knife near the house of a farmer, and cooked it in a deep ravine where the fire could not be observed." For guerrillas in all parts of the state, feeding on wild hogs was a common occurrence. Andrew Walker recalled that while out in the brush with George Todd's band, they could not go into the houses of supporters for food because there was snow on the ground and their horses would leave tracks that would guide the Union troops to them. Then "a lucky thing happened. It had not been an uncommon thing, in pretty weather, for hogs to stray into camp; and it so happened that . . . a big grunter plowed his way to us through the snow." Walker caught the hog, fellow guerrilla Jim Little skinned and butchered it, and the guerrillas cooked the pig without being discovered.[29]

While the brush was teeming with food, the fields and rivers were also full of food from which the guerrillas could graze. The planted fields were full of corn, potatoes, other vegetables, and fruit. These fields would be picked clean by large campaigning armies, but the relatively small number of guerrillas and their supporters—roughly the same number of people were living off the land during the war as had been before the war—meant the land could produce ample foodstuffs for the guerrilla war's participants. In addition to plucking an occasional ear of corn from a field, guerrillas would also pluck food from nature. Gregg recalled that on their return trip from acquiring caps for the guerrillas' guns, as Quantrill and Todd were "going down the river, the next day they came upon Blunt and Bledsoe fishing from a skiff on the Missouri River." They had the freedom to fish for their dinner, and when the opportunity presented itself, guerrillas also hunted wild game. At one point during the war, Hildebrand "saw some deer on the side of an adjoining hill . . . selected a nice buck and shot him dead on the spot." He and his fellow guerrillas dressed and cleaned the meat and ate a dinner of venison that night.[30]

At various times and places during the war, however, the Union army challenged the rebels' ability to continue to feed themselves. At first, the Union army had merely chased the guerrillas with patrols hoping to catch them, or to catch their supporters in the act of feeding the guerrillas. Eventually, however, they found it to be a wiser policy to go directly to the guerrillas' source of food. In its earliest forms, the attempts to limit the guerrillas' access to food were difficult, if not impossible to enforce. In April of 1863, one Union officer ordered that when his men arrested "heads of families under the preceeding [sic] instructions you will compel all persons on the farm to desist from all labor of every kind except the necessary household duties for boarding the family." In theory the policy would prevent rebel women from feeding any extra persons, like a band of hungry guerrillas, who might show up and ask for food. Eventually, it was clear that this half-measure was not enough; as long as women were in the household, food would be produced. Besides well-known examples like General Order No. 11, in the last two years of the war the Union army tried to banish the rebel women who were feeding the guerrillas on a household-to-household basis.[31]

The guerrillas immediately responded to the Union policies that made the conflict a war over food production. In 1863 James Callaway, a pro-Union militiaman living in Linn County, was visited by Holtzclaw and his band. Holtzclaw clearly laid out the rules of engagement to Callaway. He told him that when the pro-Union militia "went out scouting [they] must live off [their] own friends and let his sympathizers [and] Rebels alone." After all, this was how the guerrillas operated. Holtzclaw said to Callaway that "some of his friends had been choked for taking care of him [and] feeding him and that this had to be stopped . . . he fed his men and horses on his friends and that he did not interfere with Union men only to take contraband of war from them."[32]

Bands of guerrillas were capable of visiting the households of Unionists at the same clip as their women were being banished. A variety of sources from the provost marshals' records to the county histories to the *Official Records* illustrate the ability of rebel guerrilla bands like Holtzclaw's and Jackson's to fight this war for the sources of food. This had a range of effects on the shape of the war. In some places, the guerrillas and the militia actually formed a truce, along the same terms as those described by Holtzclaw in his visit to Callaway. In Chariton County in 1864, Holtzclaw, Jackson, and Anderson struck up a deal with the leader of the militia there, William E. Moberly. The guerrillas would not attack the militia and the militia would leave the guerrillas and their supporters alone. Elsewhere, the war became something of a de facto stalemate, at least on the question of logistics.[33]

While the war between the guerrillas' foodways and the regular Union army's system of supply was fought to a draw in Missouri, Northern forces were able to defeat the regular armies of the Confederacy on the logistical front. The historian Emory Thomas illustrates the paradox of this agrarian society's inability to feed its soldiers, especially as a factor in General Robert E. Lee's decision to surrender his Army of Northern Virginia at Appomattox Court House on April 9, 1865. Thomas says that "when Lee's tattered veterans reached Appomattox they were half-starved"; however, "after days of continuous fighting the rebels still had sufficient ammunition to fight on." Bringing his point home, Thomas says, "At the end the supposedly agrarian nation had supplied its principle army with no food, but there were seventy-five rounds of manufactured ammunition for each man." An army of farmers, fighting within the borders of their own country, had been starved into submission by an army of well-fed, so-called industrial wage-slaves and clerks fighting hundreds of miles from their homes.[34]

Preceding his surrender to General Ulysses S. Grant, General Lee was presented with an alternative action: guerrilla warfare. When General Lee announced his decision to his officers, the bright, young artillery commander, Brigadier General E. Porter Alexander, who was utterly depressed by the thought of surrender, interjected that they should "scatter in the woods [and] bushes either to rally upon Gen. Johnston in North Carolina, or to make their way, each man to his own state, with his arms, [and] to report to his governor," essentially transitioning from a conventional force controlled by the centralized power to hundreds of local guerrilla forces. While he was himself a dedicated Confederate officer who was committed to the conventional way of making war, Alexander knew that the type of warfare waged by the Confederate Army of Northern Virginia made its very existence unsustainable. He clearly believed that while they had sucked up all of the resources in that part of the country, fighting in smaller units, closer to their homes, would allow the Confederates to be better fed and supplied so that they could keep the war going. In the end, Alexander believed that "if there is any hope for the Confederacy it is in delay," a sentiment that was the major touchstone of guerrilla strategy.[35]

Lee had serious reservations regarding this plan, some personal and others logistical. As one scholar asserts, Lee feared that the use of guerrilla tactics "would bring anarchy, [as] Lee told an artillerist just before Appomattox, because the soldiers 'would have no rations & they would be under no discipline.'" Indeed, Lee was himself too old to become a bushwhacker, meaning his men would be without their dear grandfatherly commander. Lee was vulnerable and his ego was exposed, for this comment about discipline can be read another way. Staring at his choices—surrender or guerrilla warfare—Lee's decision may have had as much to do with his own fate as with the fate of his men, his army, or his country. He realized that his army could continue to fight on without him; the war would go on without him. If his men scattered into the hills, Lee would become like all of those old men in Missouri who suddenly found themselves irrelevant.[36]

More important than the influence of vanity upon Lee's decision was his thoughtful analysis of the logistical reality of fighting on. Continuing his explanation behind his refusal to order the men into the brush, Lee said, "They would have to plunder & rob to procure subsistence. The country would be full of lawless bands in every part, [and] a state of society would ensue from which it would take the country years to recover." However, this comment is too often read as a critique of guerrilla warfare. Certainly, many modern scholars of guerrilla studies would agree with the Confederate general: no matter their initial motivations or principles, guerrillas ultimately devolved into lawless thugs, with their war turning to utter anarchy. However, Lee's comment is better understood another way. Whether he understood it this way, it was a direct critique of conventional warfare. Lee was right in his assessment of northern Virginia; it had been ravaged by war, lacking in any kind of food that would allow for the orderly supply of food for his men. Many of them would turn into scavengers, seeking food at any cost. In fact, it was likely that some of them had already turned to less than legitimate ways of procuring a meal or shoes or clothing. However, this was not the result of guerrilla warfare. This was the result of conventional warfare and its destructive nature.[37]

This final debate over guerrilla warfare illustrates once and for all that there was not separation between battlefield and home front. Although Lee and his fellow Confederate commanders idealized this division and imagined a war in which violence was contained, their inability to come to terms with the reality that this war was a household war cost them dearly. It is possible that the Confederacy, in the form of General Lee and his Army of Northern Virginia, was defeated on the battlefield and not destroyed from the inside out by fissures in Southern society. But even Lee, it would seem, in his last moments as the commander of the Army of Northern Virginia would have to acknowledge that such distinctions were false ones. Just as the fighting and dying worked to determine the outcome of the war, so too did factors born of the interior of the Confederacy play a direct role in the conclusion of hostilities. There was no getting around it: the battlefield and the household were the same place.[38]

Guerrillas like Hildebrand knew that no such separation existed. Hildebrand recalled that "unlike my enemies, I had no commissary department," and yet he was fed by his supporters until "he was as plump as a stuffed turkey." In addition to lacking the logistics of a formal army, Hildebrand rejected other essential qualities of formal warfare like its tactics. He said, "I adopted the military tactics not in use among large armies." Moreover, because of this difference in his style of warfare, his "plan was the most successful, for in the regular army the rebels did not kill more than one man each during the war." The informal structure of his supply line gave his supporters the ability to better feed him, which clearly translated into success on the battlefield. Unlike Lee's Army of Northern Virginia, Hildebrand was not forced to surrender because he was hungry. Like many of the guerrillas, he never surrendered.[39]

CHAPTER 5

The Rebel Style

ON THE AFTERNOON OF OCTOBER 27, 1864, Union soldiers wheeled the dead body of the infamous rebel guerrilla Bill Anderson—or, as he was known, "Bloody" Bill Anderson—into the town of Richmond, Missouri. They stuck his wild-haired corpse in a chair and propped him up in front of the courthouse, where a roistering crowd of townspeople, including a dentist who part-timed as the local photographer, gathered to yawp and gape. Here, dead, was the man who over the previous summer had killed untold numbers of Union men; here, cold, was the man—some said murderer—who since June had both mutilated soldiers and waylaid civilians. At some point that afternoon the crowd parted shoulders and elbows long enough for Dr. Robert Kice, Richmond's aforementioned dentist-photographer, to take a famous image. Anderson's likeness is as macabre today as the corpse must have been for the gawking villagers then: bearded, bucktoothed, arch-eyebrowed and wide-eared, a crazy mane obscuring the two bullet holes in his head, there he is, propped up with a revolver across his stomach, gripping it at his belt, posed but poised to maim again.[1]

And there he is: killed, in his guerrilla shirt. The shirt is homemade, and garish for being homemade, hand stitched in flowers of all shapes and sizes and colors. It is an oddly bedazzling garment for any man to wear, let alone a man of notorious repute for mayhem.[2]

The objectification of Anderson's body points to a conflict deeper than the political dispute between Southern-sympathizing Missourians and the

Union. This was a clash of societies with divergent concepts of manhood. For the Union men who killed Anderson, stripped his body down to his colorful shirt, and displayed his corpse, he was a different type of man: he was a guerrilla. Demonstrated through his warfare, the guerrilla's nature was woefully out of step with that of "civilized" men. In fact, Union officers described the guerrillas as they did Native Americans during the Indian Wars. The guerrillas were "cowards," "fiends," and "savages," labels that were only confirmed by their exotic and unusual appearance. Yet, for the men who were guerrillas, their seemingly irregular look signified important components of a distinctive manhood born of their slaveholding society west of Mississippi. Analysis of the guerrilla's appearance will expose the place where their quests for love and immortality intertwined. It was there, where dependence on their women and their deep-seated belief in masculine independence converged, that the guiding force for their particular brand of warfare originated.[3]

To better understand the connection between appearance and manhood, we must consider the social relations on which the two societies built their different systems of war making, and how clothing reflected and facilitated these systems. The conventional system of warfare was the product of an increasingly industrialized, centralized, and bureaucratized state. A soldier within this system wore the conventional military uniform, which was clothing of the same color and cut worn by every man in the army, with only slight alterations denoting their rank, their unit, and their branch of service. Conventional military clothing quite literally established a sense of uniformity, creating a highly visible bond between a man and the other men to his right and left, men that may have been strangers before they found themselves together in the army. It was this male-male bond, then, that served as the social underpinning of the conventional army.[4]

Guerrilla manhood was primarily defined by the relationship between women and men. Just like the antebellum household head, the guerrilla thought of

Bill Anderson. There he is: killed, in his guerrilla shirt. (Courtesy of the State Historical Society of Missouri)

himself as an independent man, free from the influence of or dependence on other white men, but of course he was reliant on the dependent members of the household, most notably white women. When the war came, one guerrilla remembered that this sense of independence held true no matter the cost. He said that they still "preferred the free but more hazardous life of independent soldier," over the safer but more regimented life of a regular army soldier. Nor would they don the fashion of conformity, as another guerrilla added: "I do not remember ever to have seen a bushwhacker wearing a Confederate uniform." Instead, the guerrillas wore clothing produced by their women. Not only were these clothes, in particular the guerrilla shirt, representative of the female-male bonds that fused them to their community, but the unique look allowed each man to stand out among his peers.[5]

The conventional armies did not begin as the homosocial, uniform organizations they would quickly become. When volunteers for the Union and Confederate armies left home for war, most did so with homemade uniforms on their backs. Women all over the North and South made military uniforms in a wide variety of colors and cuts for their men. These women, and the men who benefited from their looms and needles, had a vision of the war that was limited to their immediate worlds, which were often comprised of their local communities, a narrow understanding of the war that could be seen in the irregularity of the uniforms, which varied greatly from one locally raised volunteer unit to the next. But whether it was confusion in battle, unit rivalries, problems with supply, the integration of replacement soldiers, or a general lack of discipline, the mishmash of uniforms worn by men in these national armies had to go, so, following the creation of the formal supply lines, the Union and Confederate governments sought to institute a much more "regular" and homogenized look for their soldiers.[6]

The geographic location of this guerrilla war was an important factor in the centrality of women to the war effort as well as the style of clothing with which they outfitted their men. When young men left their homes along the western border of Missouri to protect their neighborhoods from jayhawking Kansans in the years preceding the war, they did so with whatever clothes their women had made for them. As the border war became the Civil War in 1861, the Confederate Army and its affiliate the Missouri State Guard were unable to provide a substantial defense of the border. In the formal army's stead, young men remained at home to protect their vulnerable communities, and their women began to make shirts for their men that were especially suited for the extended duty outdoors. It is unclear who made the first guerrilla shirt, or who wore it, but it quickly became popular among the men in Quantrill's band. Andrew Walker offered insight into the guerrillas' style throughout his memoir. He recalled that by the spring of 1862, the guerrillas were affecting "but one garment that might be distinctive; a handsome, embroidered overshirt . . . was worn at nearly all times, by each and all of us."[7]

Women responsible for creating guerrilla clothing designed a shirt that was unlike any other military garb of the day. In today's parlance, the guerrilla shirt would be considered an overshirt, but in the mid-nineteenth century this was just a shirt. Further, what we would see as an Oxford shirt or a button-down today was actually called a "shirt-jack." The neck of the guerrilla shirt was cut low in the front, ending in either a sharp V-shaped point or more of a U shape. Sometimes there was a rosette anchoring this point. The collar was usually faced with ribbon of bright color, and ribbon also outlined the pockets and sometimes the tail of the shirt. There were two large pockets, one on each breast. The shirt was typically made from a fabric that was fairly thick, sometimes flannel or butternut, material that became the backdrop for beautiful and elaborate needlework stitched by the men's mothers, wives, and sweethearts.[8]

The shirts were emblematic of the guerrillas' style more generally. The greatest influence on their style was the look of the frontier hunters who had straddled the fringes of the white and Indian worlds since very early in the European settlement of the Americas. Some of these white hunters had so merged the two styles that they were derided by other European Americans as nothing but "white Indians." Antebellum hunters wore what one scholar calls "a composite of European and Indian style," saying that "the hunting shirt was a loose frock that reached halfway down the thighs. . . . In the front folds of the shirt hunters kept small rations of provisions." The general appearance of the hunters was also influenced by the cultural exchange. Furthermore, "like Indian men, American hunters let their hair grow long and dressed it with bear grease, plaiting it into braids or knots." Just as Indian hunters painted their bodies and attached ornaments to their hair, "American backwoodsmen heading into battle frequently adopted a similar style of ornamentation."[9]

Like the wives of those backwoodsmen who outfitted them during the frontier wars, when the Civil War swept into the border women became the quartermasters of the guerrilla war effort, with their domestic skills becoming highly valued military tools. Before the war in Missouri, women produced clothing for themselves, their men, and their children. When their brothers were learning how to use firearms and ride horses, girls were learning how to spin, weave, and sew. In mastering their skills, women used every possible material to make clothes for their families—wool shorn from sheep raised on their farms, small amounts of homegrown flax and cotton, and whatever textiles could be purchased or otherwise procured from local marketplaces. Because the climate of Missouri, prone to rapid fluctuations on the thermometer and barometer, took its toll on clothing, and because the nature of combat, typically taking the form of an ambush or a running fight, often forced guerrillas to flee their hideouts and their supporters' homes in such haste that they left pieces of clothing behind, or when the clothes that the guerrillas left home wearing wore out or were lost, they returned to their women for replacements.[10]

As quartermasters, women showed a real genius in adapting their design of guerrilla clothing to deal with the environment. Guerrilla shirts, in particular, were made by women to provide young men with protection from the elements. In the summertime the guerrilla shirt offered an extra layer that protected them against the bloodsucking mosquitoes that infested their haunts in the timber bottoms of Missouri, yet it was not as thick as a jacket or coat, which would cause a man great discomfort in the heat. Of course, if the heat was unbearable, men could easily shed their guerrilla shirts for the plain cotton shirts they wore below. During the winter, an extra layer was even more welcome, especially one that was made from a material that was fairly sturdy. On the run as they so often were, the guerrilla shirt provided men with insulation from the wind and cold air that could chill any man on a midnight ride.[11]

In order for the guerrilla shirts to offer such protection from the elements, women made the shirts from heavier materials, wool being the most common. Quantrill "wore a guerrilla shirt made of brown woolen goods," during the raid of Lawrence, Kansas, in August of 1863. His shirt was made of "butternut," a wool yellowish-brown in color that was the most commonly used textile in Missouri and in other parts of the occupied South throughout the war. It is likely that the guerrilla shirt worn by Jesse James in the 1864 photo was made of butternut. Other wool-based materials, like flannel, were used to make guerrilla shirts as well. Wool was so commonly used because it was accessible, and a shirt made from wool could be produced entirely at home. The availability of wool can be seen in the number of sheep owned by Missourians in 1860. The 3,581 households of Jackson County owned

10,462 total sheep. Howard County, which was located in the central part of the state and became a hotspot for guerrilla activity in the latter years of the war, was perhaps more representative in terms of sheep ownership, the 1,740 households in the county being home to 19,345 sheep.[12]

While most guerrilla shirts were made from wool, other materials that were either bought or stolen from merchants were also used. During the summer of 1863, a woman named Mollie Grandstaff was arrested by the Union Army. She was charged with receiving and concealing stolen property, but she was obviously making clothes for the guerrillas as well. Showing an understanding of the relationships that undergirded the guerrilla war effort, the Union Army tracked Grandstaff down because of her romantic connection to a guerrilla who was killed with Grandstaff's likeness on his person. They found her in Jackson County, at the Gray household, and where they also found the remnants of a bolt of calico that was recently stolen from a local Unionist merchant and forty shirts that had recently been made for the guerrillas. Naturally, the majority of shirts were made of the stolen material.[13]

No matter what was used to make the shirts, women designed the guerrilla shirt to offer several functional advantages over the clothing worn by soldiers in the regular armies. The shirt was especially beneficial in the fast-paced, mounted combat of guerrilla warfare. On each side of the breast a large pocket was sewn in which the guerrillas stored ammunition, powder, and caps, next to personal items like a photograph of the woman who made the shirt. Often, the guerrillas carried preloaded six-shot cylinders that could be quickly swapped out with the spent cylinders in their revolvers. Soldiers of the Union cavalry like those occupying Missouri stored these same implements in pouches attached to their belts. The action and movement of combat could cause these containers to shift and move, making the materials in these cases more difficult to reach.[14]

Beyond the practical functions of the guerrilla shirt, the embroidery on the shirts articulated the bond between a particular guerrilla and a female supporter. The images of men wearing their different guerrilla shirts are evidence of the way that the decoration of each shirt was used to represent a singular connection. Whether it is Jesse James's shirt, the shirts of John and Thomas Maupin, or George Maddox's shirt, the variety of forms taken in the shirts reflected their unique bonds with their mothers, sisters, sweethearts, and wives.

To communicate the beauty of the connection between themselves and their men, rebel women attempted to recreate the most beautiful things they

Jesse James as a boy during the war. He most likely didn't join the fight until 1864, and it is likely that this picture portrays him at that point in his life—the very beginning of an infamous career. The collar of his shirt does not come to a point, as so many of them did. Rather, his collar is a large oval, bordered with black or dark ribbon and with small white flowers stitched every couple of inches or so. His pockets have a similar design. He wears a white shirt or shirt-jack underneath that is buttoned to the top with a flowing black necktie accentuating the look of this fresh-faced gentleman killer. (William E. Connelley, *Quantrill and the Border Wars*)

The portrait of Dick Maddox shows a man with a dark beard, long curly hair, and a scar on his face. He resembles the fearsome Blackbeard of popular imagination or even his own comrade "Bloody" Bill. Maddox's guerrilla shirt has a darker collar than some others. It also appears to have a dark ribbon sewn across its shoulders and down its sleeves. He does not wear a necktie but keeps his shirt buttoned very high. (William E. Connelley, *Quantrill and the Border Wars*) knew: flowers. These women were aware of the great symbolic value of flowers and that a "language" of flowers existed, with each type of flower standing for a different idea or emotion. For instance, daisies symbolized innocence, violets stood for faithfulness, pansies signified thought and remembrance, and red roses represented love. Using this language, women spoke to their men and about their men to anyone who laid eyes on the shirt. They used green thread to stitch long vines of garland that looped around deep-cut collars and across large pockets. Along the garland, rebel women used red, blue, yellow, purple, and white thread to stitch the roses, bluebells, daisies, violets, and dogwood blossoms. For those women who did not have access to homegrown wool and had to purchase cloth as well as all of the different colored threads, it cost them between $15 and $20. This was a hefty cost for a shirt, unless the message it carried was priceless.[15]

Of the shirts that appear in surviving photographs, none are as intricate as the one worn by Anderson on the day he died. Flowers of varying sizes and colors created a border around the collar of the shirt, covered the pockets of the shirt, and even decorated the cuffs of his shirtsleeves. The flowers stand out, not only because they appear in such a great quantity but because the black material from which the shirt was made offers an outstanding backdrop for their bright colors, not unlike real flowers springing out of freshly tilled earth. These stitched flowers may have been strung together by a vine of garland, but the quality of the black-and-white photograph prevents us from knowing for sure. What is evident, however, is that whoever made the shirt for Anderson had hands that were both talented and loquacious.[16]

Itself a labor of love, the guerrilla shirt worn by Anderson offers a starting point for understanding the connection between his deep affection for his women and his quest for immortality. Few guerrillas left written evidence of the significance of immortality in their lives. However, a wartime ritual not only shows that the concept of immortality was present in the minds of the men serving in the guerrilla ranks, but of immortality's inextricable entanglement with feminine love. Like men of the conventional armies, Anderson and many of his fellow guerrillas had their pictures made. Sitting for a moment or two while the lens absorbed their likenesses, the guerrillas created what words could not, a lasting and indelible image of themselves at this all-important time in their lives. The practice of having one's picture made shows that these men wished to be remembered as fighters, and in giving the image to a sweetheart or female relative, they wished to be remembered by the women they loved. These men might have had the morbid fantasy that someday feminine eyes would take in the frozen image of her man, dressed in the clothes she had made for him and holding the weapons he used to kill the men who threatened her. Once his likeness was made, the guerrilla need not worry about his legacy. He would be remembered as a man.[17]

Romantic love was important as an expectation and goal, but, in its place, female love for Anderson came first from his sisters. While we do not know if he ever gave one of his sisters a photograph of himself, it is quite possible that one of his sisters was responsible for the beautiful shirt that Anderson wore on the day he died. Having lost both parents just before the war, the Anderson children were reliant upon each other. When both Bill and his younger brother Jim left home to fight in the brush, Mary Ellen, Josephine, and Jane must have been deeply affected. In 1860 the girls were only fourteen, eleven, and eight respectively. Not only were their brothers putting their own lives at risk, their absence made their sisters that much more vulnerable. The mutual reliance, the emotions brought on by missing their older brothers, and the general stress of war could easily have inspired the creation of the ornate guerrilla shirt worn by Anderson.[18]

During the summer of 1863, the Union general Thomas Ewing went after rebel women like the Anderson sisters because they were the source of logistical support for the guerrillas. Ewing, as shrewd an observer of the guerrilla system of warfare as any Union officer, saw that material support traveled along highly gendered lines of blood, affection, and friendship best seen in the short-lived General Order No. 10. With this logic in mind, Ewing arrested the Anderson girls, Charity McCorkle Kerr, Nannie Harris McCorkle, Susan Crawford Vandever, Armenia Crawford Selvey, Susan Munday, Martha Munday, Mrs. Lou Munday Gray, and the aforementioned Mollie Grandstaff. He put these women—the sisters, cousins, wives, and sweethearts of a few notable guerrillas—in a makeshift prison located in the Kansas City neighborhood of McGee's Addition.[19]

Union counterinsurgency measures were undoubtedly interpreted by the guerrillas through the lens of manhood. The guerrillas' reaction to these measures was further exacerbated when an accident seemingly undermined the very foundation of guerrilla manhood. On August 13 the makeshift prison for women collapsed, killing four women outright and seriously injuring many others. Josephine Anderson, who was fourteen at the time, was killed. Sixteen-year-old Mary Ellen Anderson was crippled for the rest of her life. The fall broke both of Jane Anderson's legs, injured her back, and cut up her face. She was only ten years old. John McCorkle, who had a sister killed and a sister-in-law seriously hurt in the prison collapse, expressed the sentiments of many of his guerrilla brethren. According to him, the recent tragedy was "the direct cause of the famous raid on Lawrence." McCorkle claimed years later that the guerrillas had plenty of reasons for going to Lawrence. Men from Kansas had burned down their homes, killed their fathers, and stole their families' property—all things the guerrillas would later inflict on the residents of Lawrence. However, for McCorkle and no doubt Anderson as well the cause that outweighed all others was that their "innocent and beautiful girls had been murdered."[20]

News of broken and lifeless female bodies set off an alarm in the minds of the guerrillas, an alarm not unlike the ones that had been triggered in men over and over again, generation after generation, up and down the American frontier as it crept westward through time. It seems that the guerrillas had not only adopted the frontier hunter's style but had taken up his warfare as well. The guerrillas envisioned themselves as the rangers of olden days who rode across the landscape unfettered by anything save their homes and families, whom they were protecting either through the direct defense of the settlements or in their strikes against Indian villages and European outposts. This type of warfare was not limited to battlefields but was taken into the very households of the enemy. Dwellings were burned. Food was taken and eaten or destroyed. Enemy men, simply because they were men, were by definition combatants and were often killed whether they were armed or not. Attacks were not limited to men but extended to women and children. Though guerrilla warfare was influenced by this model of frontier warfare from the outset of the Civil War, it had held closer to the limits of nineteenth-century conventional warfare in respect to the treatment of women. Now with the knife taken to their women, a shift occurred in the way in which these men viewed themselves as men, and along with it the shape of the guerrilla conflict would change as well.[21]

Like white frontiersmen reacting to Indian attacks on their homesteads or Indians reacting to attacks on their villages, the guerrillas determined to take the war to the closest enemy settlement and destroy it. On August 21, 1863, a large body of guerrillas under Quantrill raided the Kansas town of Lawrence, during which Anderson demonstrated that he had begun to see himself in the same vein as the frontiersmen who likewise had been unfettered by the regimentation of the regular army. There is really no way of knowing how many men each guerrilla killed, because most guerrillas did not offer details on the raid, even if they contended that their actions were justified. According to one account, Anderson told two Lawrence women, probably two recently widowed women, that his "two sisters, with three other ladies, were crushed to death," in a prison collapse. Another account claims that Anderson said to an onlooker, "I'm here for revenge and I have got it."[22]

Just months after he did more than his share of widow-making at Lawrence, Anderson took a bride. Over the winter of 1863–1864, he met a woman in Texas and fell in love. Her name was Bush Smith, and she could have easily been the seamstress behind the creation of the shirt that appears in the 1864 posthumous photograph of Anderson. Besides her name and her relationship with Anderson, little is known about this woman. For lack of a better phrase, she has been the subject of historical rumors. With scant evidence, historians assert that Smith was a prostitute who worked in a saloon in Sherman, Texas, a town close to the guerrillas' camp. The saloon in question was owned by Jim Crow Chiles, a man from Jackson County who was not only known to the guerrillas but likely had relatives among Quantrill's men. Regardless of Smith's occupation or historical reputation, there is enough evidence that she and Anderson formed a strong relationship. They were wed in the spring of 1864 before the guerrillas returned to Missouri.[23]

A guerrilla wedding like the Anderson-Smith nuptials would not only see women turn out in fancy dresses, but the men would also dress in their finest clothes. The groom may have worn an outfit like the one he wore on his death day: a white hat with a large black ostrich plume covering his head, a guerrilla shirt, a blue waistcoat, and a well-tailored, dun-colored frock coat. Standing beside Anderson, his fellow dandies were decked out in fine jackets, coats, and hats, each man accentuating his individuality. Walker remembered that such fine clothing was not simply worn at weddings, but that the guerrillas "always, unless in exceptional straits, wore the best of clothes," like "A rather large slouch hat ... and boots, with spurs." While much of their clothing was made by women, the guerrillas had to purchase or steal their accessories from local merchants. Occasionally women purchased these accessories for the guerrillas. In the case of the Spencer women of Johnson County, they bought "seven pairs of boots and three or four hats," for a group of male relatives out in the brush. The most conspicuous of these things, fine hats with feathers, were a sought-after item. The guerrilla Joseph Bailey made sure to note in his memoir that after a skirmish he took a hat that was decorated with an ostrich plume from a man he killed. He wore this prized trophy for a brief time, until he left it behind fleeing the home of his sweetheart.[24]

For the guerrillas, clothing was important to conveying their individuality when they faced inward, toward members of their own community. However, when Anderson and his warrior-groomsmen turned outward, away from their congregation and toward their enemy, clothing became a weapon for fighting the war. Nearly as quickly as the war began and the Union Army conformed to blue uniforms, the guerrillas began to wear blue jackets and coats stolen from their enemies or taken off the bodies of the Union soldiers killed in combat. Walker attested to this addition of the blue uniform to the guerrilla wardrobe, saying that while they never wore Confederate uniforms, they "very often wore plain citizen's clothes, more often Federal uniforms." He went on to say that even though the guerrilla shirt "was worn at nearly all times," often "a Federal cavalry coat was worn over it."[25]

Wearing their blue coats out in the brush, the guerrillas easily tricked Union patrols. Walker recalled one instance early in the war in which Union troopers surprised the guerrillas and gained the upper hand, only to be confused and deceived by the disguise of the guerrillas. Immediately following their initial volley toward the guerrillas, the Union patrol rode closer, and as Walker said, "Seeing so many of us with blue uniforms, it occurred to them that we must be another of the several Federal scouting parties that were out after us." In the moment that the patrol hesitated, the guerrillas opened up on them. Walker remembered that "the captain shouted excitedly: 'Don't shoot here, don't shoot here.'" Todd, who was leading the guerrilla band, yelled back, "'Who are you?'" The Union captain replied that he was a Union officer. The guerrillas fired again. Clearly confused, the Union captain shouted out again, exclaiming, "'I am not Captain Todd, the bushwhacker, neither am I Captain Gregg.'" According to Walker, when the fighting was done, nineteen of the fifty-two Union troopers lay dead, without the loss of a single guerrilla.[26]

An important part of guerrilla strategy, the blue uniform that the guerrillas wore over their distinctive guerrilla garb was also a trophy. Following the skirmish with Union troopers, Todd's guerrillas probably scoured the corpses of the nineteen dead troopers for things of value, while the few men without blue jackets almost certainly wrestled uniforms from the unwieldy, mortified bodies. After losing his own clothes in a close escape from the Union troopers who beset his winter hideout, Walker recalled that he procured his Union garb in just this way. Following another fight with Union troops, a group of guerrillas that included Walker came up to the body of a dead Union soldier. The dead man was, according to Walker, "just my size and well dressed. I traded clothes with him on the spot; and I looked like a soldier I can assure you, with his brand new uniform, cavalry boots, blouse, and overcoat." For Walker, this man's clothes were not just a useful disguise.

He clearly admired the man's clothes, perhaps a reflection of how he viewed this now dead soldier. Just as a hunter wearing a buffalo coat conveyed a certain message to other hunters, by wearing a blue jacket a guerrilla was boasting to all who saw him that he had bagged a Union trooper.[27]

The widespread wearing of these trophies by guerrillas throughout the war haunted Union officers, who saw guerrillas everywhere they looked. In a May 7, 1865, report to his commanding officer, Major B. K. Davis revealed that his "men have come near shooting each other several times lately, and are liable to be outwitted and deceived by Bushwhackers, who you are aware are frequently dressed in Federal Uniform." General E. B. Brown, in a report to the headquarters of the Department of Missouri, reiterated the critical nature of the confusion created by the guerrillas' use of Union uniforms. He said that "this week a foraging party from Springfield entered the SW part of Henry Co. and while moving about in the night were mistaken for a party of bushwhackers." While no one was injured because of the misidentification, Brown said that the origin of the problem was that "nearly every 'bushwhacker' . . . has a sky blue overcoat regulation pattern."[28]

To deal with the new dimension of warfare being employed by the guerrillas, Union officers came up with counterinsurgency cues and fashion. Colonel James Ford observed that "the guerrilla and bushwhacking parties all have [more or] less clothing and uniform on." To avoid confusion and either succumb to a guerrilla attack or friendly fire, Colonel Ford told the officers under his command that when they see a group of fellow Union soldiers, give "some preconcerted signal when still afar off, and by some particular motion of a squadron guidon, a particular wave of the cap, sword, &c., you can never make the mistake of attacking other scouting parties." These signals were easily learned and imitated by the guerrillas, forcing the increasingly bewildered Union officers to develop more subtle means of communicating their identities. In an order from Adjutant General Edward Berthoud to the entire Fourth Sub-District of the Border, officers were told to alter their men's clothing so that "a bade of red cloth, flannel, or calico will be worn on their hats. After next Monday a white bade will be worn in the place of the red one."[29]

The problem of misidentification that bothered Union troopers did not seem to plague the guerrillas. In fact, except for one mention by William H. Gregg that Al Wyatt and Boone Scholl—the latter being named after his cousin several times removed, the legendary Daniel Boone—might have been accidentally shot by their own men because they were dressed in Union jackets, there is nothing in the written record that indicates a pattern of guerrillas mistaking other guerrillas for Union troopers. This could simply be a matter of sources. The Union Army, the massive bureaucracy that it was, turned out a huge number of reports, making their records more comprehensive than did the guerrillas, who produced almost no written documents during the war. Given the nature of the guerrilla-guerrilla exchange hypothesized here, the Union sources would not even be able to comment on such a happening. One can also say that the guerrillas who recorded their wartime experience in memoirs would not be inclined to acknowledge a pattern of mistaken identity within their own cohort. All of this said, given their propensity to dress in disguise and combined with only one mention of mistaken identity, there is enough evidence (or a lack thereof) to conclude that the guerrillas had much less trouble distinguishing friend from foe even when the friend in question was not known by the guerrillas firsthand.[30]

It took a guerrilla to know a guerrilla. The social location of the guerrilla equipped him with the intuition to read his fellow guerrillas' performance even as they passed as Union troopers or dressed in a sort of bushwhacker drag. In addition to creating a culture, or a way of seeing, the identity of the guerrillas also generated subtle mannerisms and visual cues that could be read by other members of their community. Indeed, the very impulse to throw on the blue jacket and try to pass as a Union trooper created a mechanism of deception that would alert other members of the guerrilla in-group. Union officers, however, understood uniforms to be an outward expression of a man's natural identity, making them easy dupes. In the culture of the conventional army, friends wore uniforms of a particular cut and color, enemies wore uniforms of a different color, and noncombatant men and women wore nonmilitary clothing. The formal army way of seeing was so strong that even when they knew what the guerrillas were doing, Union officers still could not adjust their perspective; they were as attached to the conventional uniform as *the* indicator of identity as ever.[31]

The guerrillas also played on assumptions regarding the gendered nature of clothing. Although the instances were exceptional (and perhaps even apocryphal), guerrillas were known to slip into women's dresses, skirts, bonnets, and shawls. Harrison Trow was helped into women's clothing by some female friends in an attempt to escape discovery by Union troopers. In this instance, the masquerading guerrilla was caught and exposed. Trow also reported that Cole Younger dressed in an old sunbonnet and a riding skirt to reconnoiter a Union post. He duped the Yankee soldiers into believing he was an old woman until, on the way out of town, Younger reached into his basket, pulled out a pistol, and shot down a perplexed Union trooper. Jesse James was sent on a similar mission to perform reconnaissance on a Kansas City brothel filled with Union troopers. James, "arrayed in coquettish female apparel, with his smooth face, blue eyes, and blooming cheeks, looked the image of a bashful country girl, not yet acquainted with vice, though half eager and half reluctant to walk a step nearer to the edge of its perilous precipice." According to Trow, the cross-dressed James then interviewed, quite successfully, with the madame of the bawdy house and was asked to return that night for her first shift as a painted woman. Arriving after dark, James, still dressed as the curious and rebellious farm girl, brought with him a handful of guerrillas, who ambushed twelve lustful Union soldiers.[32]

Trow, Younger, James, and the other guerrillas so queered warfare that they fractured the reality of the Union soldiers without any cost to their own identity as men. For the guerrillas, unlike their male counterparts across the war, cross-dressing was not a source of shame or something to be explained away. Infamously, Jefferson Davis struggled to restore his reputation as a man after being captured by Union troopers while he tried to sneak away in his wife's clothing. It was a moment that was not only emasculating for Davis but went a long way toward destroying whatever remnants of Southern manhood had survived defeat on the battlefield. Furthermore, with men unmanned, the whole gender system of the South was destabilized by the Confederate leader's decision to toss his wife's shawl over his shoulders and slip out into the darkness. Quite to the contrary, however, the guerrillas owned their gender-bending deception. They seemed quite proud of the moments when they squeezed into a dress and covered their long, curly bushwhacker locks with a bonnet, even emphasizing these instances in their autobiographical histories. Certainly it helped that they were rarely caught in their compromising state of dress and were able to get the drop on their enemies, but even when they were undressed and their disguise pulled away, they were not humiliated.[33]

Whether they wore a guerrilla shirt, a lovely riding skirt, or a Union officer's coat, it was all just vengeance dressed up. If the guerrillas' pride remained intact when they wore women's clothing, they certainly felt no shame in wearing Union cavalry jackets. It was not that the guerrillas did not care. They did. The guerrillas not only understood the meaning of clothing, they knew its significance better than their enemies and perhaps most men of their era: they decoupled clothing and its antebellum or conventional meanings from their essence as men. More and more the guerrillas came to embody the concept of revenge, and clothing only affected their vision of manhood insofar as it helped to facilitate their ability to achieve reprisal against their enemies. Furthermore, as they used clothing to transcend military and gendered lines of identity as they were traditionally understood while simultaneously maintaining their own manhood, the guerrillas tried to communicate something to their enemies about the overall nature of war: death is all around you, anyone can be a guerrilla, and anyone can be a killer. Although there was truth in this message, it was told with a great bit of theater and cannot be trusted outright. From the guerrilla perspective, it would be great for their intended audience—Union invaders—to come away thinking they were in some hellish freak show where nothing was what it seemed and there were no rules. However, like all good ringmasters at the center of the circus, the guerrillas disarmed their onlookers with some measure of buffoonery while they tugged this way and that way on wires unseen by their helpless spectators-turned-dupes.[34]

While it is impossible to know all of the visual cues that the men who fought as guerrillas read in each other, there were some aspects of the guerrillas' appearance that were distinctive and therefore worth pointing out. Guerrillas were known for their long hair and their penchant for facial hair, making them conscious of these aspects of personal style in others. In their portraits, we see that some of the men were too young to grow proper beards, but all who could grow facial hair grew it and most of the men had their hair long, although it was sometimes covered by a hat. Walker described the guerrillas' and especially Quantrill's use of facial hair. He said, "In order to escape recognition by day, the guerrillas changed their personal appearances . . . especially by changes of the style of beard." Walker observed that "Quantrill's beard grew faster than that of any other man I ever knew, and he remodeled it often. I do not remember ever to have seen him without a mustache . . . and he seldom wore chin whiskers, but made the most of the fruitful possibilities of sideburns."[35]

McCorkle described the guerrillas' personal style in contrast to that of the regular Confederate soldier. As the guerrillas headed south during the late fall of 1862, they came into contact with "regular" Confederate forces in Arkansas ,where McCorkle bumped into an old friend, a Missourian named Henry Brookins. According to McCorkle, "Brookins and I had agreed not to have our hair trimmed nor to shave until the war was over. I had kept my promise and when I saw Brookins, he had his hair nicely trimmed and cleanly shaved except a long mustache." Upon seeing his conservatively groomed

"Bloody" Bill Anderson as he looked in life. His likeness is
beyond menacing. He embodies the liminal darkness of the
guerrilla, possessing so many characteristics that would seem
to clash with each other but instead come together to make his
fearsome and wild appearance. (Courtesy of the State Historical Society of Missouri.)

friend, McCorkle said that "with my long hair which was then below my
shoulders and with my flowing beard, I walked up to him, caught him by the
mustache and said, 'Henry, you lied to me. Where is your hair?'" According
to McCorkle, Brookins told him that "they would not let us wear long hair
in the South; if we would not have it trimmed they would throw us down
and cut it off for us."[36]

If the regular army style reflected the stability of the formal system of
war, then it would seem that the guerrillas were wearing, modeling, and
performing the instabilities of their theater of war. In the photograph for
which Anderson sat while he was among the living, his long, black, curly
hair is like a woman's, but his beard is of the piratical sort. On the upturned

brim of his black hat is a silver star denoting military rank, while the hint of a plume more befitting the hat of an eighteenth-century "macaroni" can be seen peeking out just above his hat. Anderson's very posture is somewhere between that of a general and barroom cardsharp, with one hand firmly gripping his lapel while the other is relaxed, resting over the edge of a nearby chair back and revealing a gold ring on his pinky finger. He wears the black or blue velvet coat of a gentlemen farmer, the type of wealthy agrarian who needs a brace of revolvers like the one around Anderson's waist. In short, he is a fop, but deadly.

This picture of violent burlesque was only accentuated by the addition of the gory trophies displayed by the guerrillas. A quintessential image of their bloody pageantry was on display on October 11, 1864, when Anderson and his men rode into the Missouri town of Boonville to meet the ragtag invasion force of "butternuts" led by Confederate general Sterling Price. Price's army was far from uniform, but aside from the occasional involvement of the Cherokee forces in Confederate operations in the western theater, a more striking disparity in two parties of Southern-sympathizing troops was likely not seen during the war. The general—a Missourian, Mexican War hero, and former governor of the state—planned his invasion of the state with the idea that if he could capture St. Louis, the North would lose its taste for war and vote Lincoln out of office. Without the resources to achieve his goals, the invasion was ill fated, and by the time Price reached Boonville, he had given up hope of capturing St. Louis. When the guerrillas came to meet the general, they were not dressed in the humble, monotone clothes of other Southern soldiers but "in black or dark suits, and had their hats fantastically decorated with ribbons." Seemingly in contrast with the flowing rainbow of ribbons, the saddles and bridles of the guerrillas' mounts were decorated with human scalps that twisted and bounced to the rhythm of the horses' canter.[37]

In the months leading up to this moment, trophy taking of this kind became a more prevalent part of the war for the guerrillas, signaling the evolution of guerrilla manhood into something that combined the traditional forms of frontier manhood with the more refined form of Southern manhood. The end result was an even more acerbic and primitive form of braggadocio than had existed among the strutting men of western Missouri before the war—or even in the war's earliest days. The July 7 open letter from Anderson to two Lexington newspaper editors and several Union Army officers offers a rare chance to get into the head of the guerrilla captain. The epistle demonstrates that Anderson's war was an experience to which he had devoted much thought. From beginning to end, the letter describes the war as a contest of masculinities.[38]

At a pivotal point in the letter, Anderson said, "Burris, I love you; come and see me. Good-by boy; don't get discouraged. I glory in your spunk, but damn your judgment." Such a goad can be seen as evidence of an arrogant and heretofore successful guerrilla. However, such an observation overly simplifies Anderson's letter, especially this particular portion, reading it only for its tone and nothing more. Under the surface of this taunt, Anderson was acknowledging that his foe was formidable. Anderson could only celebrate his victories over Burris if his opponent was worthy; he could only exult in his drubbing of this "boy" if he saw some man in him. This Burris, however, had made choices he could never make. Furthermore, in critiquing Burris' choices, Anderson, perhaps in a moment of reflection, must have known that his own actions likely confounded Union officers—or, perhaps, he was not that thoughtful. What is clear from the letter is that Anderson believed that he had bested Burris and had earned the right to taunt his vanquished foe in the public forum of the arena of Missouri's guerrilla war. Although they were both men—both champions of a cause—"Bloody" Bill was telling anyone who would listen that they were not the same, and that they were certainly not brothers.[39]

Anderson articulated that it was attacks against Southern women— women just like his sisters and his wife—that were at the root of this difference. Further down in the same letter, Anderson addressed a portion to Union general E. B. Brown, the commander of Union forces stationed in Lafayette County, where the general had ordered the arrest of a number of rebel women. Anderson scolded Brown, saying that he believed him "to be a man of too much honor as to stoop so low as to incarcerate women for the deeds of men." To Anderson and his fellow guerrillas, for Brown, Burris, the other Union officers, and the whole Union Army "to stoop so low" was to move away from the most important tenet of the guerrillas' understanding of manhood. These two groups of men were sliding farther away from one another on the spectrum of manhood.[40]

In the wake of his sisters' arrest, the prison collapse, General Orders No. 10 and 11, which both targeted women, and the continued arrest, confinement, and banishment of rebel women throughout the state, the concern on behalf of Anderson for the fate of Southern women was well founded.

This attack on the very interior of the rebel community was an indication of what some Union officers had in mind for Missouri's Southern-sympathizing community. An August 15, 1864, letter from Union General Clinton Fisk to Major General Rosecrans, who was the commander of the Department of the Missouri at the time, discussed Fisk's strategy. Fisk said that "nothing short of holding the bushwhacker aiders and abettors responsible with their lives and property for these barbarous acts will ever drive out the murdering villains." These terms used by Fisk were not unfamiliar in the lexicon of United States military officers in the nineteenth century, being reminiscent of the way in which they talked about dealing with the Indians, that other group of people whose fighting style reinforced and perpetuated stereotypes and cultural misinterpretations among many army officers.[41]

Ironically, the guerrillas only embraced frontier-style warfare more as their opponents sought to eradicate them for doing so. At the one-sided Battle of Centralia, which took place on September 27, 1864, a large body of guerrillas that included Anderson and his men marked the bodies of some 125 Union troopers they killed, nearly the entire Federal command in that battle. The day after the battle, a Union colonel, Kutzner, arrived at the scene. He reported that in a field three miles outside of Centralia, the guerrillas with "great superiority of numbers and arms broke through the line, completely surrounding the troops, giving no quarter and mutilating bodies." A Lieutenant Clarke recounted the details of the mutilation. He reported that "ears were cut off, and all commissioned officers were scalped . . . the privates were cut from one wounded soldier while living and thrust in his mouth." All signs point to the targeting and assaulting rebel women as the source of this ghastly bloodletting.[42]

On October 11 those scalps and those pieces of men taken at Centralia dangled from the bridles of the guerrillas' mounts and ribbons fluttered about their heads—the picture of guerrilla manhood. The man who wrote about the guerrillas at Boonville, an outsider to the rebel community, was drawn to the bloody scalps and saw the guerrillas on parade not as staunchly independent men or highly accomplished warriors but as a group of savages indistinguishable from one another. He was only seeing evidence of one half of guerrilla manhood, the trophies taken. Those ribbons, fluttering so close to the scalps, created such a grotesque juxtaposition that it must have seemed that the guerrillas were making light of their bloodletting: it was merely a joke to them. Though the writer could not comprehend them, if he had he would have seen that those streamers of colored thread suggested another kind of prize, a trophy given. Those ribbons dancing so whimsically in the air were like flags announcing the presence of trophies hidden from view, prizes representing the other half of guerrilla manhood.[43]

Inside their clothes and close to their persons, the guerrillas held onto warped inversions of the ribbons and scalps. The guerrillas carried with them locks of their women's hair bound together by ribbons and twine. These tokens were tucked away in the pockets of another trophy that was given to the guerrillas and escaped the eye of that man at Boonville, their colorful guerrilla shirts. Some guerrillas, notably Anderson, seemed reticent to expose their shirts, symbols of intimacy that they were, to the world outside their community. Like the dainty locks of hair, the shirts were gifts from and pieces of their women. And like the love infused in them, the shirts marked the powerful but vulnerable part of their war, the part that had to be protected from ill-willed outsiders.[44]

To see the guerrillas as they saw themselves and as they were seen by their female kin, independent men eternally bound to their women, we must weave together two seemingly dichotomous lines of thought: ribbons and bloody flesh, Southern-sympathizing women's hair and Union men's scalps, feminized shirts and jackets of dead men, trophies given and trophies taken, things hidden and others brazenly displayed, the invisible and the visible, love and immortality. We need not ignore the complexity of these men and their appearance. If seen by an outsider, they might have appeared patched together, that they were men out of focus, and out of fashion, shape-shifting, liminal; they were murderous, walking send-ups of dandies, each with an Indian eye for style. Yet it is important to remember that when they saw each other out in the brush or their women laid eyes on them as they trotted out of the brush toward their homes, each man, each guerrilla was seen as he saw himself. They were Bill, Jim, Arch, and Jesse. They were brothers, sons, sweethearts, and husbands. Most of all, they were men.[45]

When Anderson tumbled from his horse on October 27, he had a scalp hanging from the bridle of his horse and a lock of hair from his wife and another from a sister in his pocket. His killers found these bits of feminine hair when they stripped him down to his guerrilla shirt, a sort of unmasking by which his true identity was revealed. In their final act as the creators of his shirt, Anderson's women had marked him not only as a guerrilla and a man, but also as a trophy. He was the trophy of all trophies taken by Union soldiers in Missouri. Because such a trophy had to be shared, he was photographed and his death image passed around the Union Army, then, generations later, passed down to historians. The continued relevance of this haunting image suggests that Anderson achieved some measure of immortality. His killers knew this picture would be seen by many eyes for many years, and they hoped that Anderson's strange appearance would paint him as a savage, a hope that has been realized in the work of many historians. However, in revealing his shirt and photographing it, those Union troops unwittingly tied one strand of guerrilla manhood to the other, thus completing the fabric of masculinity. Not only does the surviving image deepen and color Anderson's niche in the history books, but it plainly shows that he wore his heart on his sleeve.[46]

CHAPTER 6

The Rebel Horseman

IN THE SPRING OF 1865, William Clarke Quantrill left his stomping grounds in Missouri for Kentucky, where both he and his horse would die. William E. Connelley, one of the first historians of the guerrilla war, drew a direct connection between the death of Quantrill and the death of his horse, Charley. In his book *Quantrill and the Border Wars*, Connelley claimed that the guerrilla chieftain's "horse became a part of Quantrill, and the guerrillas believed he absorbed the nature of his master and became a guerrilla." They thought that the horse was "the best guard in camp and sounded many an alarm that saved the guerrilla band." Connelley was sure that the "horse did absorb the nature of Quantrill," because "[the horse] became vicious. . . . He would strike, bite, kick, and squeal if approached by others." However, while Quantrill and his band were resting one day in Kentucky, the guerrilla blacksmith, Jack Graham, set about shoeing Charley. In the process of paring the horse's hoofs, Graham struggled with the horse, leaving Charley hamstrung, necessitating that the animal be put down. When he heard of the accident, Quantrill read it as a sign that his own death was near. Indeed, the guerrilla chief was mortally wounded shortly after his beloved horse was ruined. In hindsight, it was simple to see why Quantrill understood Charley's death as a prologue to his own demise: without a horse, a man could not be a guerrilla, and in the brush a man who was not a guerrilla was as good as dead.[1]

At the center of both the myths and reality of the guerrilla war was the mounted man. The guerrillas imagined themselves as chivalric knights in the same mold as Sir Walter Scott's dashing heroes of medieval Europe, but they could only do so as long as they were astride charging steeds. There was nothing romantic or dashing about trudging on foot for miles along rutted roads, through mud, over hills, and across streams; marching was beneath these young men from the best families of Missouri. Tapping into the romantic imagery of Scott, Hamp Watts—a young guerrilla who fought with Bill Anderson—painted quite the image of his cohort. He remembered that "when in line, mounted on the finest of horses, the band certainly gave a 'Knightly' appearance." More than just an attempt to embody the characters of a fabled past, the use of horses made the men who fought as guerrillas into elite soldiers for their time and place. Going to war on thoroughbred (and even Arabian) horses quite literally made the guerrillas superhuman. Whether they were fighting foot soldiers or novice cavalrymen, the guerrillas' mastery of their animals gave them an incredible advantage in speed, strength, size, maneuverability, and power on both the tactical and strategic levels of warfare. Horses made the guerrilla war possible, made the guerrillas men, and propelled them into realm of legend.[2]

Despite the seemingly fundamental nature of horses to guerrilla warfare, historians have not examined the role of horses in the guerrilla war in much depth. Some historians have remarked that the guerrillas were universally mounted. However, what that fact might have meant in terms of the way the guerrillas fought or the bearing horses might have had on the outcome of the war in Missouri has never been studied in any significant way. When the subject is broadened to the role of the horse in the Civil War more generally, military historians contend that the horse became a less decisive factor in the American Civil War than it had been in previous conflicts, at least tactically speaking. There are some works, though, that attempt to understand the significance of the horse within antebellum culture and suggest that the horse remained important in the war, but only as a romantic symbol of chivalry. Indeed, the horse was an important symbol for the guerrillas, but it was hardly an empty one. By embracing important components of antebellum manhood, notably mastery and horsemanship, the guerrillas turned a cultural icon into the great tactical and strategic advantage of their warfare.[3]

To fully understand the significance of the horse in Civil War Missouri, the deep currents of horse culture in the white South must be examined. Beginning in the colonial period, settlers from England took advantage of the horse's many uses in places like Virginia. These settlers were well aware

"BABE," 1864

(Drawn by himself—in 1913)

A drawing of Babe Watts as he imagined himself astride his horse. This is the closest thing we have of a picture of what the guerrilla may have looked like in mounted action. It makes clear how important the horse was to guerrilla identity. Of special note is the heart on Watts's saddle. Clearly he loved this animal. (Watts, *Babe of the Company*)

of the benefits that could be yielded from the horse in farmwork, transportation, and warfare. Further, the exact circumstances of the society being created in the colonial South heightened the importance of these activities. A rural, agrarian world with a sprawling but sparse population surrounded by enemies was very much in need of all the services provided by the horse, and the solidification of African slavery as the primary form of labor only increased this need. As Southern society developed, it moved westward.

With their slaves in tow, white Southerners from Virginia pushed through Kentucky and eventually into Missouri in pursuit of cheap, fertile land. As they migrated west, they perpetually created communities along the frontier and the same factors that led colonial Virginians to bring the horse to the New World remained in play. Throughout the antebellum period and into the Civil War, Missouri was still a mostly rural, agrarian, slave-based society that had dealt with successive external threats in the forms of Native Americans, abolitionists from Kansas, and eventually Union soldiers.[4]

The horse was equally important as a source of transportation as it was a source of energy in farm production. On the farm the horse could be used as a draught animal to bring in the harvest or take goods to market. Horses could also be used to supply the energy for a mill. Perhaps their most important role on the farm was in pulling a plow to turn the soil and put a crop in the ground. Early in the history of colonial Virginia, English settlers used hoes rather than plows for the job of planting. Some historians have asserted that this was the result of Native American influence, as Indian women used hoes to break up the soil. It is just as likely, however, that the different farming techniques existed because settlers were having a difficult time maintaining a horse population in the New World. By the end of the seventeenth century there was a drastic increase in the number of working animals in the colony, and English settlers returned to European methods of farming in the production of their tobacco and other products. Oxen and mules were used to pull plows. However, the utility of the horse made them the most attractive option for plowing, as they could be unhitched and just as easily used for fast transportation across the vast countryside.[5]

Horses were critical to the protection of society in the South from external threats, especially along the frontier. These animals were used by men for ranging along the frontier in an effort to protect white families from Indian attacks. Beginning during the seventeenth century, bands of so-called rangers began to appear up and down the colonies, both in the North and in the South. In the colonies of the North, these men ranged on foot, while in the colonies of the South they traveled and fought on horseback. There are two possible reasons for the difference in approach. First, the landscape of Piedmont Virginia, where the first Southern rangers appeared, was more wide open and the settlements were separated by a greater distance than in the heavily wooded, and more densely populated northern colonies. Second, a "horse culture" existed in Virginia that did not exist in Puritan New England.

Whatever the reasons for the origin of the mounted ranger in Virginia, the tradition of mounted ranging went with them as they moved west. While they were hardly the only mounted rangers in Missouri, Daniel Boone's sons were the torchbearers of the mounted ranger tradition in Missouri. They famously rode on patrol from one end of the Boonslick region to the other and back, protecting whites from Indian attacks during the first few decades of settlement, a feat that was only possible on horseback.[6]

Also beginning in the colonial period, horses were used to protect the white community in the South from an internal enemy. Faced with the difficult task of trying to control the population of enslaved blacks who could disrupt society by running away or rising up in armed revolt, white men—slaveholders and nonslaveholders alike—established a system for protecting white families called the "slave patrol." After dark, the time when whites were most vulnerable and slaves had the most freedom of movement, a group of white men in a given neighborhood gathered together to patrol the countryside. A scholar and expert on the slave patrol says that "horses were essential in rural areas because slave patrols met in a central location, traveling from their individual residences, and then moved from plantation to plantation," and that "patrollers also relied upon horses for purposes of intimidation," as "a group of men on horseback, at night, could terrify slaves into submission." Without horses, the potentially unruly slave population would be otherwise uncontrollable.[7]

Mastery of the horse was an indicator of manhood. In addition to its important role in the serious aspects of Southern life, the horse played a central role in Southern recreation. In this arena, men used skills that were otherwise practical only in the most extreme circumstances of life. Horse racing was the most exciting of these leisure activities. It had its origins in colonial Virginia and came with Southerners when they moved west to Kentucky and Missouri. While horse racing was the sport of the planter class in its early existence, by the time it reached Missouri, men from all segments of white society took part in the competition, with the stakes of a race reflecting the status of the men involved. With speed and daring being essential to the sport, horse racing allowed a young man to show off his prowess as a horseman. Horse racing challenged the men in the saddle to push themselves and their mounts in ways that replicated the circumstances of a military venture. Older men could exhibit their prowess vicariously by having their son, a hired man, or a slave race their horses, or simply by betting on the horses of their friends

Significance of Horse Ownership through Comparative Analysis

State	Number of Horses
Missouri	361,874
Kentucky	355,704
Virginia	287,578

Missouri Guerrilla Co.	No. of Horses
Jackson Co.	6,502
Howard Co.	6,226
Chariton Co.	4,962
Boone Co.	9,292

Guerrilla Households	No. of Horses
Morgan Walker Hhld	25
Avg. Guerrilla Hhld	7

Tabulated from *Agriculture of the United States in 1860: Compiled from the Original Returns of the Eighth Census* (Washington, DC: Government Printing Office, 1864)

and family. Of the young men who were born and raised in this world and went into the brush, Joseph Bailey—a guerrilla himself—said, "As a rule they were ... superb horsemen."[8]

By the beginning of the Civil War, Missouri society was a horse culture. The large population of horses at the state level reinforces the idea that the horse was significant to white culture in antebellum Missouri. The state had a horse population of 361,874 in 1860, while the total number of white people in Missouri was 1,063,489 just before the Civil War. This created a ratio of one horse to three white persons. Virginia had substantially less horses at 287,578, while the white population was roughly the same as Missouri at 1,047,299. The ratio of horse to white person in Virginia was high, being a little bit more than one to four, but not as high as it was in Missouri.[9]

Within the state, the area in which guerrilla warfare took place had a disproportionately high horse population. In 1860 Jackson County had 6,502 horses. This number was comparable to other counties across the South better known for their horse culture. The importance of the horse in the South and horsemanship there were reflected in the number of horses owned in a specific area. Turner Ashby, who many thought was the greatest horseman in the South, resided in Fauquier County, Virginia which had 6,721 horses in 1860. In addition to Jackson County, several other Missouri counties that were hotbeds of guerrilla warfare compare favorably with counties where the significance of the horse in antebellum culture has been more tightly woven into their history. Howard County, where Clifton Holtzclaw resided, had 6,226 horses, and neighboring Chariton County had 4,962 horses in 1860. Chariton's neighbor to the south, Saline County, had 5,493 while Boone County had a whopping 9,292 horses just before the Civil War.[10]

When we look at the specific households that produced the guerrillas and supported their war we see an even greater emphasis on the horse. For instance, the Morgan Walker farm, from which Quantrill's guerrilla band originated, was home to a large stable of horses. According to the 1860 Federal Agriculture Census, Walker owned twenty-five horses. This was quite a bit more than his neighbors. The average number of horses owned by households in the Fristoe supply line was a little more than six. The Walker household had only six white members, meaning there were nearly five horses for each white person. Within the average household of the Fristoe supply line this ratio was much lower, but it was still relatively high compared to most other households of the day. The ratio was nearly one to one, as there were an average of seven white people in each household. Walker certainly had horses to spare for horse-based guerrilla warfare, and the ample number of his equine property made it possible for the guerrillas to constantly trade tired horses for fresh ones. While not nearly the size of Walker's herd, each household in the Fristoe supply line had a favorable horse to guerrilla ratio. With less than one guerrilla emerging from each household, the ratio was about six horses to every one guerrilla.[11]

Such a wealth of horses suggests an element of class among the guerrilla ranks. Given their cost, a horse—especially a good horse—was expensive enough that their ownership was limited. Over the decades of American settlement and expansion, equine ownership had become more democratized since the landed gentry of colonial Virginia began dabbling in horse racing. Nevertheless, the number of horses across the nation never amounted to a one-to-one ratio in horses to citizens. Among the myriad associations with the horse, the simple fact that a man could afford to do so made it attractive to go to war astride a horse. It is just as likely that horse ownership made it difficult for a man to surrender his horse to march and fight on foot while another man—a peer in the antebellum period—shouted orders down at him from atop his mount. When given a chance, the guerrillas often told allies and enemies alike that their cohort came from the best families in the state and their horses were symbols of this status. Indeed, in their minds a man on horseback was still above a great many people.[12]

The horse offered a platform for men to demonstrate their martial prowess. For men who were born in the lower ranks of society or found themselves as hired hands at the outset of the conflict, horsemanship was a way of showing their comrades that they did in fact belong in the guerrilla ranks. For instance, at the Morgan Walker farm two such hired men hopped on horses and used them effectively against enemies of the Southern household. In the fall of 1861, Morgan Walker "hired Jim Little . . . to range from place to place over the county to get news of the movements" of any invaders, be they jayhawkers or Union troopers. Sure enough, Walker's trusted man was able to sniff out a group of marauders and sound the alarm well ahead of their arrival. Not too much later, Quantrill would also prove himself to be a peer of the Southern menfolk. After his show of self-sacrifice, admitting to the death of the Union trooper during the fight at the Thompson house and making him a target of Union hostility, Quantrill showed his adopted community that he had the mettle to back up his talk. He was a horseman, and when the Union came after him with a squad of soldiers, he rode them out of their saddles.[13]

Quantrill was joined by other horsemen. To the young men who went into the brush and became guerrillas, it went without saying that they did so upon horseback. Horses were such an essential part of the guerrilla war that few guerrillas who left a memoir mention leaving home on a horse. Instead, they seem to have thought that the reader would make that assumption on their own, just as they and their families had assumed that fighting on horseback was the only way for young men to fight. Of the guerrillas who do mention leaving on horseback, the information was conveyed in a very matter-of-fact tone.[14]

The relationship between horse and man was transcendent. Once in the brush with their mounts, the guerrillas prepared the horses for their particular brand of combat. Most of the horses brought into the war had the intrinsic talent to be a bushwhacker mount, but the guerrillas nevertheless tested them. Walker recalled that "on coming into possession of a new animal, the first thing a bushwhacker would do was to break him to leaping fences, logs and gulleys, and traversing rough ground." This was done "so that they would not fail [the guerrillas] in an emergency." A practice run like the one described above would help the horse and rider get in step. The two beings became one, and the man was elevated to a greater sense of self. Now he identified as a horseman.[15]

As their "training" suggests, the horse was highly valued for its ability to move quickly across the countryside in combat situations. Speed and mobility were the most manifest of the tactical benefits derived from the horse. The horse enabled the guerrilla to enter combat situations with lightning quickness, often surprising and overpowering their enemies. Gregg described this tactic as it was used by the guerrillas early in the war. On February 22, 1862, Quantrill's small band of fifteen charged into Independence, Missouri. As Gregg remembered, as they sprinted into the town "of course there was a collision and while we lost two men and the enemy held the town, we had the better of the fight." Gregg recalled another instance when he and the guerrillas under his command used the speed of their mounts to attack their enemies. During a night battle, with Union troops bearing down on them, "Gregg ordered his men back from the crest of the ridge, giving a chance to see the enemy by sky light." There they waited. Eventually, "as soon as the enemy came in view, Gregg ordered a charge. The enemy was surprised and were hurled back at least half a mile."[16]

Speed and mobility were also used by the guerrillas to escape their enemies. The scatter technique was especially popular among the guerrillas. Harrison Trow recalled that "it was a part of Quantrill's tactics to disband every now and then." Trow remembered Quantrill saying that "scattered soldiers . . . make a scattered trail. The regiment that has but one man to hunt can never find him." Reducing the band to its smallest unit, the individual mounted man, allowed each guerrilla to harness the full potential of his animal's speed and mobility. Unfettered by formation, individual horses could outrun the more structured groups of Union horsemen, who tried to maintain their tight formations throughout the chase, and those free-wheeling horsemen, who scattered throughout the brush, riding in every direction, added confusion to the already challenging task facing their Union pursuers. Union General Thomas Ewing was all too aware of the deadly nature of this tactic. He said of the guerrillas, "When assemble[d] in a body of several hundred, they scatter before an inferior force; and when our troops scatter in pursuit, they reassemble to fall on an exposed squad, or a weakened post." Because of their ability to put distance between them and their pursuers, the guerrillas turned a successful retreat into an even more successful counterstrike.[17]

The horse made the guerrilla harder to kill. A mounted guerrilla was able to make the most of his one life. Essential to the guerrilla war strategy was an effort to string out the conflict, to make it a long, costly, and morale-deflating proposition for their Union enemies. At the risk of stating the obvious, in order to undertake such an initiative, the guerrillas had to keep up the fight, which in turn meant that they had to avoid dying. Because of both the limitations of many of the firearms used against the guerrillas—most notably the rifle musket, which required twenty to thirty seconds to reload after firing—and a densely wooded landscape that provided a seemingly infinite number of hiding places, the speed of these horses allowed the guerrillas to get out of a number of deadly scrapes. After the Union turned toward the bloodier strategy of no quarter in the spring of 1862, the horse became even more valuable. When the enemy's central purpose was killing—rather than conquest, pacification, or assimilation—then the greatest act of resistance became survival. For this reason, the horse was more important to the guerrilla than his gun.[18]

Knowing on a deep level that it was possible to escape even the direst situation could instill a spirit of invincibility in the heart of the guerrilla. At its best, this cockiness manifested in poise and coolness during a deadly firefight; it gave men the courage and daring to charge into the flank of a larger enemy force. Quantrill, when he was confronted in 1861 with the possibility that a price would be put on his head and he would be pursued by dozens to hundreds of Union troopers, he did not shrink at the long odds confronting him. Instead, he remarked to Andrew Walker, "They can't catch me." Furthermore, given the uncertainty of war—any war—and the guerrillas' own perception that they were waging a war against long odds, this aspect of self-assurance in their collective personality created a positive outlook on their day-to-day existence. This did not wipe away fear but minimized it. Although it is very difficult to gauge the guerrillas' collective morale throughout the war, it seems that they were generally optimistic. Dark humor and a devil-may-care attitude permeates the small amount of wartime record that exists and appears frequently in the postwar narratives.[19]

Confidence can quickly become an overinflated sense of self, especially for young men. For the guerrillas this most often materialized in the form of the occasional suicidal charge (suicidal in *our* minds, but probably not in theirs!). However, arrogance first appeared in the guerrillas' negligence. Early in the war, they failed to put pickets out when they ate and rested at their supporters' homes. Gregg recalled the first time Quantrill and his band lost their horses. On March 22, 1862, Quantrill's small band of twenty men was ambushed and trapped at the Tate house in Jackson County. Gregg said "when Quantrill and his men made a dash . . . [they] escaped with the loss of their horses." After the Tate house the men had to stop fighting, scatter on foot, and find new mounts. Perhaps they were able to find new horses too easily, because they did not develop a strong sense of value for the animals. Gregg said that from the Tate house debacle "to about the middle of April, it was a series of surprises for Quantrill and his men, in each case losing our horses, which was a great drawback." This realization was the turning point. After this stretch, the guerrillas did not "lose horses in any considerable number, but often beat the enemy out of theirs." Perhaps they realized that when they lost their horses, they were all but useless as men in the brush. A lost horse was not only a loss of the ability to fight as a guerrilla, it was also a loss of confidence. Without those powerful feelings of self-belief, a man went scrambling desperately to find a new mount, something to make him whole again.[20]

The bond between the guerrilla and his horse was unique even among other men who fought on horseback during the Civil War. This is not to say that cavalrymen on both sides did not form strong relationships with their mounts, only that these individual relationships were secondary to the primary purpose of the cavalry. More and more, the horse was being thought of as just a conveyance for transporting men to reconnoiter or screen for the army, carrying them quickly to the battlefield, and moving them across the battlefield. In this context, the horse was one part of the government issued equipment provided to a cavalryman. Furthermore, the army was responsible for the upkeep of the horse either directly or indirectly and if a horse was ever shot out from under a horse soldier, he was not doomed; the army would merely provide him with another mount. The horse was not intended to facilitate masculine independence or even a real freedom of movement. Instead, cavalry horses were only good if they allowed the men who rode them to maintain formation, execute orders, and keep formal army discipline in the face of battle. Both armies were even working to decouple the soldier from his horse in combat. In other words, officers found that cavalrymen were much more effective fighting on foot than on horseback.[21]

The guerrilla fully embraced his horse's individual personality. Four decades after the war, Gregg wrote about his war horse, Scroggins. In a piece which was intended to be a chapter for his memoir, he tried to explain why this horse, out of all the horses he rode during the war, was so unique. Gregg recalled one battle in which Scroggins proved an invaluable asset to his rider. Gregg wrote that, "Scroggins and I led the attack, twenty feet being as near as I could get to the embankment . . . and when that close, the enemy would rise and fire at me." It was just then that "Scroggins would drop to the ground on his 'belly' and lay there until the firing had ceased when he would rise up again." Neither the horse nor the rider were hit in the fight. Even more important to Gregg than the horse's performance in battle was that Scroggins had protected his wife during their "wedding tour" to Texas. Gregg recalled that when his wife was asked by a friend if she was scared during a firefight that occurred on the ride south, Mrs. Gregg said, "No . . . I was on Scroggins." Lizzie Gregg held great admiration for the horse, and Scroggins became something of a stand-in for Gregg, there to protect his wife when he could not. Gregg left Scroggins in Texas with his wife when he returned to the war on another mount, essentially leaving part of himself there to look after his young bride.[22]

Horses began to demonstrate their personalities in a variety of ways. They took their horses into the brush for their speed and strength, but once in the brush the guerrillas discovered unintended benefits of having their horses with them. For instance, Gregg, while riding through the night tried to take his horse over the Smith's Fork River. When he and his horse approached a covered bridge, the horse refused to enter it. Gregg originally thought it was because the bridge was too dark and the horse would not go where he could not see. In fact, it was just the opposite. According to Gregg "a flash of lightening disclosed the trouble, the bridge was full of sleeping militia." Bailey also found his horse to be helpful at night, remembering that he and his comrades stopped posting a guard at night once they realized that their horses were up to the task. The horses could detect someone at a much greater distance than the men ever could. If the horse detected someone, it would give a snort or display "a listening attitude."[23]

The advantages provided by the horse were not without their costs. In addition to the fact that without horses the guerrillas were unable to defend their homes, horses required upkeep. The animals needed substantial food, water, and rest. Without enough of any one of these things, horses would decline in performance and get a guerrilla killed. Bailey stated that to feed and groom the horses was their first care, as the men depended on the horses' speed and endurance for survival. He even claimed that he and other guerrillas would go hungry to feed their horses. There were many offhand references by Bailey and other guerrillas about watering their horses, something they seemed to do whenever possible. Resting their horses was also important. Any chance they could, they let their animals rest. If they were too tired, horses were traded out for fresh ones. This often occurred, with the original animals being returned to their owners after a short time.[24]

While the rebels in Missouri were dealing with the old problems of caring for their animals, the Union occupying forces were trying to master new technology that had yet to be used in warfare. To try to subdue the rebels, Union forces were now using both the railroad and the telegraph, two new technologies that enabled the overall strategy applied by the Union forces to the occupation of Missouri. The garrisoned towns established across the state by the Union were, many times, towns with the railroad running through them and/or with a telegraph office. From these centers of men, matériel, and information, the Union army hoped to control the countryside by sending patrols out to places where the guerrillas were reportedly located. Information came into a garrison via rider, railroad, or telegraph, and in response, the commander sent out the appropriate number of troops in the direction of trouble. Post commanders could also send requests for more troops or matériel out to other nearby posts or even the department headquarters in St. Louis. If they were granted their request, the desired men or matériel would then arrive via railroad.[25]

Union men placed their faith in the massive institution that was the army's logistical infrastructure. Exploiting the benefits of the railroads and telegraph lines, the occupation plan for Missouri was strong. The system was designed so that the Union army could control local communities while maintaining the advantages of being a part of larger statewide and national efforts to defeat the rebellion. Theoretically, an outpost in the middle of Missouri was connected to the centralized war machine in the North. This was the first time a policy like this had ever been implemented, and in this sense it was the first modern attempt at a counterinsurgency strategy by an industrialized power.[26]

The guerrillas quickly showed just how tenuous the lines of communication and transportation for the Union occupation were. Once they realized the advantage that the telegraph lines gave to Union officers, guerrillas made sure to cut them whenever possible. The disruption of Union communications allowed guerrillas to attack one outpost without fear of troops from another coming to their comrades' aid. Further, Union officers, who had become reliant upon the lightning-quick communications between outposts, were forced into the uncomfortable practice of sending out runners, who were vulnerable to ambush by guerrillas. Guerrillas also made sure to rip up railroad tracks and burn railroad bridges whenever possible. This limited the ability of the central hubs in places like St. Louis to resupply the outposts across the state. In short, by attacking the lines of communication and transportation, the guerrillas isolated each garrisoned town, forcing the Union troops in a specific town to fight a local war against the rebel communities, who controlled the surrounding countryside. Each post was a Union island in the middle of the angry rebel sea.[27]

Even when they were able to use their technology against the guerrillas, it took special circumstances for it to be effective in direct ways. A raid on the town of Laclede made by Clifton Holtzclaw and his band of guerrillas offers a useful illustration of the ways in which horse-based warfare was successful against the type of warfare preferred by the Union army. On June 18, 1864, Holtzclaw and some fifteen other men stormed into the northern Missouri town from the west. The speed of their attack allowed the guerrillas to take the town with minimal resistance, though two incidents occurred. While they rounded up the pro-Union townspeople into the town square, a man named David Crowder took a pot shot at the guerrillas from inside a building, hitting Jim Nave and wounding him. Nave quickly turned and shot Crowder, killing him. Another townsman, Jonathan Jones, ran from the guerrillas, despite their warnings. He too was shot and killed. With the other residents of the town under guard, the guerrillas began taking contraband from the people, whom they thought to be affiliated with the Union occupation force.[28]

Someone was able to escape the guerrillas, however, and head toward the Union garrison at nearby Brookfield. Holtzclaw and his men would have the town to themselves for only a short while. The guerrillas relieved some ten citizens of nearly $4,000, a few pistols, some liquor, and other assorted valuables, in addition to several fine horses. While his men looted the town, Holtzclaw issued a warning to its inhabitants, that "if any of his southern friends were abused . . . he would deal with them severely, killing two for one." Perhaps even as the guerrilla chief proclaimed these words, Lieutenant Billings, in charge of the Union post at Brookfield, was being informed of the guerrillas' presence in Laclede. Billings took immediate action. Only two and a half miles away, Billings knew he had a chance of catching and killing the guerrillas. All that mattered now was speed. He put a soldier on every horse he could find, and along with a Lieutenant Lewis, Billings led the mounted soldiers toward Laclede. Before he left, he put the remainder of his force, those without horses, on a train that ran between Brookfield and Laclede.[29]

Two conflicts unfolded at Laclede, one atypical of guerrilla–Union trooper interactions and the other a more common happening. The former was a running fight between the locomotive and a group of guerrillas. Whether through sight, sound, intuition, or perhaps the observational skills of their horses, the guerrillas were alerted to the impending arrival of Union troops. Nave, who could not ride as a result of his wound, was loaded into the back of a buggy that had been used by the government to deliver mail. The hack was driven by another guerrilla, with a third man riding "shotgun." It was escorted by two more guerrillas on horseback. The mail hack-turned-ambulance departed in the direction of Locust Bottoms, to the west of Laclede, and just as it lumbered out of town, the train from Brookfield rolled into Laclede. Seeing the guerrillas rolling down a road that ran parallel to the railroad tracks, the engineer sped up in pursuit. According to a Union report, as the engine chugged up behind them, the guerrillas "had some distance to go by the side of the track, before they could turn, off [sic]." The guerrillas in the hack, even though it was moving as quickly as it could, had no chance in a head-to-head race with the engine. Crawling with Union soldiers armed with rifles and shotguns, the engine pulled up alongside the hack. From atop the train, the soldiers fired into the guerrillas like some grotesque version of a buffalo hunt. All of the guerrillas were hit. Nave was killed, the two other men on the hack were wounded, and both escorts were mortally wounded. Here the full force of the Union logistical leviathan wrecked the guerrillas who found themselves in its path.[30]

In the brush, however, the mounted and unfettered guerrilla was better than his blue-clad foe. While the remarkable running fight took place along the railroad tracks, Holtzclaw scattered the remainder of his men in all directions. They each rode out of Laclede as quickly as they had sprinted into the town. Lieutenant Lewis was tasked with the job of pursuing Holtzclaw and his men, and a Union report describes his pursuit: "Lewis heard of [the guerrillas] from place to place . . . they had just gone on such a road but a short time . . . but after riding in that direction 8 or 10 miles, would hear of them in another direction." After two days of tracking the guerrillas, Lewis and his men traveled around sixty miles and found themselves right back where they started—"within 2½ miles of Laclede again." They never saw a guerrilla. One Union officer said of Lewis's efforts, "This trip has again proven to me the perfect folly of chasing bushwhackers." Man for man, there was no contest.[31]

As the confrontation between Union soldiers and Holtzclaw's guerrillas showed, only in the most irregular circumstances did the rails provide the Union army with a direct tactical advantage. More often than not, horses, the way in which the guerrillas used them, and the local nature of guerrilla warfare nullified the benefits of the railroad to move men and materials quickly from one place to another. Confined to the static location of the track on which it rolled, the train and everything along its tracks could simply be avoided when the circumstances required that type of action. Horses, as has been shown, did not have such limitations. The freedom of direction enabled the guerrillas to take Union companies like Lieutenant Lewis's away from their source of supply and ride them around in circles until they gave up. Furthermore, the guerrillas had little use for the strategic advantages that the railroad offered. Their conflict was a local one and therefore a tactical one, at least in the way that commanders of the formal armies understood the meaning of tactical. The guerrillas had no need to move large groups of men from one end of the state to another. Their horses worked just fine getting them around their neighborhoods, from one rebel household to the next.[32]

While there was no guarantee of success, the Union army realized that their only chance of combating the guerrillas was to beat them at their own game, a game played on horseback. During summer 1864, Union general Clinton Fisk told the commander of the Department of Missouri that he was "adopting the bushwhacking tactics," and that he would "now bushwhack them." General Fisk wanted his men to surprise the guerrillas and charge upon them with such speed and power that they would not be able to retreat. A Union colonel articulated how important mounted troops were in combating the guerrillas. He said, "One main object of my being here is as I understand it is to clear the country of guerrillas. To do this it will be necessary to have some cavalry for scouting." Left with infantry, this officer would only be able to hold the garrisoned town in which he and his men were stationed. Foot soldiers could not range across the countryside at the same speed as cavalry, and they would fall easy prey to the mounted guerrillas.[33]

All of the horses immediately accessible to the guerrillas gave them an advantage over Union forces in the area. A lot has been made of the material advantage the Union army held over Confederate forces during the Civil

War, and it has been assumed that the same material superiority existed in Missouri's guerrilla conflict. Based on all of the scholarship comparing the differences in Union and Confederate resources, there is no reason to doubt that the formal armies of the Confederacy suffered a disadvantage. In Missouri, however, the Union army seemed to be always in need of horses. In an all too common report, a Union officer requested "that at least one hundred (100) more cavalrymen be sent to me as soon as practible [sic]." His command's duties were "so heavy that . . . it will unfit [the horses] totally." There were a large number of requests for all the materials required to keep horses alive as well. Union general E. B. Brown complained of "the scarcity of forage in [his] District, and the fact that the speculators have control of large quantities, which they hold at twice its former value." Another Union officer requested "one hundred and fifty thousand feet of inch lumber to build sheds for the horses" during one winter. Without the shelter the "horses will soon be wholly unfit for service." To rival the world of their enemies that had been built by and for horses, men in the Union army tried to construct a parallel world which would support their mounts, a task they found to be difficult, if not entirely unsustainable.[34]

To supplement their horse supply, the Union army took horses from the Southern-sympathizing population of Missouri. The Union army considered the horses to be contraband and took them from Missouri citizens who were suspected of being sympathetic to the rebellion. While they wanted to take horses from disloyal citizens as early as 1862, Union policy in this early stage of the war prohibited them from doing so, although the examples of Walker and Younger show that Union troops did not always abide by such restrictions. By 1863 it seems that Union policy had changed so that horses could be liberated from Southern farms for use as Union cavalry mounts. One order that permitted the taking of horses from rebels was General Order No. 58, which prevented Southerners who were related to Confederate soldiers from moving stock out of the state but allowed it to be taken by the Union army. The Union forces replenished their horses in this way. Taking Missouri horses had just as much to do with quality as it did quantity. Missouri horses had great pedigree and most horses in the area could be traced back to fine stock in Kentucky or had been bred from Arabians. The Union soldier Wiley Britton commented that their horses were collected mostly from Missouri and Kansas because they were better for service in that area than those raised in northern latitudes. Horses from a state like Ohio were just not good enough.[35]

Guerrillas, not to be outdone, responded to the shift in Union strategy by taking horses from Union men in Little Dixie. Holtzclaw and his band were prolific in removing horses from local pro-Union militiamen, robbing them of their ability to combat the guerrillas in any practical way. In July 1863, around the same time that Holtzclaw's band had visited W. H. Sidner's house in Linn County, the guerrilla captain was on a mission to collect from each Union militiamen his horse and gun. While they did not end up taking Sidner's horse because it was a nag, they would take a gun and a horse from his neighbor, a Mr. Haiters. They then went to another house, a Mr. Buckman's, and took another horse. Each horse taken from these militiamen was a two-horse swing in the war for horses.[36]

Women took action to help the Southern side win this equine battle and protect themselves and their homes. The guerrilla community had to find a balance between those used for the war and those used for farmwork. The high horse-to-white person ratio allowed for some flexibility in the usage of the animals. For instance, it is doubtful that any cavalry unit in either formal army ever had the six–to-one horse-to-rider ratio that the guerrillas had. This high ratio created a situation in which some horses could be left at home while a substantial number were still available for combat. Horses left on the farm gave women the ability to do jobs they might not have been able to do otherwise. Knowing this, the men felt more comfortable leaving their women on the farm while they went off to war.[37]

Sometimes rebel women took initiative in holding onto their horses. Britton said, "It is a rare occurrence now to find a family with more than two or three horses . . . which are generally either old or blind. Families sometimes try to keep their horses concealed in the woods, but this is not very successful." If they really wanted to hold onto a few horses so that they would not be taken, rebel women took drastic steps. Britton observed that "the great temptation to keep good, vigorous animals . . . has in a number of instances, led to the putting out of the eyes of desirable horses." Britton could not help but feel for "a mother with half a dozen children around her and her husband away in either the Union or Rebel army, might . . . permit a young son . . . to destroy the sight of 'Charley,' the good, reliable family horse." With a blind horse, rebel women would "cultivate and gather the crop . . . [and] take the grain, wheat or corn, to the mill, and to fetch back the flour or meal."[38]

Rebel women and their blind horses provided for themselves, their families, their men, and the sighted guerrilla horses. Women used their horses to plow and plant seeds for the majority of the crops needed to keep their families alive, but they also planted crops meant to be fodder for their horses. Hay was the dominant food for horses in antebellum Missouri. On the Fristoe supply line, the rebel households each grew an average of 5 tons of hay a year. They also averaged the production of 63 bushels of wheat and nearly 2,000 bushels of corn a year, all food that could be used to feed their plow horses and the guerrillas' mounts. Further east, the rebel households in the Holtzclaw supply line grew an average of 10 tons of hay a year, according to the 1860 Federal Agriculture Census. They also grew nearly 100 bushels of wheat and 1,300 bushels of corn on a yearly basis, plenty for rebel women, men, and horses to live off.[39]

Rebel women, in making their horses unfit for combat, knew that their men had an advantage in finding rides elsewhere. Sidney Jackman, a Confederate officer who used guerrilla tactics more often than not recalled that after a year and a half they "knew well how to acquire horses." This sentiment was echoed elsewhere, albeit not as succinctly. The guerrillas were constantly acquiring and trading horses. They tried to hold onto their favorites, but the exigencies of war meant that horses were lost, stolen, and killed. However, within the rebel community there were ample horses, and one only need to move on to the next barn if one's current mount was unsatisfactory.[40]

Besides the clear advantage in the number of horses owned by rebellious Missourians over those that were readily accessible to the Union army, there were reports that the guerrillas may have been bringing in herds of horses from outside. In one of his final reports, Union "detective" and "scout" Harry Truman claimed to have a bead on five guerrilla bands: Quantrill's, Holtzclaw's, Jim Jackson's, David Poole's, and Jim Anderson's. According to Truman, Union officials had to act quickly, as the guerrillas had "some thirty head of horse" that they were bringing down from northern Missouri. He told his superiors that the "stock can be captured if you will make a move on it soon." It is unclear whether or not Truman took part in the surrender of any of these men, but his intention to get the men to surrender before they could get the fresh horses into action comes across very clearly.[41]

As important as the horse was during the war, it would become legendary during the postwar period. Many of these legends were crafted by John Edwards. Noted Guerrillas, his so-called history, turned Gregg, Younger, Quantrill, Todd, Anderson, and others into heroes on the level of the champions and near-gods of classical Greece and Rome. While it was nominally about Quantrill, this passage by Edwards offered a rather revealing description of the guerrilla as an archetype: "He was a living, breathing, aggressive, all-powerful reality—riding through the midnight, laying ambuscades by lonesome road-sides, catching marching columns by the throat, breaking in upon the flanks and tearing a suddenly surprised rear to pieces; vigilant, merciless, a terror by day and a superhuman if not supernatural thing when there was upon the earth blackness and darkness." Whatever criticism has been directed at *Noted Guerrillas* for its "lost cause" message, literary flourish, and mythologizing, this passage should not be completely dismissed as fanciful imagery. The midnight rider Edwards sought to describe *was* more than a man. This all-powerful reality was two separate beings fused together—man *and* horse.[42]

Chapter 7

The Rebel Gun

On the night of March 22, 1862, William Clarke Quantrill and twenty or so guerrillas were trapped in a burning house surrounded by a few hundred Union troopers. After a brief firefight, the guerrillas voted to try and make a break from the house for the safety of the woods. Cole Younger remembered that at that moment "Quantrill said quietly, 'Shotguns to the front.'" John McCorkle recalled the guerrilla chief ordering the men who only had revolvers to "stoop and jump as far as you can, shooting with both hands." When the men were ready, Quantrill threw the front door open and sprang from the building. With his revolver he shot a Union soldier and kept right on running through the Union line. Immediately behind Quantrill came six men with shotguns, including Younger. These men fired their spread of buckshot into the Union troopers to their left and right, either hitting them or forcing their heads down. Just behind them were men like McCorkle, who fired their pistols with each hand as they sprinted through the gap in the Union cordon. According to Younger, "In less time than it takes to tell it, the rush was over." With a few shotguns and pistols, the small band of guerrillas was able to take on a much larger Union force and live to fight another day.[1]

The guerrillas adopted a weapon that allowed them to combat long odds. At first glance, the guerrillas and their pistols would appear to be outmatched by the Union troopers and their rifles. Where the leaders of the conventional armies found merit in the long arms, the young men who fought as guerrillas rejected the superiority of the rifle musket. Rather, they considered several factors when selecting a weapon—whether it could be wielded on horseback, its effectiveness in close-quarter fighting, and whether or not it gave a man the best chance to defend his household against all comers. While many young men held onto the shotguns and rifles that they brought from home when they first entered the brush, they acquired revolvers as soon as they could. The revolver was not a long-range weapon, being accurate only to a short distance, but the handheld weapon carried six rounds that could be fired in rapid succession. In other words, the guerrillas chose a high rate of fire and versatility over long range and accuracy. Such a unique weapon would have to be mastered, however, and in the process of mastering their revolvers the guerrillas would become masters of themselves, something that distinguished them from other men who participated in the war.[2]

The image of Civil War soldiers armed almost exclusively with revolvers is very different from the iconic image of men armed with rifle muskets lined up to fire en masse at their enemies. Despite the remarkable armament of the guerrillas, little historical analysis has been brought to bear on the significance that these weapons had on the guerrilla conflict. The works that give the most attention to the firearms used in the guerrilla war are the oldest histories of the conflict. These historians were the first to assert the guerrillas' preference for the pistol. Unfortunately, they do little more than offer anecdotal observations of the potential firepower such a weapon might give the guerrillas. Nor has the discussion been moved forward since then, perhaps because military history has been pushed to the fringe of academia. Staying as far as possible from military history and all its elements, the most modern studies of the guerrilla war do not discuss weaponry. Despite their focus on the amount of violence committed in the guerrilla conflict, scholars show little interest in the actual tools of that bloodletting. By looking especially at Quantrill's band as a representative group but also including the guerrillas of central Missouri and a few other outliers, we will examine fully the relationship between the tools of violence and the men who wielded them.[3]

The story behind the selection and use of these tools began long before the war. From an early age, boys in the South learned how to use firearms effectively. The rural landscape of the South made the gun important on a variety of levels, from recreation to warfare. Hunting was an important part of the Southern lifestyle, and not just as a source of food. Skill in hunting could increase a young man's masculine prowess in the eyes of his peers, and the isolated nature of living conditions in this rural place also made

Cole Younger as he appeared during the war. He was described as broad and powerful in his body, and his face would seem to confirm his stature. (William E. Connelley, *Quantrill and the Border Wars*)

the gun important for personal defense. The constant fear of slave rebellion meant white Southerners were always on guard, keeping guns close at hand. Southerners also fought Native Americans throughout the colonial period and into the antebellum period and took on foreign powers in the French and Indian War, the American Revolution, and the War of 1812—and they were the first to volunteer to fight the Mexicans in the war for Texas independence and the Mexican-American War. There always seemed to be another war in which men from the South would need to fight.[4]

Missouri boys were no exception when it came to the youthful inundation into the South's gun culture. Younger's childhood experience with firearms was typical for boys raised in and around Jackson County. In his autobiography, Younger recalled that he mostly learned to shoot by hunting. He said that "wild game was plentiful on my father's farm on Big Creek near Lee's Summit." Perhaps exaggerating a bit, Younger said, "I cannot remember when I did not know how to shoot. I hunted wild geese when I could not have dragged a pair of them home unaided." Embellished or not, Younger's point is well taken. For boys in antebellum Missouri, learning to shoot was as fundamental as learning to walk.[5]

The significance of firearms went beyond the practical need to shoot one's dinner; they were an important feature of white manhood in the antebellum South. In the first place, white men, unlike slaves or women, were generally the only persons allowed to carry firearms, marking their status above these dependent groups. Through the use of a firearm a man displayed the quality of his character. It was for this reason that men like Younger learned to shoot at such a young age. Being skilled with a gun was no small talent, as the respect of other white men in the community was a necessary ingredient in the making of a man.[6]

Guns became instrumental in creating masculine independence for white men in Missouri. They were used to keep dependent members of the household in line and keep those from outside their communities out. They also allowed white men to establish and maintain their independence from one another; on a fundamental level, guns made each white man equal. No white man could infringe on another unless he was willing to face the harsh consequences of powder and ball. The sentiment of a phrase made famous in the postwar period could not have been truer in the antebellum South: "God made men, but Samuel Colt made them equal."[7]

Young men in Missouri were familiar with the range of new weaponry available to men. Relatively speaking, they had the most recent encounters with hostile Indians, and in 1838 men from Missouri, born in the South, had also driven the Mormons out of the state. By the time of the Civil War, men from the state of Missouri, knowing firsthand how important western lands were for future generations of slaveholders, made up large contingencies of the forces that took part in the antebellum wars of expansion. The original American families that settled in Texas and later fought for the independence of Texas from Mexico came from Missouri, and Missourians made up the bulk of Alexander Doniphan's expedition during the Mexican-American War. Also, the army sent to conquer the Mormons in Utah originated in Missouri.[8]

More than any other reason, boys turned to their guns because of the border war with the abolitionists who had settled in the Kansas territory in the 1850s. The history of the border conflict is well known and will not be revisited here, but it serves to illustrate the need for violence or the threat of violence to maintain such a fragile system of labor as race-based slavery in the mid-nineteenth century. The challenge of keeping people enslaved was made more problematic by the presence of jayhawkers. Crossing over from Kansas with the intention of liberating black men and women, killing their owners, and otherwise robbing or destroying other property, jayhawkers offered the most immediate reason for young white men of the Civil War generation to pick up their guns in the years, months, and days leading up to the war.[9]

The Younger household was attacked by jayhawkers in just such a way. According to Younger, when his father was "in Washington attending to some business regarding [his mail contract], a raid was made by the Kansas Jayhawkers upon the livery stable and stage line for several miles out into the country, the robbers also looting his store and destroying his property generally." While they may have been waiting for their father to offer guidance as to how they should act, such an assault would no doubt have led the Younger boys to think of how they might defend themselves. They were likely more vigilant, carrying guns at all times while awake and leaving them loaded and nearby their beds while asleep. They may have even done what Andrew Walker, Quantrill, and Jim Little had done and patrolled their neighborhood on the lookout for jayhawkers.[10]

Right around the time of the border war in Missouri, Samuel Colt's revolver was becoming a more common sight in the hands of the various kinds of men who were using violence to make their way in the West. Colt received his first United States patent for the "revolving gun" in 1836. Because of where he was born, Colt was exposed at an early age to the seemingly limitless possibilities of industrialization. Exposure to industrialization in general and the time spent working in his father's textile mill served as fertile ground for ideas. However, the seed of inspiration was planted during his brief time away from Connecticut, working as a sailor. While watching the waterwheel of the ship turn, Colt observed that each individual paddle passed at the exact same point every time. With the idea that soldiers always wanted more firepower in the back of his mind, he now knew how to give it to them: he would make a gun with multiple barrels that would rotate like the waterwheel. The first batch of revolving firearms was sold to the United States army in 1837 to fight the Seminoles in Florida. Every soldier who used the weapon fell in love with it. After a brief hiatus from the gun business, Colt again sold revolvers to arm the Texas soldiers during the Mexican-American War in 1846, during which time it became incredibly popular.[11]

After the Mexican-American War, the cap-and-ball revolver became a standard issue firearm for the United States cavalry. The bulk of the United States cavalry was stationed in the West during the 1850s at places like Fort Leavenworth, located just on the western side of the Missouri River in the Kansas Territory. The people living around the fort, both in Kansas and

Missouri, became accustomed to seeing the troopers and their armaments. Some men, like Quantrill, who had recently moved out to the West, saw the weapons in action, and the experiences of the many other Missourians who also served as soldiers in the same war led them, and their rivals across the border, to purchase the guns during the border war or at least see the their benefits.[12]

Despite knowledge of the revolver's capabilities, it was not universally owned before the Civil War. When they left home for the brush for the first time, many young men brought with them whatever firearms they had at home when the conflict began. These were typically weapons that had great utility before the war, like shotguns and rifles that could be used for hunting as well as personal defense. When Andrew Walker went out to "bushwhack them Feds" with a slave, they "took two double-barrel shotguns." When John McCorkle and his cousin George Wigginton left home to join Quantrill, McCorkle had "a rifle and eight cartridges and George [had] a double-barreled shotgun." When Samuel Hildebrand began his guerrilla career, he took "Kill-devil," his rifle. Hildebrand, McCorkle, Wigginton, and Walker were all experienced with shotguns and rifles and were comfortable with them, which explains why they took them out into the brush.[13]

The guerrillas made good use of their rifles and shotguns. In his first action under Quantrill, McCorkle's rifle came in handy. In a joint effort with some regular Confederate forces to take the town of Independence on February 22, 1862, McCorkle found himself next to Confederate colonel Upton Hayes. Hayes saw Union soldiers taking positions behind a stone fence and knew that if something was not done quickly, the Confederates and guerrillas would be pinned down. McCorkle remembered that Hayes "said 'John, you are the only man with a long-range rifle. Make those fellows take their heads down.'" McCorkle took aim and "fired, but the first shot fell short. I fired the second shot and they all fell off the fence and didn't stick their heads up anymore."

Hildebrand also had success with his rifle. He went into the brush alone and stalked a man named McIlvaine who was a part of the pro-Union militia that had done so much harm to Hildebrand and his family. After watching McIlvaine's field for days, his target came out to make his rounds. Hildebrand recalled McIlvaine "stopped to whet his scythe," about one hundred yards away. When McIlvaine was done, he "for a moment stood resting on the handle. [Hildebrand] fired, and [McIlvaine] fell dead."[14]

A nineteenth-century drawing of Hildebrand's long-range kill-shot of his enemy McIlvaine. Despite the crude quality of the image, it illustrates Hildebrand's skill with his rifle and demonstrates an alternative form of killing to that of the pistoleer. As he was a stalker and an assassin, there was still a level of intimacy to the way in which Hildebrand killed, despite the distance between him and his target. (Samuel Hildebrand, *Autobiography*)

Some guerrillas held onto their rifles and shotguns for the length of their service in the war and even used them as their primary weapon. Hildebrand was the most notable of these men. As a result of his preference for "Kill-devil" over the revolvers he carried, Hildebrand's fighting style in southeastern Missouri was very different from that of Younger and the guerrillas on the western border. Hildebrand stalked his prey like a hunter, moving quietly, slowly, and patiently across the landscape. The guerrilla boasted in his memoir that he "could always hit a spot as large as a man's hand at that distance [100 yards] with old 'Kill-devil.'" He would position himself about that far from his target and wait until he showed himself or walked into his line of fire. Hildebrand claimed that his rifle only failed him once, and otherwise he hit just about everything for which he aimed, rather like Robin Hood. Hildebrand may have been full of himself, as he consciously tried to construct this noble image of his wartime action, but it seems beyond dispute that he fancied his own rifle and seemed to benefit from his familiarity with it.[15]

Even if they kept their long arms, most guerrillas found revolvers to be more favorable and acquired them as soon as possible. Andrew Walker said, "Everyone, unless a fresh recruit, wore two six-shooters," which were "Colt's cap-and-ball pistols." He recalled that "at the beginning of the war, many of the men were armed with sabers as well, and many provided with long firearms." However, "in due time all implements of war, save pistols and knives, were put aside." Some, like Younger, left home with a revolver. In his memoir, he said that "armed with a shot-gun and revolver, I went out into the night and was a wanderer." McCorkle does not state the exact moment when he picked up and began using a revolver, but it is likely that it happened in the wake of the successful attack on Independence. The guerrillas and Confederate forces captured all the Federal arms kept in the town and also took back whatever arms had been taken from Southern sympathizers by the provost marshal. It is more than likely that the revolvers were the first to be snatched up by the victors.[16]

There were a few reasons why the guerrillas picked up and armed themselves with revolvers as quickly as they could. The rapidity with which the guerrillas could fire multiple rounds was a clear benefit that was also increased because the small size of the revolver meant that each man could carry anywhere from two to six, and perhaps even more than six revolvers. The small, handheld size of the revolver also meant that they were a perfect complement to their mounted style of fighting. With reins in one hand and a pistol in the other, the guerrillas could ride upon their enemies, discharge a relatively large volume of fire, and ride off again out of the effective range of musket fire. Moreover, some of the revolver's downside was nullified by the environment. The lack of range, for instance, was less important in the densely wooded areas that covered much of Missouri. Shear volume of fire also made up for any issues with accuracy from which the revolver suffered.[17]

In addition to the benefits the revolver offered them, the ability to choose and acquire their own firearms was essential to guerrilla manhood, which dictated that these men had a choice, a say in their fate at almost every instance. They were volunteers, fighting for themselves, their families, and their property, and no one had the right to force another man to arm himself in a certain way, especially when it was each man's responsibility to furnish his own equipment. In the brush, the location of power in terms of how he might arm himself was within the individual man, no matter his position within the guerrilla band. Each man came to his own conclusion that the utility and effectiveness of the revolver made it the best possible weapon in the brush.[18]

Freedom of choice was still open to the influence of peers. Older guerrillas mentored their younger kinsmen regarding the appropriate armament for their bloody work. When the guerrillas were fighting in small groups, it was necessary to know what arms the other members of the cohort were carrying and with which ones they were proficient. Any guerrilla would prefer that his brothers and cousins were armed as well as they could be; he might need any one of these men to come to his aid. Likewise, most guerrillas felt accountable to their cohort. The group then, in addition to the individual, had an interest in the superior handheld firepower that the revolver could unleash.

The location of power in the guerrilla ranks was very different from where power resided in the regular armies of the nineteenth century. Within the system that relied upon the regular armies, power lived at the top of the political structure or at the apex of the formal army and was held by a relatively small number of men. Politicians cared about winning wars, but they rarely knew exactly which weapons the soldiers preferred. Arming their men almost universally with rifle muskets had reflected the status quo in the formal military since the use of firearms became popular. For soldiers' weapons, the belief was that bigger is better. Furthermore, the increased range of the rifle was an attractive feature to the men in charge. Revolvers, when they were issued, were reserved for officers drawn from the middle and upper classes of society, who were therefore deserving of the autonomy that such a weapon provided them.[19]

Equipping soldiers with firearms other than the muzzle-loaded rifle musket could threaten the authority of the officers in charge of the regular Union and Confederate armies. In addition to the positive feelings for the rifle, generals and politicians also had negative feelings about other firearms. These feelings became more and more evident as the war went on and as innovation led to the creation of a wider range of firearms. The firearms most desired by soldiers—repeaters—were the guns that received the most criticism from officials. There were two major criticisms against the rapid-fire weapons. First, repeating firearms, whether revolvers or lever-action carbines, did not have the long range of the rifle. This decrease in potential range diminished the length of the reach of the field general. Second, leaders feared that the rapid-fire capabilities of repeaters would lead soldiers to fire as often as they pleased. In addition to the claim that soldiers would waste ammunition, officers were afraid that the repeaters would engender a greater sense of independence in their soldiers and lessen their own authority and control in battle.[20]

The relationship between the soldier and the firearm in the formal armies of the Civil War was such that it corroded his identity as a man. The experience of the formal army soldier was something like that of the experience of the increasingly industrialized workforce in the North. Just as land ownership and the ability to raise a crop and generate a competency were indicators of manhood in rural America, in urban areas before the Industrial Revolution the skill necessary to become an accomplished artisan was closely associated with manhood. A boy could hope to apprentice under a master, learn a trade, and become a master artisan himself someday. With the Industrial Revolution, skill was taken out of factory work. Stripped of their expertise, men were also stripped of an important part of what made them a man. Southern proslavery politicians and critics of the Northern system would call these men "wage slaves"; they were slaves to the factory master and to capitalism itself. The pursuit of profit had made them cogs in the factory machinery. Not unlike the working class in the North, or even the pieces of the rifle-musket he carried—the trigger, the hammer, the spring, the cap, the stock—the soldier was a piece of the formal army machinery. He was only as good as his ability to stand, load, aim, fire, and reload, a task that anyone could do regardless of education, background, ethnicity, or age, at least between eighteen to thirty-five. In the formal armies, the rifle mastered the man.[21]

Like the relationship between an artisan and his tools, the guerrilla was the master of his firearm. Fitting in the palm of a man's hand, the revolver was a much more natural extension of his person than the cumbersome rifle-musket. Among the guerrillas, there seemed to be almost no division between a man and his weapon; the relationship was natural. In fact, Samuel Colt had designed his revolver to fit well into the palm of the typical nineteenth-century young man. His model for the revolver's sloping handle was the handle of a plow. Farming being the most common profession among the guerrillas, the plow would have been their most common tool in accomplishing a competency. When a young farmer picked up a Colt Navy revolver for the first time it would have felt much the same as the plow they had held in their hands as they toiled over the fields. Additionally, the shape of the handle made the recoil of the weapon easy to absorb and actually assisted in the recocking of the pistol to fire the next ball. As the round was projected

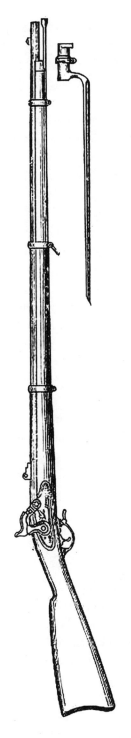

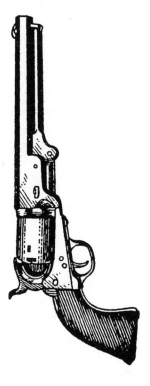

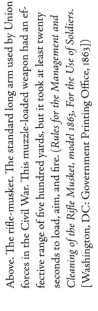

Above. The rifle-musket. The standard long arm used by Union forces in the Civil War. This muzzle-loaded weapon had an effective range of five hundred yards, but it took at least twenty seconds to load, aim, and fire. (*Rules for the Management and Cleaning of the Rifle Musket, model 1863, For the Use of Soldiers.* [Washington, DC: Government Printing Office, 1863])

Right. Colt's "Navy" revolver. This weapon was deadly up to around fifty yards, although longer shots, like Cole Younger's seventy-one-yard shot, have been recorded. Despite its short range, the revolver could discharge six rounds with lightning speed. Notice the sloped, plow-handle grip that would have felt natural in the hand of the young farmers and hired hands who became guerrillas. (William E. Connelley, *Quantrill and the Border Wars*) out of the barrel of the revolver, the barrel of the weapon rose slightly, but rather than jerk its operator's hand upward, the entire gun rotated and slid backwards so that the hammer was in reach of the thumb, making it easy to recock. This smooth action gave each man additional autonomy. To be accountable for one's actions and free from the sway of other men was the goal of all nineteenth-century men, but only masters embodied these traits. The guerrillas did not need, or necessarily want, an officer to tell them when to fire and reload, and the guerrillas often moved about alone or in small groups, choosing freedom over security. The guerrillas were masters of their trade; they were artisan killers.

Men had to work to become proficient with their guns. The guerrillas' prewar knowledge of firearms was important to their skill as soldiers, not only in the direct and obvious way—they were experienced marksmen with rifles and shotguns—but also because they were familiar with the process through which a man became skilled with a particular firearm. It took practice. According to John Edwards, who knew Younger personally, he "spoke rarely, and was away a great deal in the woods. . . . He had a mission to perform—he was pistol practicing." As Younger acquired skill with the firearm, he blossomed into a fully mature guerrilla. As Edwards recalled, "Soon he was perfect, and then it was noticed that he laughed often and talked a great deal." Edwards's romantic depiction of Younger's practice with firearms was likely founded on some amount of truth, but it also signified the relationship between the mastery of the pistol and what it meant to be a man. There was a direct correlation between Younger's skill with the revolver, his self-confidence, and the acceptance of his peers. He was now a man as the guerrillas understood what it meant to be a man.[22]

Fighters like Younger had a great deal of free time. Unlike the regular army soldier, their time was their own, disciplined only by the war they were fighting. While this freedom has often been remarked upon by historians in connection to a perceived lack of discipline among the guerrillas, it seems that it was beneficial to the personal development of fighting skills. In contrast, the "well-disciplined" soldiers of the regular army were given little instruction with firearms or the time to practice their shooting. Also, the guerrillas had the means to practice, meaning they had access to enough powder, caps, and ammunition to expend some in an effort to become better marksmen. The expense of these materials in the regular armies were often cited as a primary reason as to why soldiers did not practice shooting more often.[23]

Just like their overall independence, the freedom to practice with their firearms was built on the work of other members of their households. Unlike the regular Union and Confederate armies, the guerrillas did not have the same industrial resources to produce shot, powder, and caps. Ammunition, in the form of lead shot, was one aspect of the war effort that was produced within their supply line. Multiple sources assert that southwestern Missouri had lead mines that were accessible to the guerrillas. Sidney Jackman recalled being sent to Granby, Newton County, for lead, and Wiley Britton, a Union soldier stationed along the border, also confirmed that guerrillas often went to Granby, which was a mining town, for lead.

Perhaps the most interesting reference to this area of Missouri as a source of lead used to make the guerrillas' ammunition came from McCorkle. He recalled that on one trip south he and some other guerrillas went through Newton County, where the "Redding boys" extended their hospitality to the men. The 1860 census reveals that John and Edmund Redding were a millwright and a blacksmith, respectively. It is likely that they not only had access to lead but perhaps even used their skills in metal work to produce ammunition. Once lead was acquired in its raw form, it then had to be melted and molded into shot. This might have been done out in the brush by some men, but it was probably safer and more convenient for it to be done within the confines of the household by rebel women.[24]

While lead could be pulled out of the earth, percussion caps could only be produced in an industrial setting to which the guerrillas did not have direct access. Caps had to be either stolen or purchased. There was the story that Quantrill and George Todd dressed up as Union officers and purchased caps in this disguise from the Union army in Hannibal. While the story seems somewhat fantastic, it was so commonly told by a number of reliable sources that there must be some truth to it. Rebel women also worked to acquire caps. McCorkle recalled that his cousins had an underground network for acquiring caps. His cousin Will Wigginton was imprisoned in Alton, Illinois, but escaped, and rather than return home, he served as the point man in buying caps for the guerrillas. Once the caps were purchased, he passed them along to his sister, Mollie Wigginton, who then smuggled the caps across the river into Missouri and took them back to the family home, where guerrillas like her cousin McCorkle and her brother George were supplied with them.[25]

Powder, too, had to be procured from beyond the rebel supply line. William "Hawkeye" Livingston, a guerrilla chieftain who operated in northeastern Missouri around the Palmyra and Hannibal area, was able to get a substantial amount of powder and hide it at a supporter's house. According to a slave woman named Virginia, who testified against the guerrillas,

"5 or 6 persons came out from Hannibal—Kinney—Bright [and] Barron women were amongst them [and] took dinner at our house they had 8 kegs of powder- one box revolvers—1 box cartridges [and] a can of fluid to burn cars with." Virginia, who was the slave of Samuel Caldwell, the patriarch of a large, wealthy family who supported Livingston and his band, went on to say that "Mr. Green [and] son, Larkin Caldwell, old man Caldwell, Wm Armstrong [and] Wm B Caldwell drove the wagon to the fence [and] unloaded it [and] put it under the haystack." Her testimony not only helped the Union troopers to find the stolen powder but illustrates the process through which guerrilla forces supplied themselves with powder.[26]

Well supplied and trained, the guerrillas quickly became artful with the revolver. In one instance, early in the conflict, immediately after his relentless training with the weapon, Younger displayed this mastery. While out on patrol, the guerrillas heard of a group of Union soldiers raiding the neighborhood around Independence. While they were initially unaware of the odds, the guerrillas quickly discovered that their band of thirty-two was more than doubled by the Union's eighty-four. Outnumbered, the guerrillas attacked anyway and were able to best their foe. During the confrontation, Younger claimed that "my persistent pistol practice showed its worth when one of the militiamen fell, 71 yards away, actual measure." While that was beyond the effective range of the weapon, and an incredibly uncommon shot, it nonetheless illustrates that some of the guerrillas had become absolute masters of the revolver.[27]

Younger's famed shot was not merely representative of his proficiency with the firearm, it also speaks to the significance of the mastery with firearms to the guerrilla's manhood. The story, which was first recorded by Edwards in *Noted Guerrillas*, points to the prowess of Younger. It is not a story about the advantages of the revolver but rather how, in the hands of a man, the revolver can transcend any supposed weakness like its limited range. Even though the guerrillas had chosen a weapon that they knew had limited range, being able to hit a target at a relatively great distance was still a gauge for measuring themselves. It was as if the guerrillas and their defenders were saying that they did not judge themselves by the same standards as musket-carrying soldiers, but even if they did, they were better. So integral was the story to the guerrilla narrative that it reappears in several guerrilla memoirs. It was a point of pride that Younger could make such a shot because it spoke to his character as a man. To Younger and his cohort, no hapless member of a rabble could make such a shot; only a man with clarity of purpose and virtuous skill could hit his mark at that distance.[28]

Whatever has been romanticized about the guerrillas and their revolvers, from the view of the Union troopers tasked with killing these men, the revolver did much to level the playing field whenever the guerrillas were outnumbered. Britton was very observant as to the advantages and disadvantages possessed by his enemies. Britton said of the guerrillas that "it is not thought now that they can get together more than three or four hundred men in that section." But he knew, as did most other Union officers and men by 1863, that the guerrillas had a way of overcoming the odds against them. He continued, "But considering that every man is almost loaded down with repeating rifles and revolvers, this force is equal to a thousand of our best troops." Britton suggests that a guerrilla was worth three Union soldiers in head-to-head combat.[29]

Repeating firearms, like the revolver, were more significant in shaping Civil War combat than the rifle musket. The assumption of historians had been that rifle technology, which made rounds fly straighter and farther, was the cause of the high battlefield casualties during the war. This conclusion was a legacy of what many officers and soldiers took away from the bloody conflict, but in the 1980s this assumption was put to the test. The idea that the rifle musket forced a change in tactics is, as one historian says, "demonstrably false." The typical Civil War firefight took place in such close proximity that the increased range and accuracy of the rifle musket over the smoothbore was all but nullified. The duration of these fights, which were often much longer than those of the Napoleonic Wars, meant that the higher frequency with which a soldier could fire his weapon was more important than whatever perceived increase in accuracy the rifle offered. The real revolution in firearms came in the form of repeating weapons.[30]

The guerrillas were fond of remembering themselves as always outnumbered and successful despite the bad odds. A group of fifty-two Union soldiers were riding up on what looked like just two guerrillas when, according to Walker, "the Yanks fired a volley at us. . . . As the Federals came plunging up the slope they received a volley—not from two men—but from a dozen, much to their surprise." Here the guerrillas' disguise as Federal troopers lured the Union soldiers in closer and prevented them, unsure for a bit whether these were their friends or enemies, from getting their bearings. In the meantime, more guerrillas dressed in blue and armed with revolvers rode up and fired another volley into the Union soldiers. Walker does not report the Federals firing again after their initial volley, as they were either confused or without rounds in the barrels of their guns or, most likely, both. Not waiting around, the guerrillas fired a third volley, and finally the Union soldiers returned fire. After that, "a hot engagement followed, lasting twenty or thirty minutes." Only after they had driven the Union patrol off a bluff into a creek did the guerrillas realize their "pistols were empty, and had to be reloaded before we could pursue them." In the end, according to Walker, the guerrillas killed nineteen of the fifty-two Federal soldiers.[31]

There were a great many instances when the benefits of the revolvers were evident, but perhaps none more so than on the guerrillas' retreat out of Kansas following their raid on Lawrence. Greatly outnumbered, guerrillas under the leadership of Gregg faced wave after wave of Union troopers in hot pursuit and drove them back time and again. As Gregg remembered it, "Quantrill ordered Gregg to cut out sixty men and, hold the rear until the main command had crossed a small river one mile away," but "before Gregg had completed his skirmish line, the enemy, now twelve hundred strong was upon him, and, the battle was on." After an hour of fighting, Gregg's line was being pushed into the main force of guerrillas "when our little army less than one forth the enemy, faced about, charged the Kansans and drove them back." After holding the rear for five hours, Gregg was relieved by Todd and his command of around the same size. With their six cylinders and their multiple pistols, the guerrillas were able to keep a consistent fire going. Some men likely fired until their revolvers were empty then rode behind their fellow guerrillas, switching places to reload while their mates blasted away into the sea of Union soldiers flooding upon them.[32]

The wide use of revolvers was not limited to those guerrillas along the border but pervaded the whole of the guerrilla movement. In central Missouri, Holtzclaw's band was armed with revolvers and was purportedly quite deadly with them. A local history of Linn County recounted a fight near a place called Muddy Creek in which Holtzclaw demonstrated great confidence in his men because they were armed with revolvers. According to the history, "Holtzclaw stationed Joe Gooch and Jim Jackson on the road, with instructions to draw the militia into a trap or ambush. The bushwhackers numbered less than twenty-five men; the militia probably one hundred and fifty." Nevertheless, "Holtzlcaw placed his men in a line behind trees, with the design of drawing the Federals into the woods and subjecting them to a fire from his pistols, the most unerring and deadly." While the Federal commander, who separated his unit into two groups, sending half after Gooch and Jackson and the other half around the flank instead of charging headlong after the bait, was able to avoid the ambush, it shows just how the revolvers changed the odds for the guerrillas.[33]

With the exception of the earthworks thrown up in garrisoned towns and brick and stone buildings that were turned into fortresses, Little Dixie was a heavily wooded landscape that was open to the fast, frantic horse-and-revolver warfare of the guerrillas. Garrison towns took up an almost negligible amount of real estate and could only hold the Unionists who fled to the towns' safety along with the Union soldiers stationed there. In contrast, the vast majority of the countryside was controlled by the guerrillas; it could not be walled up and fortified. Instead, the Union soldiers would have to come out from behind their walls to engage the guerrillas. When they did, they entered a world that was dominated by the revolver, a world in which any advantage their rifle may have had was often nullified and each disadvantage was frequently amplified. As long as the guerrillas avoided the fortified towns, they could hold their own on the battlefield against Union troopers.[34]

Out in the brush, the revolver became handy in smaller, sometimes one-on-one engagements. While escorting his bride to Texas with some forty other guerrillas, Gregg was a part of just such a fight. Gregg said, "We met seven federals at the foot of the mountain, six of whom we killed, the seventh one taking the road south toward Gibson, followed by Capt Gregg." With the reins of his horse in one hand, he fired at the man with the other. Gregg recalled that he "fired eleven shots, hitting his overcoat nine times." In distinctive western humor, Gregg recounted that he "and [this] man would shoot awhile and talk awhile." Gregg said, "He never fired at me but I could see the bead on his pistol." After six miles of this, Gregg spotted a large body of Union cavalry and returned to the bridal party and continued south. While he may not have killed the man, it is evident that in this sort of chase or running fight the revolver was an irreplaceable weapon.[35]

Due to the guerrillas' success with revolvers, there was a great demand for them on both sides of the war. Guerrilla captains like Holtzclaw would try to round up whatever guns were held by Union men in the regions in which they operated. In summer 1863 James Phillips, a Union man, reported that his neighbor, William Brinkley "lives a mile [and] a half from me. He is a Union man. Brinkley said that the Rebels got a gun and revolver there." One at a time, Holtzclaw hoped to disarm the Union population of Linn County just as the Union forces there had attempted to disarm the South-sympathizing population. These firearms, especially the prized revolvers, would also be used to arm his men.[36]

Union officers in Missouri did their best to both keep their soldiers armed and keep up with the guerrillas' arsenal of revolvers. In summer 1864 a Union major Matlack sent a report to General Fisk in which he said, "General, our muskets with not one revolver are poor arms to fight bushwhackers with. Can we not be better armed?" While Matlack's command was clearly in need of revolvers, there is evidence that some units had acquired revolvers as early as 1863. A May 1864 letter from Assistant Adjutant General Stegar to the chief ordinance officer, Lieutenant Baker, requested:

> Three thousand (3000) rounds ammunition cal.
> Two thousand (2000) rounds ammunition Revolver Navy size
> One thousand (1000) rounds ammunition Revolver Army size
> One thousand (1000) rounds Ammunition Buckshot Cartridge

This implies that the armament of Captain William Smith's command— the unit to which the ammunition was being sent—was comprised of Colt revolvers, both the Army and Navy models, as well as muskets. This request was similar to others sent in the last two years of the war in that a significant chunk of ammunition requested was either .38 or .44 caliber, the sizes of rounds needed for the Colt Navy and Colt Army revolvers respectively. While the United States government supplied many of these hand-held firearms, some of the Union officers may have taken pistols for their men out of those collected from dead and captured guerrillas, or found in the homes of guerrilla supporters. A Lieutenant Mooney said to his commander "you did not say anything about pistols I wish you would advise me as to whether I can get any—there is plenty of Bushwhackers pistols here if I can Draw them."[37]

Though the Union forces adopted the revolver as an important part of their armament, the majority of Union soldiers in Missouri continued to be armed with rifles and carbines. In fact, despite all the advantages that the revolver gave the guerrillas, rifles were deadly enough when it came to killing the guerrillas who were shot down in the field. Both "Bloody" Bill Anderson and Todd were knocked to the ground for good by rifle rounds. At Fayette, perhaps the worst defeat encountered by the guerrillas, it was well-aimed rifles that littered the streets with the bodies of fourteen guerrillas. At Laclede, the train chasing down the hack-turned-ambulance was crowded with shotgun- and rifle-wielding troopers who poured their deadly fire into the wounded man and his escort. In short, the Union army acquired revolvers, but its strategic and tactical culture was too difficult to change in such a drastic way that it could discard rifles and begin the fluid, hell-for-leather, high-firepower, low-accuracy, and individualistic warfare that the revolver enabled.[38]

Keeping the rifle as the central weapon in the Union armament helped Union troopers to maintain their distance between themselves and their targets. This distance could be measured in feet and in peace of mind. A basic tenet of nineteenth-century tactics was the use of firepower in the tactical defensive to keep the enemy at bay, keep them at a distance. It may not have been conscious, but due to the benefit of hindsight and modern psychology, we know that killing at a distance is less traumatic, less damaging than killing at the tip of the gun barrel or at the knife's edge. Riflemen firing together at distant targets may or may not know if it was their round that knocked a guerrilla from his horse. Nor did a rifleman or sniper have to stare into the eyes of a man as life faded away. This was anonymous killing.[39]

Out in the brush a man had to become a fighter. When most of the guerrillas first left their homes to enter the brush, they likely imagined their service as that of a soldier. They would fight differently, but they were doing their part in the war effort. However, the choice of the revolver over the more conventional rifle marked the difference between a soldier and a fighter. There was no going through the motions of killing; he had to embrace the up-close, nasty, and gruesome business that came with fighting a war. For the soldier, time in uniform was service to his nation. Whatever being a soldier entailed—marching, fighting, serving as a stretcher bearer or nurse, loading and unloading supply trains—it fulfilled their wartime duty. For the guerrillas, being enrolled and serving out the conflict in the brush was not their objective; their objective was to fight their enemies, kill them, and win the war. All the other parts of waging their war were ancillary to the supreme act of getting into a fight and winning it. Hildebrand summed up this mindset the best when he said, "But fight I must, and fight I did! War was the object, and war it was. I never engage in but one business at a time—my business during the war was killing enemies."[40]

Being the fighters that they were, the guerrilla tried to get in as close to their enemies as possible so that they might do the most damage. Like a pugilist trying to get within the reach of a taller, larger opponent and knock him out early in the round, the guerrilla knew he had to get inside of effective rifle range, unload as many shots at his enemy as he could, and put that enemy down before he could extract himself and regroup at a safe distance.

Grappling in an intimate space was not only the most effective use of their weapons, but it reaffirmed the guerrillas' identities. Only a fighter—a man whose fearless and belligerent mentality led him to thrive in a brawl—could persist in such an environment for years. This was not just the attitude of a few guerrillas; nearly every man in the brush developed a bellicose character.

This type of point-blank killing carried with it a deeper psychological wounding. One could not hide behind the wall of anonymity that eased the psyches of conventional army soldiers who fired en masse and killed at a distance. The guerrillas would know that they had killed and they would take in the moment in which their victim's life ended. Looking into a man's eyes as the light of his life flickered out was traumatic, even for hardened killers, affecting them for as long as they lived. Whether it was a conscious or subconscious decision, when the guerrillas chose to use the revolver they also chose to get close to their enemies. They chose to become intimate with those they were trying to kill. They chose to sidle up next to death. In this way the guerrillas' war was indeed a personal war, in which they knew their enemies and their enemies knew them, if only for a second.[41]

Killing in the guerrilla war has been misunderstood. The fact that these men—Younger, McCorkle, Holtzclaw, Jackson, Anderson, Quantrill—killed at such an intimate distance has been used as evidence that killing meant nothing to these men—or, perhaps worse, that they relished it. There is an implication that exists in the literature that during the Civil War soldiers of the regular army had an aversion to violence or at least had a hard time adjusting to it, whereas the guerrillas seemed to dive right in to the bloody work. They walked up to their neighbor's door, or the door of some other unlucky person, and shot them down. They invaded the private spaces of others and killed them at such close range that they could have used a knife. It took no skill to kill in this way, only a thirst for blood and a fractured mind.[42]

Killing was serious work. Rather than think that killing was a casual act for the young men to perform, perhaps it is time to think differently about the ramifications of such intimate killing. It is possible that there was a psychopath or two in the bunch, as those with damaged minds exist everywhere. For them killing may have come easily and they may have enjoyed it. For the others, though, the vast majority of the guerrillas, killing carried a great significance. It took skill, both physical and mental. A man had to first master his weapon, and then he had to master his mind to deal with the consequences of his wartime trade. Killers carried a heavy burden, and these young men, who were much more familiar with death than we are today, were well aware of the weight. Knowing what they knew, knowing that the weight of their actions would hang around their necks like a millstone, knowing that there were consequences to their actions that far outweighed those of the draftee taught to fire at targets in the distance, they still chose the revolver.[43]

When the war ended, a great many of the guerrillas put down their revolvers to pick up their plow handles once again. Certainly killing left a great many scars on the psyches of these men, but they were able to cope with the lingering reminders of their bloody deeds. Like the vast majority of men who saw combat, especially in such an intimate environment, the return to peaceful, civilian life was not necessarily smooth, but over time a great many men made as full a return as a killer can make, many becoming leaders of their communities. Younger touted this fact in his memoir, saying that "when the war ceased those of the guerrillas who were not hung or shot, or pursued by posses till they found the hand of man turned against them at every step, settled down to become good citizens in the peaceful walks of life . . ." Among the examples offered by Younger were:

Henry Porter [who] represented one of the Jackson county districts in the state legislature, removed to Texas, where he was made judge of the county court, and is now, I understand, a judge of probate in the state of Washington . . . and W.H. Gregg, who was Quantrill's first lieutenant, has been thought well enough of to be a deputy sheriff under the administration of a Republican. Jim Hendricks, deputy sheriff of Lewis and Clark county, Montana, is another, but to enumerate all the men of the old band who have held minor places would be wearisome.[44]

Younger tried to put his own revolvers down after the war. He recalled, "I returned to Jackson county in the fall of 1865 to pick up the scattered ends of a ruined family fortune. I was 21, and no man of my age in Missouri, perhaps, had better prospects, if I had been unmolested." Younger's situation was not all good, but it was a tenable one as he wrote in his memoir that "my dead father's fortune had been stolen and scattered to the winds; but our farms were left, and I had been given an opportunity to till them in peace . . ." This peace would not last, however. He offered no precise details explaining his turn to outlawry. In fact, Younger never really owned up to being an outlaw in the first place, with the exception of the Northfield raid that ended in his capture. Instead, he presented quite a few hypothetical reasons as to why a man *might* want to keep up his fight against the government through the robbing of trains, banks, and payrolls. He mentioned the Drake Constitution, which disenfranchised men who sympathized with the South after the war and greatly curbed their rights, and posses of pro-Union men who sought to avenge wartime deeds. Younger asserted that one such posse was after him. Reading between the lines, it seems that the political climate of Missouri and the direct threat to his life caused Younger to set down his plow and pick up his guns.[45]

This decision to return to the gun was uncommon. Not to discount Younger's decision as without merit, only another man who had his rights and wealth stripped away and had been hunted by a posse can sit in judgment of Younger. It is important to keep in mind, however, that a great many Southern men lived under the burden of the Drake Constitution. Some men might have remained peaceful even in the face of threats to their lives. Younger, however, believed that there was an appropriate response to these antagonisms that was an alternative to his otherwise peaceful postwar existence. We do not know exactly when he returned to his profession as a pistoleer, although it seems mostly likely that he had joined up with the James brothers in 1868 for robbery of the Nimrod L. Long & Co. Bank in Russellville, Kentucky. For nearly a decade until the failed Northfield raid in 1876, the James-Younger gang successfully robbed banks and trains throughout Missouri, Kentucky, and other parts of the Midwest and South. Their primary tools for this profession as thieves and murderers were disguises, horses, and their guns.[46]

Younger became a fighter, an identity he could not shake. In the act of becoming the master of his firearm, he changed, he became something different—*someone* different—from the gentlemen farmer he had been raised to be. Additionally, he moved beyond the scope of the citizen-soldier. The metamorphosis from the innocent and privileged boy Thomas Coleman Younger into the artisan-killer—the fighter—was a complete one. The Colt Navy and his ability to use it became an essential part of his identity as a man. For all the freedom it gave him, with the revolver came the weight, a burden that any man who chose to kill should have to carry, a weight that Cole Younger, the man, the guerrilla, the master pistoleer, the artisan killer, and the outlaw would struggle under his entire life. Whether it was jayhawkers, Union troopers, pro-Union posses, northern bankers and railroad men, Pinkerton detectives, or his own critics, Younger was looking for a fight. In the end, he knew of no other way.[47]

CHAPTER 8

The Rebel Bushwhacker

ON SEPTEMBER 28, 1864, Union lieutenant colonel Dan M. Draper rode out of the brush and into a small clearing just two miles from the town of Centralia, Missouri. He described what he saw in his report as "a scene of murder and outrage at which the heart sickens." Indeed, the battle at Centralia was the peak of violence for arguably the most brutal theater of the Civil War. Draper deduced that Union major A. V. E. Johnston, with about 125 men, had followed the guerrillas' trail from town "to where they were, and when he came in sight dismounted his men." The guerrillas, who were in the woods around the field "soon came on a charge. When 150 yards distant the major ordered his men to fire . . . when within 100 yards the men began to break, many of them not firing the second shot, and none of them more than that." Seeing the bodies splayed out and piled upon one another, Draper reported that his comrades "were beaten over the head, seventeen of them were scalped, and one man had his privates cut off and placed in his mouth. Every man was shot in the head." As his horse walked among the littered remains of Union troopers, Draper was left to wonder what kind of men these were who could be so vicious.[1]

Draper's report suggests the guerrillas used and understood violence in ways that were different from those of men in the conventional armies. Generally speaking, men of the Civil War generation were expected to kill in war. Drawn from across the North and South, millions of men were forced to fit the formal Union and Confederate armies' conception of what it meant to be a man. These men, the vast majority of whom had never killed before (and would never kill again), were then marched out onto the formal field of battle, often times hundreds of miles from home, where they were expected to kill one another. Lined up, they fired en masse at one another while exposing themselves to the fire of their enemies. As men of the conventional war were pushed and crammed into a preconceived idea of manhood, they were stripped of important pieces of what had made them men before the war. Freedom and independence were traded in for rote disciple and submission. For instance, if a man in the ranks of one of the formal armies had trouble conforming to this conventional type of soldiering and hightailed it for some safer place, he did so under the threat of death. In contrast, the men who fought as guerrillas remained at home to wage a war within their own communities, where they employed more personal and intimate forms of violence. They also maintained their personal autonomy: they could recklessly charge headlong into an enemy line without any orders to do so or skedaddle in the face of superior numbers and return to their homes without fear of being shot by their comrades. Extracting them from two sources, antebellum manhood and the necessity of their war, the guerrillas married two behaviors at the extreme ends of the spectrum of male conduct: brutal violence and seemingly gutless running and hiding. In so doing, they created a paradigm of masculinity that worked for them.[2]

Violence has long been recognized as an essential part of guerrilla identity. Through a gendered lens, we must examine the men at Centralia who committed so many gruesome acts of violence to see if they were in fact the agents of chaos or if they continued to be agents of their society. According to the first interpretation, the "savage" nature of the guerrilla war took normal men—peaceful, church-going farmers—and turned them into guerrillas, a wretched lot of barbarous murderers and thieves who then turned on their own society. The other possibility is that, while prevalent, violence was also well understood by the men who fought as guerrillas. That is not to say the guerrillas applied it without passion. Even when it resulted from hot tempers or rage, however, violence was purposeful. Although it may have looked different from the killing and maiming of the conventional war, it was no more or less brutal. Certainly, the guerrillas did not imagine their violence to be anomalous. As nasty as guerrilla violence was, the human destruction that took place at the Sunken Lane, the Battle of the Crater, and the Wilderness (to name a few) was no less brutal or murderous. Just as before the war, when the fist, knife, pistol, rod, rifle, and whip were employed by white men to maintain the fragile structure of their slaveholding communities, the guerrillas believed that their pistols and scalping knives would help them to protect their communities and save their world from annihilation.[3]

For the guerrillas, their first great departure from conventional Civil War manhood was not that they killed but rather that they could break and run in the face of the enemy. The guerrilla Hamp Watts offered the philosophy of "irregular" warfare as simply "He who fights, then runs away, will live to fight another day." In contrast, the commanders of the formal armies tapped into strong currents of courage, bravery, and personal honor that pushed and flowed just beneath the surface of the dominant concepts of antebellum white manhood. By killing, standing firm while in harm's way, and dying for the cause, a man believed that he could retain or even bolster his personal honor. If Watts's little rhyme was corrected to fit the philosophy of the formal army, it would read, "A real man fights, and does not run away, and may not live to see another day." Within his own community, the guerrilla may have been the man's man, but when viewed through the lens of the conventional war, he was a coward.[4]

Outside of just trying to save their own skin, the guerrillas had a number of reasons for fighting their war outside of the orbit of the conventional armies. Indeed, scholars have shown that the violence of war eroded the foundations of manhood. For the men who marched to war in blue and gray, the reality of this new kind of warfare was dehumanizing, destroying any romantic notions of war they might have held and turning them into nothing but cogs in the machinery of war. Nevertheless, many men held fast to their understanding of what it meant to be a man even as they faltered before their own expectations. They were enslaved to their rifles, beaten down by the hierarchy of the army, shocked by the randomness of death, pulled unwillingly into the chaos of war, and most of all they were unmade by their own fears. Powerless in the face of war, soldiers of the formal armies were crushed as men.[5]

Avoiding the disillusionment of the formal armies, the guerrillas went into the brush. It has often been remarked that the environment of Missouri was perfectly suited to this type of warfare, but it was also suited to the economic pursuits of the white men and women who settled throughout the Missouri River counties in which guerrilla warfare would become most prevalent. These people, coming from agrarian communities across the slaveholding states, wished to use slave labor to plant and harvest cash crops. In order to do so, they needed the fertile land that could be found

A hand-drawn map of a guerrilla neighborhood. This map, from the papers of Thomas Ewing, offers a bird's-eye view of the geography of a guerrilla battlefield, in particular the interrelated nature of the guerrilla household and the brush. There was no clear distinction between the two spaces. The map also shows how perceptive a guerrilla hunter Ewing was, fully demonstrating his grasp of the nature of the guerrilla war as a household war. (Courtesy of the Library of Congress. Special thanks to LeeAnn Whites, who originally found this map)

along the great river and all of its tributaries. The grass of prairies did not spring forth from the most fertile land; rather, tall trees and underbrush close to the waterways signaled that their roots lay in earth rich with minerals. With this knowledge the settlers, who sought to plant tobacco or hemp or even small patches of rice, cotton, and sugar cane, settled in and around the timber bottoms along the rivers, creeks, and streams cutting this way and that and ultimately spilling into the Missouri. They planted their crops on the lower lands with great success and built their homes where the wood could easily be cleared or where the dense forest gave way to a meadow.[6]

Bushwhacking was a seasonal activity in Missouri. A bushwhacking season ran during the same period as the growing season, beginning in the spring about the same time as the planting of crops and ending with the harvest. The brush was a living thing. The guerrillas could only use the brush to their advantage when it was there—lush, green, and leafy. During the first two winters of the war, most of the guerrillas stayed in Missouri. During the second winter, however, the guerrillas who hung about their old neighborhoods found it hard to hide from Union troopers. From then on the men would follow the brush line down into the South at the end of the fall and retrace their steps to Missouri in spring. By 1864 Union commanders, like General E. B. Brown, would brace for the guerrillas' return, saying in a March 29 letter, "I expect before the leaves are out that the whole country will be prepared for its own defense."[7]

These woods were both fascinating and haunting, but for the young men who became guerrillas this was their world. They were quite familiar with the brush and quite at home there. This was true of their knowledge of the woods generally, but they had a very specific knowledge of the landscape that surrounded their homes and communities. Every path was well known to these young men as they had used them to play, hunt, travel, and work since they could remember. They did not need a map to know where they were, nor did they understand geography in that way. The bird's eye was not their perspective of the world. They viewed the world from the ground on which their horses' hooves trod. To them these roads, cuts, and traces were extensions of the household from which they came and led them toward the household to which they were headed.[8]

In point of fact, the brush itself was an extension of the rebel household. This was a measured and quantifiable truth revealed in the agricultural censuses of the day, as they listed the amount of acreage owned by these rebels. The real estate was broken into two types, improved and unimproved land. The former took the shape of the farms that one would see as they traveled along a country road while the latter was the brush, the wild areas of Missouri yet to be tamed by the farmer's ax and plow. A Union general articulated the connection between the households and the brush when he said that "no better region than this could be selected for guerrilla warfare. The topography of the country and the hearts and consciences of the people are adapted to the hellish work." The people and the land were one and the same. As the general explained, "There is scarcely a family but what has its representative in either Price's invading force or in the corps de bush. Men and women of wealth and position give their entire influence and aid to the knights of the bush."[9]

The young men of Missouri knew the potential advantages that the woods gave them. Andrew Walker led the first group of young men into the brush and introduced William Clarke Quantrill to the particular advantages of the landscape. As Walker put it, in Quantrill's initial attempts to escape the Union troops out looking for him, he "began dodging among the *fastnesses* of the vicinity." Quantrill was able to avoid capture because he had darted among the natural strongholds and havens of the landscape. To the guerrillas, the brush was a fortress, a safe place that they might enter to protect themselves from the groping and grasping of Union patrols.[10]

Early in the war, Union troopers recognized the potential of the brush as a sanctuary to the guerrillas. Captain W. S. Oliver, a Union officer tasked with ending the guerrilla resistance on the border, observed that Quantrill "has defied pursuit, making his camp in the bottoms of the . . . Blue [River], and roving over a circuit of 30 miles." A bit later in the spring, during the fight at the Tate house where the guerrillas had stopped to eat and rest and were surprised and surrounded, a good number of the guerrillas were able to retreat into the safety of the woods. A Union colonel, Robert Mitchell, who was on the scene said, "The men in the house who were not wounded then burst out the weatherboarding at the back of the house and ran for the timber immediately in the rear." While two men were shot down, "the others escaped, and though the woods were carefully scoured, no traces of them were found."[11]

In response to the increasingly unwieldy population of men in the brush, the Union army created a policy that was intended to either push the guerrillas out of the war or at least force them into the same shape as the obedient soldiers of the conventional armies. On March 13, 1862, Union general Henry

MAJOR-GENERAL HALLECK, COMMANDER-IN-CHIEF.

Henry Halleck, the commander of the Department of the Missouri, known by the sobri-
quet "Old Brains," which was a nod to his intellectual proclivity and perhaps his conspicuously large, balding head. A scholar of military law, he was nevertheless stumped by the
problems that the guerrillas and their households presented to the formal, conventional
army. After seeking the assistance of his close friend and renowned legal scholar Francis Lieber, he decided to declare that no quarter would be granted to the guerrillas in his
department, setting a precedent for dealing with guerrillas across the South. (*Harper's
Weekly*, November 30, 1861)

Halleck declared that no quarter would be given to the rebel guerrillas operating in his Department of the Missouri. Instead, they were to be shot on sight. If captured, they were to be summarily executed. Halleck's order has been understood as a response to the guerrillas' own policy of no quarter, or what was popularly known as "flying the black flag." Even with the inherently sketchy details of the early days of the guerrilla war, an investigation of the primary sources first demonstrates that there was no single policy to which the guerrillas operating across the state adhered and, second, that the guerrillas often did take prisoners, paroled them, or attempted to exchange them. More to the point, neither of Halleck's orders in which he called for the Union to unfurl the black flag in Missouri mentioned anything about the guerrillas refusing to take prisoners as a reason for the policy. Halleck was much more concerned with the guerrillas' involvement in railroad destruction, telegraph wire cutting, and bridge burning than any act of killing. He even said, "Bridge burnings are the *most* annoying features of the war." For Halleck, these "annoying" tactics were enough to warrant the black flag because they disrupted the logistical foundation of his conventional war.[12]

In his attempt to contain guerrilla warfare, Halleck actually outlawed normative, peaceful manhood. Working from the template that was provided for him by his friend Francis Lieber, the general developed a guide to help Union officers determine which combatants were worthy of protection under the laws of war and which ones should be shot on sight as outlaws. According to Halleck, the keys to identifying a guerrilla were through his clothing and whether or not he had a legitimate, meaning conventional, source of supply. As opposed to a regular Confederate soldier who wore a formal uniform and was supplied by the quartermaster's supply line, a guerrilla was a man with Southern sympathies who was lacking in these two respects but was presumably taking part in the war nonetheless. A guerrilla found out in the brush with his beard, long hair, Colt Navy revolvers, and flamboyant clothing was easy enough to identify. Taken at face value, however, the Lieber-Halleck guide for identifying a guerrilla could also be read by Union officers to include men with Southern politics who were at home on their farms, trying to stay out of the war.[13]

Without much incentive to remain peaceful, Halleck's order backfired and his problem and the problem of Union officers on the ground increased exponentially. The guerrillas felt the consequences of the new Union policy almost immediately. One week after the order was declared, Quantrill's

Francis Lieber, author of the "Lieber Code," or General Order No. 100, which offered a legal framework for making war against the South. The impetus for creating the code was the guerrilla war that Lieber's friend Halleck faced in Missouri early in the war. Halleck needed a legal basis for dealing with the guerrillas, their supporters, and the guerrilla household more generally. Lieber's guidelines for dealing with the men who became guerrillas were straightforward: they had no protection from the laws of war and should be summarily executed. (Lewis R. Harley, *Francis Lieber: His Life and Political Philosophy* [New York: Columbia University Press, 1899])

guerrillas learned of the new Union policy. William H. Gregg remembered that "at this date we had sixty men, twenty of whom had come to us only the day before, and when the order was read and explained to them, these recent recruits left us." Though he and a few others remained in the brush, Gregg recalled that the men who had just left "did not stay away long however, as the federal troops began murdering by wholesale, old men and boys." Faced with the choice of dying at home or taking to the brush where they still might die but would at least have a fighting chance, most men chose the brush.[14]

Bushwhacking quickly became even more unmanageable for the Union across the state. Despite the Union policy of no quarter, the guerrillas continued to try and play by the rules of war, at least initially. In the summer of 1862 Quantrill's band of guerrillas captured a Union lieutenant who they attempted to trade for their friend, Perry Hoy. The Union commander at Fort Leavenworth refused to make the exchange. In August of 1862 the guerrillas read in a newspaper that their friend, Hoy, was executed. Without absolving the guerrillas of their bloody deeds, it is nonetheless quite evident that Hoy's death, coupled with the shocking realization that their very identity had been outlawed, was felt by the guerrillas on a personal level. When Quantrill read the graphic account of Hoy's execution, in which it was reported that one of the executioners made sure to blast a hole in the prisoner's head and that afterwards the band played "a lively air," Gregg "saw a change in Quantrill's countenance." He remembered that "the paper fell from his hand, without saying a word, [Quantrill] drew a blank book from his pocket, penned a note on a leaf, folded and handed it to me, saying 'give this to Blunt.'" The note read: "Take [Lieutenant] Copland out and, shoot him, go to Woodsmall's camp, get two prisoners and shoot them." The next day the guerrillas rode to Olathe, Kansas, and killed ten more men. After that, they killed one more prisoner, who had been captured following the bloody business at Olathe. At least nominally, fourteen men were killed for Hoy. It seems just as likely, however, that the guerrillas killed so many to avenge the impending loss of their own lives, already forfeited for fighting in the brush or for being Southern-sympathizing white men, an identity they inherited.[15]

Union troopers had to go into the brush and get the guerrillas. This was a task very different from simply riding up to the home of a suspected Southern-sympathizer and arresting him, burning his house down, and/or shooting him down for being a suspected guerrilla. On July 3, 1862, Union Major Eliphalet Bredett filed a report that reflected the type of challenges that were faced by Union scouts in the brush. His report shows that he began his scout by arresting all the Southern-sympathizing men at their homes around the town of Sibley, Jackson County, before they went into brush. Bredett was aware that the guerrillas were in the bottoms. After surprising a few men in "the bottom below Sibley" and taking them prisoner, he "patrolled the timber and brush below Sibley to the distance of 8 miles . . . in consequence of which two bushwhackers, driven by my line toward where those of Lieutenant Vance should have been, found nothing to intercept them and made good their escape." After this patrol, he sent additional scouts out into the countryside and noted that "two of these above Sibley had each a shot at two bushwhackers running through the brush." Bredett also observed that "the day had been intensely hot, and the men underwent much suffering, which they bore with cheerful subordination."[16]

As the war went on, scouts like Bredett's became futile. Union Captain John Wyckoff documented several scouts under his command with results that were representative of these patrols and their typical outcome. Wyckoff's report read:

> June 1, 1864, Sergeant Millerons and 20 mounted men . . . saw considerable signs but no guerrillas; marched about 25 miles. June 2, 1864, Corporal Overstreet and 14 mounted men . . . marched 25 miles. . . . Mo. June 3, 1864, Sergeant Hart and 10 mounted men . . . on scout to Kingsville and the brushy region northwest; found considerable signs of guerrillas; marched about 30 miles and returned to Camp Holden, Mo. . . . June 5, 1864, Sergt. David M. Key and 19 mounted men . . . saw some signs but no guerrillas; marched about 70 miles and returned to camp at Holden, Mo. . . . June 6, 1864, Sergeant Combs and 14 mounted men . . . on scout on Crawford's Fork of Big Creek and the brushy region northwest of Kingsville, Mo.; searched the brush; found signs of a few scattered guerrillas, and returned to camp at Holden, Mo. . . . June 8, 1864; marched about 50 miles.[17]

Scouts could not find the guerrillas in part because the guerrillas actively ran and hid from these Union scouts, avoiding a fight whenever they were at a disadvantage. In late summer 1862 John McCorkle recalled a period of time in which the guerrillas under Quantrill's command were constantly hunted and constantly declining battle. Being camped, McCorkle recalled that "our pickets informed us that there was a regiment of militia from Lexington approaching. We immediately mounted and rode about ten miles up the Sni and started to cross the prairie to Blue Springs and when in about a mile of Blue Springs, we met a man who told us that there was another regiment of Federals coming from Blue Springs after us." So again they turned their column and "crossed the Sni and, as we started up the bottom, we ran almost into Jennison's Kansas regiment.... Quantrill gave the command to counter-march." Headed back across the Sni, the guerrillas then tried to cross a large prairie to Big Creek. Prairies were dangerous ground as they were wide open, so "Cole Younger was detailed to fall back with twenty men and act as rear guard to Quantrill's force." A Union scout was in pursuit, but the guerrillas were able to cross the prairie to the safety of the brush on the other side, where they set up an ambush that, according to McCorkle, cost the Union nine men and the guerrillas only one.[18]

The Union army's persistent scouting and the guerrillas' relentless dodging brings to light the question of aggression. In respect to their larger strategy, the Union army took an aggressive stance in this war, while the guerrillas' posture was defensive, at least in a strategic sense. Of course, there are exceptions to the strategic defensive stance like the raid on Lawrence—no doubt a huge exception. The guerrillas were perpetually on the run: waking up, looking for food, ducking Union patrols, and trying to find a place where they might lay their head at night without being surprised in their sleep. A few times the guerrillas planned to attack vulnerable or otherwise crucial points of the Union defense, like the home of a Union militiaman, a lightly guarded town, a railroad bridge, a telegraph wire, or a supply convoy, and they pounced with aggression. Sometimes they stumbled across unsuspecting Union troops and made the most of it, killing as many as they could. However, most skirmishes seem to have been initiated by Union scouts regardless of who came out on top.[19]

The idea that the Union forces were on the offensive in Missouri raises another question, that of loyalty within the state. It has been argued that Missouri was loyal to the Union because the secession convention voted to remain in the Union. However, postconvention events like the Camp Jackson affair drove the population to their most fundamental levels of loyalty. Nearly the entire native-born white population outside the city of St. Louis held Southern sympathies, and even many of the native-born whites in St. Louis became outwardly sympathetic with the South. Furthermore, this shift can be seen in the oft-forgotten vote by the elected state government to leave the Union and join the Confederacy. With the war underway, Union officers never doubted the direction of people's loyalties in the state. After all, the state *required* occupation. Further, in early 1862 they issued loyalty oaths to all of the adult white men who were thought to have Southern sympathies. Johnson County, a place that witnessed only a moderate amount of guerrilla warfare over the course of the war, still had 921 men take loyalty oaths. That was nearly half of the heads of household in the county and many more than half when we consider all of the men who left to fight for the Confederate army and those in the brush.[20]

But we have also been told that the vast number of soldiers from Missouri who fought in the war fought for the Union. In the first place, while the number of men who fought for the Union has been cited as evidence of the overall sentiment in the state as pro-Union or one of torn loyalties, that number was greatly skewed by the population of St. Louis, which generated many of the Union regiments. At 160,000 people, the mostly Unionist city made up 10 percent of the entire state's population. As an urban area with a very large German-speaking population, it was very different from every other county in the state, especially the Little Dixie counties where most of the guerrilla war was fought. In the second place, joining (or more likely being drafted into) the militia did not make a man pro-Union. A report from D. J. Hynes, the chief of cavalry for the District of North Missouri, tasked with the job of hunting down John Thrailkill and company in the fall of 1864, challenges the credibility of the idea that putting on a blue uniform made one loyal. Hynes explained to his commander that "Company F, Captain Brawner, sixty-one men on duty, all in sympathy with the Southern rebellion (except the officers) . . . can, however, be relied upon to fight bushwhackers, but will not fight Confederate State Soldiers, and they consider Thrailkill and his confederates as soldiers." Then there was "Company G, Captain Bucksath, sixty men on duty, fifty of whom are German radicals, and can be relied upon in any emergency; and ten sympathizers with rebellion, who cannot be relied upon to fight against Confederate soldiers . . . Company I, Captain Rees, twenty-five men on duty, and all in sympathy with the rebellion." It was this "company which furnished the surrender of Keytesville, and some of whose number joined the bushwhackers and marched away with them. They cannot be relied upon at all." Hynes goes on, and in the end "the total force . . . consists of 227 men 93 of whom can be depended upon, and 134 whom it is very much feared are anxiously awaiting an opportunity to deliver up the post to their avowed friends, the rebel enemies of the Government."[21]

Clearly, the popularity of Southern sympathies permeated the Union army in such a way that all of the numbers lumped on as evidence of Missouri Unionism must be questioned. In terms of the Enrolled Missouri

Militia, the group from which the soldiers described above were a part, one historian lists them under the "hodge-podge of different Union troops in Missouri" and says that "there were over 50,000 such soldiers." The meaning of this number must be re-thought: if three-fifths of that group would not chase down and fight the guerrillas or Confederate soldiers, were willing to give up their posts to guerrillas whenever the opportunity arrived, and even join the guerrillas on occasion, this number cannot be used to support the claim that Missouri was for the Union. In this context the guerrillas were not outliers, as they have been portrayed; instead they were representative of their neighbors' political loyalties.[22]

Likewise, Union officers and men faced much more desperate circumstances, at least those who were loyal to the Union. From their garrisoned towns, they looked out at the brush and the rebel households encompassed by the landscape and likely shuddered at the thought of all the men and women beyond the tree line who would kill them if given the chance. It was from these bases that patrols were sent out into the unfriendly countryside to track down the guerrillas and make it back to one of these bases in one piece. While they were outside the stockades or brick-walled buildings of these towns, Union men could trust very few, if any, white persons. The brush, dark and still, was filled with potential dangers and traps laid by men dressed in citizen's garb. There was no doubt that this was a highly stressful, frustrating experience that Union men were forced to endure time and time again, so much so that Union troopers held a negative and fearful view of the brush.[23]

Out there in the brush the guerrillas would stay, moving about, dodging and hiding, until a vulnerable point was exposed. On the morning of September 20, 1864, a group of 250 guerrillas rode into Keytesville where they demanded and received the surrender of the Union garrison there. The large conglomerate of guerrillas was comprised of the bands of Thrailkill, Todd, Holtzclaw, and other infamous guerrilla commanders. So overwhelming were the guerrillas that the Union commander, Lieutenant Anthony Pleyer, surrendered without any of his 35 men firing a shot, although it must be noted that these men were of the disloyal variety of Union soldier that so plagued the Enrolled Missouri Militia. However, the episode was not without bloodshed as "the only men of active loyalty in Keytesville at that time (Robert Carman and William Young) were marched out a short distance from the town and shot." In addition to the executions of the Union men, the Stars and Stripes was ripped down from the courthouse, the courthouse was destroyed, and a Union officer reported that "Thrailkill's address to the surrendered militia in glorification of the flag of the so-called Confederate States was greeted by applause and cheering and cries of 'bully,' &c." Many of the militiamen then joined the guerrillas.[24]

A party of guerrillas comprised of some of the men at Keytesville would also pounce on another "soft" target three days later. A Union baggage train with a dozen or so wagons and an eighty-man escort heading toward Rocheport on the Rocheport-Sturgeon road stopped at the farm of a man named Goslin, where, according to one guerrilla, the guerrillas rode up a blind lane and upon exiting it spotted the Union column. Returning to the lane, they waited until a portion of the train had wandered past them, then, yelling and screaming like Indians, they emerged again, scattering the troopers. General J. B. Douglas wrote in his report to Fisk that "twelve of his men were killed on the ground and quite a number are yet missing." (McCorkle, in his memoir, claimed they killed twenty-five men.) Douglas also said that "the entire train, consisting of quartermaster and commissary stores and all his ammunition, was captured," and, concluding his report, "We are out of commissary supplies; send us some by first boat."[25]

The ambush at Goslin's Lane illustrated some of the more brutal elements of the guerrilla war, elements that contributed to the term "bushwhacker" being considered a pejorative. Union General Fisk claimed that, although not mutilated, "twelve men were brutally murdered after they had surrendered. Some of our dead were thrown upon the burning wagons which the fiends destroyed and their bodies were partially consumed." This idea that the guerrillas shot down the men who surrendered in this particularly attack is how the deaths of these men is commonly interpreted. In actuality, most of them must have either surrendered and were executed or were fleeing the guerrillas when killed. The reasoning behind this is that the dead men seemed to be comprised mostly of the teamsters who were driving the wagons. Whether their corpses were then "thrown upon the burning wagons," or if they were simply killed and left on the wagons' driver's platforms before they were set ablaze, is unknown.[26]

Goslin's Lane demonstrates the influence of race on the bushwhacker identity. Of the twelve or so teamsters shot down and incinerated, at least three of them were black. While there was not an abundance of black soldiers serving in the state, as most were sent out of the state in keeping with the stipulations of General Order No. 135, there were plenty of black men who assisted the Union war effort in positions of support like laborers, cooks, and teamsters. For a black man in this position to be caught by the guerrillas meant almost certain death. On a rare occasion a man might escape with his life for knowing a guerrilla. For most, however, because of their skin color and the fact that in the minds of the guerrillas they were out of place, they were shot down. Here the black men sitting atop the wagons that were ambushed at Goslin's Lane experienced just that fate.[27]

Although some guerrillas omitted race-based brutality from their postwar recollections, Harrison Trow left a haunting passage that takes us into the mind of the bushwhacker. In his memoir was Trow's admission that "the only prisoner I ever shot during the war . . . was a 'nigger.'" Trow explained that after capturing the black man, his prisoner revealed that he had killed his owner. The guerrilla said, "I thought I would have to kill the 'nigger' on account of his killing his master and burning his property." So, Trow remembered, "I shot him in the forehead just above the eyes. I even put my finger in the bullet hole to be sure I had him." Somehow he was still unsure that the black man was dead, so "to make sure of him, I shot him in the foot and he never flinched, so I left him for dead." The bushwhacker shot this man down because not only was he only out of place, he had actually overturned his household, making him dangerous to the household system overall, and he had to be killed as a result. Oddly enough, however, the black man lived, as Trow remembered: "This I learned several years afterwards at Independence in a saloon when one day I chanced to be taking a drink. There I met the 'nigger' whom I thought dead." The already unfathomable circumstances of their reunion took a turn to the ludicrous, when, according to Trow, "I had the pleasure of taking a drink with him."[28]

In addition to the antebellum legacy of white men using whatever means available to keep the system in order, the assassination of black men by the guerrillas points to a certain level of anxiety brought on by shifts in gender roles. Black men underwent a significant transformation during the war. They went from slavery to freedom, dependence to independence, something less than men to manhood. From the white male perspective, however, the biggest change was that black men went from being dependent, powerless, and vulnerable to the whims and whips of white men to wearing blue uniforms, carrying guns, and marching out in the open proudly as independent men. On the flip side of this revolution, white men had gone from positions of relative freedom, autonomy, and power to hunkering down in the bush without legal, political, or social independence. These bushwhackers, while secure with their gendered location relative to their women and other white men, were forced to confront the change they had undergone when black men were seen on

Harrison Trow as an old man. It was at this age in which Trow recalled the ridiculous tale of executing the black man he had captured, and then later having a drink with him. More revealing was the unabashed and lingering racial lens through which Trow saw the world as a guerrilla and as an unrepentant veteran of the brush. (Trow, *Charles W. Quantrell*)

the battlefield. This imbalance could only be remedied by taking the lives of black men. In their minds, the guerrillas had no other option.[29]

In addition to the racial component of their violence, beginning in the spring of 1864 the guerrillas began to practice the most gruesome act to come out of their war: scalping. Scholars have attributed scalping to the psychological frailty of individual men, bloody and spontaneous collective behavior, and an imitation of Indian warfare. The original meaning of scalping among Native Americans was both social and sacred. When a scalp was taken, there was a transfer of power by which the warrior who took the scalp became the master of the scalped person's living spirit. Scalps were treated with the same respect as any living being. In fact, bringing home a scalp from battle was the equivalent of taking a living captive, who then became a dependent member of the warrior's household. While they may not have fully believed that a scalp was a living spirit, whites surely understood that scalp taking was proof of one's valor on the battlefield. With every scalp that a warrior took came added recognition of his increased prowess by his community. Although the white settlers of America attempted to transform this native practice into a business, promising a bounty for the scalps of hostile Indians, scalp taking still retained much of its original meaning. It remained among both its red and white practitioners a transfer of one person's power to another and a symbol of martial prowess.[30]

Scalping appeared to have originated with Union troopers. A few guerrillas, including the irascible Cole Younger, claimed that scalping was a practice initiated by their enemies. Toward the end of the bushwhacking campaign of 1863, a handful of guerrillas discovered the grisly evidence that confirmed their fears. Evidence of their being hunted and that men were attempting to master them came to them in a bloody form, at least according to the guerrillas. Younger claimed some years after the war that "Andy Blunt found Ab. Haller's body, so mutilated, in the woods near Texas Prairie. . . . 'We had something to learn yet,' said Blunt to his companions, 'and we have learned it.'" Although the story may be apocryphal, in the Union's mutilating, marking, and trophy taking the lesson learned was that scalping was now a part of this war; if it was good for the Union troopers, it was good for the guerrillas.

Regardless of exactly how the gruesome practice began, the guerrillas themselves left but little evidence explaining why they continued to scalp the dead. What little clue we do have points to traditions in antebellum hunting as the cultural conduit through which scalping was understood. In the summer of 1864 Archie Clements, known as Bill Anderson's chief scalper, removed the hair from the corpses of several Union soldiers. So that there was no confusion as to who had done the deed or why it was done, Anderson left a brief note on one of the bodies: "You come to hunt bushwhackers. Now you are skelpt. Clemyant skept [sic] you. Wm. Anderson." Anderson's note was ironic, of course. The hunters—in this case the Union troopers—were the ones who should be taking trophies. Instead, the prey turned on the hunters, killed them, and took bloody souvenirs. By flipping the hunt on its head, so to speak, Clement, Anderson, and the other guerrillas who participated in trophy taking sought to remind their enemies that they were not pests to be exterminated but were, rather, the *real* hunters, the *real* men. In yet another turn of irony, it was mutilation such as this that would later be used by the Union to justify their image of the guerrilla as a beast.[31]

Denied the standing of regular soldiers, the guerrillas felt as if they were hunted. Being hunted was a common theme in the postwar memoirs of the men who survived their time as guerrillas and penned their recollections of the war. Gregg remembered that "Quantrill and his men had many ups and downs, they were often in the greatest of peril, foot sore, hungry and shot at from every quarter, hunted day in and, day out." In recounting the causes for the raid on Lawrence, Kansas, John McCorkle claimed that "we tried to fight like soldiers, but were declared outlaws, hunted under a black flag and murdered like beasts." Walker, in his memoir, titled his chapter describing the status quo of the guerrilla life "The Guerrillas Hunted." Certainly, describing themselves as men who were preyed upon was an attempt to gain sympathy from postwar readers, but Union documents suggest that there was some truth to their assertions. A keyword search of one of the online editions of *The War of the Rebellion: The Official Records of the Union and Confederate Army (OR)* quickly pulls up dozens of documents in which Union officers described their counterinsurgency tactics as "hunting." More revealing are the references to the guerrillas as "beasts," "pests," and "vermin," that the Union army intended to not only hunt down but "eradicate," and "exterminate."[32]

Guerrillas were not the first men to be hunted in their community. The degraded feeling and the fear of being run to ground like a deer had lived inside the hearts of runaway slaves, resistant Native Americans, shifty rogues and riverboat gamblers, Mormons, outlaws, and wayward abolitionists who all in one way or another challenged the "natural" order of the white Southern community. From the guerrillas' perspective, then, to be hunted was not as simple as being reduced to an animal, although that was a part of it. Instead, there were tangible examples of other men (or *near* men, as they might have understood them) who were subjected to the same dehumanizing treatment before the war. It was possible that some of the young men who served as guerrillas participated in hunting other men; if not, they certainly knew that these practices existed. Now, however, the Union occupation force was pursuing a strategy that attempted to turn the guerrillas into renegades.[33]

It seems rather unlikely that the likes of the Union militia men described above were that effective in hunting the guerrillas, especially given their ambivalent sense of loyalty. Instead, it was troops from outside the state who infused the form and spirit of the hunt into Union counterinsurgency tactics, most notably men from Colorado, who were considered to be the most capable guerrilla hunters. Gregg echoed the sentiments of his fellow guerrillas when he referred to the Colorado troops as "sturdy" and "brave." These men were perhaps so well suited to the rigors and nuance of guerrilla warfare because of the necessities of their lifestyles in and around the Rocky Mountains. While the guerrillas were the actual, biological descendants of men like Daniel Boone, the Coloradans were heirs to the cultural legacy of generations of frontiersmen who led the way across the West. As hunters, trappers, and Indian fighters, they embodied the spirit of those men who pushed west and were themselves master of the tools of violence. Although they were not hunting or fighting Indians, the Colorado troopers assigned to the Department of the Missouri applied the same techniques as if they were tracking deer or a Cheyenne raiding party. Employing their own version of petite guerre, these men were well matched with the guerrillas out in the brush. Furthermore, trophy taking seemed to be a natural extension of the brand of warfare being waged by both of these groups of men. While it seems unlikely that it was Union troops from Colorado who initiated the scalping, they were quite familiar with the practice as their sister regiment, the 1st Colorado Volunteer Cavalry would demonstrate at Sand Creek in November of 1864. Viewed through this lens, the scalping of Ab Haller was not so much a lesson to be learned, but a dark homage.[34]

By the time they got to Centralia, many of the guerrillas were applying the most exacting form of petite guerre against other enemy men, armed or not. Over the course of "Bloody" Bill Anderson's notorious career, the event that unfolded in the town of Centralia on the morning of September 27, 1864, was perhaps the bloodiest, and an event that confirmed that he and his cohort had slid to the far end of the spectrum of violence on which all the guerrillas were located. While Anderson's guerrillas were raiding the town—harassing Unionists, pillaging and burning their shops, and liberating the town's stock in whiskey—a train carrying twenty-three unarmed Union soldiers pulled into Centralia. The conductor stopped the train because he presumed that Anderson and his men, who were dressed in blue uniforms, were Union soldiers. When the train was stopped, the guerrillas climbed aboard, robbed the passengers, and pulled off all of the soldiers. The soldiers, who were on leave from Sherman's army in Georgia, were lined up, stripped down, and executed, shot in the head at close range. Only one man, Thomas Goodman, was spared and taken prisoner for use as a potential bargaining chip. It was not too much later that A. V. E. Johnston and his command rode into town and saw the line of naked corpses.[35]

Enraged at what they found, Johnston and his command went hurtling into the brush after the culprits. They stumbled onto their prey, some ten or fifteen guerrillas that his force of more than a hundred could easily bring down. Johnston pursued the little pack of guerrillas into an open field, where they slowed, stopped, and dismounted just before the tree line almost two hundred yards in front of them, the Union commander having ordered his men to fight on foot. Just as the Union troopers dismounted and formed a line, guerrillas poured out of the woods all around them. In these brief final moments Johnston saw more guerrillas in one place and at one time than he had ever seen before. As astonishing as it may seem to us, this also may have been the first time that the ill-fated Union commander ever saw the front side of a guerrilla who was both alive and in his natural habitat. Like many other Union officers brought low by the guerrillas, Johnston had imagined himself as the hunter. From the time he discovered his massacred comrades in Centralia, Johnston was the pursuer, the aggressor, the hunter right up until his fate was sealed. Johnston was shot in the forehead within seconds of the guerrilla's charge. His corpse was then scalped and left to rot on the field with the bodies of his men.[36]

In 1897 Frank James visited the Centralia battlefield. James, who had been a part of the ambush that day, was now an old man and a celebrity. He had survived the war and then been a core member of the James-Younger Gang, infamous for its many bank and train robberies. James had survived his turn as an outlaw, and after his brother was assassinated, turned himself in to the governor of the state of Missouri. As the *St. Louis Globe-Democrat* famously reported, "There was a surrender at Jefferson City the other day but, whether it was Frank James to the State of Missouri or the State of Missouri to Frank James, is not entirely clear." As the witty remark from the *Globe-Democrat* would suggest, there was a commanding presence about James. There was no doubt that the crowd with James at Centralia on that day made for an attentive, even awestruck audience.[37]

During James's lengthy description of the battle, he threw a bit of light onto what lay at the core of the men who had taken part in the slaughter some thirty-three years before. At some point, while walking around the old battlefield, James stopped and said, "I do not know who originated the name bushwhackers, but it is a pretty good description. We lived in the brush." He continued, "We lived in the brush but never fought from ambush." Instead he claimed, "We always gave battle in the open." It would be a mistake to read James's entire statement as a contradiction. The term "bushwhacker" got to the very essence of what made the guerrilla a unique form of man. In that word, the two seemingly opposed currents that composed his identity were rolled into one. The guerrillas fought their war hiding away in the brush (hence the "bush" in "bushwhacker") yet were brutally violent (the "whack" in "bushwhacker"). They may have been invisible, always running and hiding in the brush—or acting unmanly—but at the moment when they attacked, they revealed themselves to their enemies. In the minds of James and his cohort, the intimate and vicious violence of bushwhackers served to redeem them as men in the final conscious moment of their bested enemies' lives.[38]

Surrounded by curious onlookers, James recalled the charge of the guerrillas against Johnston's men. James said, remembering, "Almost in the

Frank James

A drawing of Frank James as he appearing during the war. Although he would become famous to the world after the war, during the guerrilla conflict he was well known among many of the guerrillas and participated in several of the most notable events of the war, such as Centralia. (William E. Connelley, *Quantrill and the Border Wars*)

twinkling of an eye we were on the Yankee line." He recalled how he and the other guerrillas were "yelling, shooting our pistols. . . . Not a single man of the line escaped." He did not talk about shooting down Union troopers who tried to surrender, or of mutilating corpses. James did however say that "when great, big grown men with full possession of all their faculties, refer to the battle as 'the Centralia massacre,' I think they are pleading the baby act." James then reminded his audience: "We did not seek the fight. Johnston foolishly came out to hunt us and he found us," and, "Wouldn't he have killed every one of us if he had had the chance?" As off-putting as his boasting may be, James knew that he did not meet the standard of manhood as it was conceived by the "great, big grown men" of the formal armies. From the old outlaw's perspective, though, it was not a standard worth meeting. The men of the formal armies, men like Johnston, struggled to meet their own ideals of honor, sacrificed so much freedom and autonomy to fit into the stiff frame of conventional manhood, and seemingly gave up so much of what had made them men before the war—and all they had to show for it were bullet holes in their heads. In sharp contrast, James had fought how he pleased and refused to sacrifice any piece of his prewar self. It seems that it was most important to James that he strove to fight, kill, and even die on his own terms, or to do so as a man. Of course, James's definition of manhood allowed a man to fight, then run away and live to fight another day . . . and maybe even live long enough to tell his own history of the war.[39]

The path to Centralia was a dark and winding one. Kneeling on the back of a recently departed enemy with a scalping knife in one hand and a fist full of curly locks in the other, the young man who had set out to defend his household from the transgressions of jayhawkers and Union soldiers was now a long way from home. When compared side by side, the fresh-faced youngster who kissed his mother before riding into the brush and the bearded man wiping the slippery blood off of his hands would seem to be very different. One began his fight with the noble intentions of avenging his hearth and home; the other toted ensanguined souvenirs ripped from the heads of his vanquished foes. Despite the visible difference between the glittery and romantic recruit and the stern bushwhacker, these men were the same.

No matter what their intentions, the road to bloody revenge was a lonesome one. As his July 7, 1864, letter implied, Anderson's war was a personal endeavor. Egotistical as he was, his belief that the war was centered on himself was confirmed by his Union enemies. Whether it was the squads of soldiers sent out to bring in particular men, the targeting of womenfolk simply because of their association with men in the brush, or the Draconian, no-quarter policies that were created by "Old Brains" Halleck that made the lives of men the primary goal of Union counterinsurgency policy, the Union must have seemed obsessed with the guerrilla as a man—and each man in the brush must have felt that the Union was out to get him personally. The Union knew their names, who their kin were, and where they grew up. Through the eyes of the guerrilla, he was the war, a reality he could choose to ignore or embrace.[40]

As the war closed in on them, reaching the innermost parts of their selves, the guerrillas found power in their own identity. Anderson made the guerrilla's bloody identity the focal point of the war. If the guerrillas were to be targeted as men—hunted even—then it was necessary to indicate to their would-be hunters exactly what type of men they were. Very rarely did Union men ever live to tell of being ambushed by the guerrillas. Often their lifeless, stripped, and mutilated body told the tale of being bushwhacked, an illustration of the reality awaiting Union troopers in the brush. Time and again, Anderson put violent manhood front and center in his lengthy 1864 screed. In the only other document we have from the guerrilla captain, the same theme dominated. On the snippet of paper that he left on the body of a recently killed and scalped Union soldier, Anderson announced that the most horrific acts of the war were the product of bushwhackers. Moreover, in signing his name to both documents—"W. Anderson"—the guerrilla captain embraced the gruesome identity of the scalp-taking, man-killing knight of the brush. In little time, Anderson's band gained a reputation for their postmortem cutting: they were *known*, quite literally, for being bloody.

Anderson had become vengeance. That is not to say that he turned into some mindless agent of chaos, detached from humanity. Anderson and his cohort may have hoped to look like anarchy incarnate; such a portrayal was intimidating, fearful, and discouraging, a fitting image for warriors. However, these men never forgot from whence they came. They never left the world of their households or their families, in either a cosmic or a physical sense. Even when, or especially when, these men suffered the death of family and friends or saw their homes put to the torch, they were not set to wander without a reference point or drift aimlessly toward nihilism. The very nature of revenge made this impossible. Anderson was reminded of his home, his family, and himself at every remove along his bloody quest. As he explained his reasons for fighting, Anderson remembered that "the Yankees sought my life, but failed to get me. Revenged themselves by murdering my father, destroying all my property, and . . . murdered one of my sisters and kept the other two in jail twelve months. But I have fully glutted my vengeance. I have killed many." Despite what changes he underwent or how far he traveled, Anderson knew exactly where he had come from, where he was, and where he was going. His path took him deep into the brush, winding back and forth through the dark Missouri bottoms to places he had never seen before, but it was not a path to nowhere.[41]

The guerrillas were not lost. These men were on a different path, a path of their own discovery, one that was cut through the dreadful landscape of war and was muddied by blood. But just like all the other trails through the brush, it began at the threshold of one household and would eventually wind its way to the doorstep of another. So they pushed on through the shadows in the hopes that they would once again see the faraway flicker of light from the hearth fire and hear the faint but familiar voices calling them in from the darkness.

The Empty Graves
of Killers

A GREAT MANY OF THE GUERRILLAS DIED along their woodland paths long before the war came to an end. Early one spring morning in 1863, Jabez McCorkle dropped his rifle on the ground; it went off, discharging into his leg, shattering his knee, and causing a gruesome wound. Lifted onto a blanket, the wounded guerrilla was carried by his brother, cousins, and neighbors into some deep, dark place near Nelson Creek, where he would be hidden from Union patrols. John McCorkle then sent for their women, and Charity McCorkle Kerr, Nannie Harris McCorkle, and Mrs. Laura Harris—Jabez's sister, wife, and mother-in-law, respectively—were soon at his side. The wounded guerrilla then faded in and out of consciousness for nearly two weeks.[1]

Jabez teetered on the precipice of death for thirteen days before he tumbled over into complete darkness on May 25, 1863. When Jabez reached for his wife, he was able to grasp her hand. When he passed on, he did so in the embrace of his whole family, with his wife, sister, mother-in-law, and brother gathered around him. His family then carried his lifeless body to the Harris place where he was buried just feet from where he had been married only a few years earlier to Nannie Harris.[2]

The death of this killer serves as the final revelation of the true nature of the men who fought as guerrillas. Although Jabez McCorkle had undergone changes like the rest of the men in the brush, he was firmly anchored to his household. He was supported from his birth to his death by kinswomen who loved him and whom he adored. When he did die, it was not on some distant field; he died at home. He did not die among strangers; he died in the arms of his family. His body was not tossed about by anonymous gravediggers or pumped full of formaldehyde by an

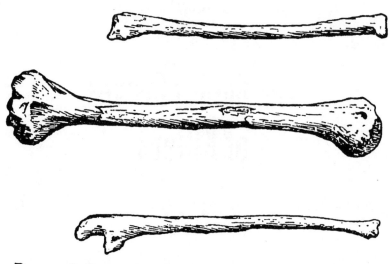

Bones of Quantrill's Right Arm now in Collection of author

A drawing of Quantrill's bones as it appeared in William E. Connelley's *Quantrill and the Border Wars*. No doubt it is an accurate rendering, as the bones had spent considerable time in the possession of Connelley. (Connelley, *Quantrill and the Border Wars*)

army doctor. He knew that his women would sit vigil over his body, washing it and preparing it for burial. This thought—that they would be looked after should they die—gave the guerrillas peace of mind; it made their imminent demise easier to swallow. Fundamental knowledge such as this was felt on a deep level; it was visceral. Intestinal fortitude freed the guerrillas to fight their war without remorse, never looking over their shoulders or contemplating their cause or methods.[3]

Like McCorkle, Quantrill passed away with his woman by his side. After Quantrill was shot down at the Wakefield farm, he was transported to Louisville, where he would slowly die. At some point during his suffering he was joined by Kate. Her presence almost certainly buoyed him, giving him the strength to leave this world with some dignity. It is unclear what effect she may have had, if any, on his decision to convert to Catholicism in his final days; she was not a Catholic. Nevertheless, perhaps in her presence he received his last rites and made arrangements for his burial. His body would be interred in a churchyard, but hidden to prevent its disturbance by enemies or grave robbers. Before Quantrill's mortal spark ceased glowing, he gave Kate some of the loot he had procured during the

During the war, rumors abounded that white women in the South, so called she-devils,
not only reveled in their possession of Union soldiers' bones but used them in rituals akin
to black masses. Representative of the pervasive nature of these rumors is this drawing,
which appeared in a popular publication and circulated through thousands of households.
(*Frank Leslie's Illustrated Newspaper*)

war. Some reports put the amount of the money at $800, while others speculate it
was quite a bit more. For a man at the very end of his life, such closure with loved
ones was invaluable.[4]

History, however, would not let Quantrill's bones rest. In 1887 W. W. Scott
escorted Caroline Quantrill to her son's resting place in Louisville. Mrs. Quantrill
believed that they were going to try to identify her son's remains and then (assuming
they were able to do so) transplant them to the family plot in Canal Dover, Ohio.
With the help of Mrs. Bridget Shelly—the church sexton—Quantrill's resting
place was located and his body exhumed. Apparently the coffin had disintegrated
along with nearly all of the clothing that the guerrilla captain had been wearing

when he died. Scott pulled the skull out of the hole, wrapped it in newspaper, and brought it to Mrs. Quantrill who had stayed back at the hotel. Scott unwrapped and showed the skull to Mrs. Quantrill—a ghastly way to be reunited with her boy. She immediately recognized a chipped tooth in the mouth of the empty head and wept. Mrs. Quantrill now wanted more than ever to have her son's remains moved back to Ohio.[5]

Scott had other plans for the remains of his boyhood friend, but the details of Scott's grave robbery are sketchy. What is clear is that he separated the skull and a few arm and leg bones from the remainder of the corpse. He then tried to offload his gory merchandise onto any interested parties. Scott first tried to sell the skull to the Kansas State Historical Society but was unable to get a decent price for his old pal's noggin. He then attempted to entice the leaders of the historical society with Quantrill's shinbones, but he failed again to find any takers. Instead, he donated them to the society. Scott was apparently able to do all this without Mrs. Quantrill ever knowing that the box she buried in Canal Dover was only bits and pieces of her son.[6]

When Scott died, his collection was passed on. Apparently, the skull was kept by Scott's son and later used in the rituals of a fraternal organization. One can only imagine what purpose the skull served or if the members of the fraternity actually knew whose shoulders the skull had once sat atop. However, it brings to mind an inverse of the reports that appeared in Northern newspapers during the war of Confederate women drinking blood from the skulls of dead Yankees. While such morose use of enemy remains was shocking and repugnant to Northerners during the war, afterwards the members of the Alpha Pi fraternity seemed to enjoy the strange cultural power that spilled from this trophy of a war that was won not by them but by their fathers and grandfathers.[7]

It was not just fraternity brothers who took and celebrated these trophies. Soon the taking and open display of such was practiced by the Kansas State Historical Society. William E. Connelley, an officer at the historical society, scooped up most of Scott's files and Quantrill's arm bones and a lock of the guerrilla chieftain's hair. Like his predecessor, Connelley tried to trade these souvenirs, but eventually he was forced to donate the bushwhacker relics to the historical society. In the wake of Mrs. Quantrill's death in 1903, the historical society put their trophies on display. Behind a glass case a visitor could see what remained of the arms, legs, and scalp of the greatest enemy of Kansas and its people. Anyone interested in making the trip to Topeka could see proof that the villain Quantrill was indeed dead and that his enemies had so defeated him that they controlled the fate of his body after his life had ceased.[8]

Eventually, in the 1990s, Quantrill's bones made it into the ground. The skull found its way below the turf of a Canal Dover cemetery close to some of his other remains. What trophies the Kansas Historical Society had displayed were buried in the Higginsville cemetery for Confederate veterans. It is tempting to conclude that it was fitting for the man from Ohio, who became infamous in Missouri and later died in Kentucky, to become a permanent part of the ground in those states, silent monuments to the fluid and sometimes confusing nature of the guerrilla war. It makes quite a bit more sense to conclude that the scattered remains represent the dysfunction of guerrilla history and the ultimate destruction of its integrity by the pushing and pulling of historians.[9]

After recounting the burial of his brother's body, John McCorkle said, "In this sad manner ended the life of my only brother, a brave, true man and soldier." The term "soldier" is not often associated with the guerrilla, whether it was the infamous Quantrill or a relative unknown like Jabez McCorkle. However, the guerrilla did think of himself in this way for one simple reason: just as the millions of other men who fought in the Union army or the Confederate army during the war, he sacrificed. And sacrifice was the most basic defining feature of soldierly service. The guerrilla placed his family in a vulnerable position, put his property at risk, and put his life on the line for a cause; as a result, there was something soldierly about him.[10]

All of this is not to say that the guerrilla should be viewed in the same light as other soldiers, nor that he should be remembered primarily for his sacrifice. Certainly, many of the guerrilla's contemporaries would have scoffed at such a thought. Even historians have taken such claims as so-called justifications; these were just pathetic attempts by outlaws to place the bloody deeds of the guerrilla war in the same context as the more legitimate and orderly conventional conflict. To fixate on the term "soldier" is to misread the McCorkle and any other guerrilla who made such an assertion. Certainly, if they could have it the guerrillas wanted the same level of respect that their counterparts received. But even the guerrillas knew that sacrifice was not paramount in the waging of their war. Rather, sacrifice was just the final element in the complex equation that was guerrilla identity, and one that was far less significant than it was for soldiers of the formal Union and Confederate armies.

Returning to the homage for Jabez McCorkle, he was a "man and soldier," in that order. A man first and foremost, the guerrilla was a complex creation. He was a physical and emotional being composed of breath, life, strength, weakness, love, hate, blood, brains, and, of course, bones, but he was also the embodiment of a violent world that had been moved to war. The basic components of his identity were formed by his household and his kin, but the process through which he became a man—the way that the guerrilla understood what it meant to be a man—did not occur until the war. With the support of their communities, they embarked on a journey through which they learned to evade, fight, and ultimately kill their enemies. It was not enough to die for a cause. Such a death, as noble as it may have been, did not achieve the ultimate goal, which was to live on and kill other men. Put succinctly: the guerrilla was a killer first and a martyr second. Soldiers could have the world below the turf; the world above it belonged to guerrillas; it belonged to killers; it belonged to those who became war; it belonged to men. Real men killed so that they might live. Indeed, they lived to kill.[11]

In Civil War Missouri, these killers were so adamant about staying above the ground that they, specters of war, continue to walk tirelessly among us. We are not doomed, however, to be haunted by them, apparitions of the past that they are, possessed over and over again by them to repeat the bloody deeds that they, as men, perpetrated. Rather, the ghosts of the guerrillas remind us that we have the ability to choose what kind of men and women we will become and that we have the power to create a world in our own image.

Appendix 1

All of the calculations in appendix 1 have been derived from a sample of 122 rebel households, the vital statistics of which have been collected from the United States Federal Manuscript Census, 1860. There were a total of 884 white people, adults and children, in these households. These households were originally identified in either the Provost Marshall's records or sifted from guerrilla memoirs. The rationale behind the selection of these households is that they were part of one of two support networks. The second chapter of this work explores the interplay between the households that make up each network and illustrates how the organic logic of guerrilla warfare extends from a single household to many households, resulting in a community defense. The Fristoe family occupies the position of the central household to the network. For these reasons this network is and will be known as the Fristoe system of guerrilla war. The Holtzclaw network is rather evenly dispersed over Howard, Chariton, and Linn Counties in the north-central part of the state. Clifton Holtzclaw and his family are the central players in this network, so it is and will be known as the Holtzclaw system of guerrilla war. In this appendix, however, as only the household is being considered, the two networks have been brought together to offer a more accurate picture of the rebel household.

Calculations I.A through I.C present the average age of the male heads of household, guerrillas, and women (age 13 and up) in 1860 from the sample of households previously mentioned.

    I.A   Average age of the male heads of household in 1860

          45.1 years

    I.B   Average age of the guerrillas in 1860

          21.07 years

    I.C   Average age of the women of these households in 1860

          30.6 years

Calculations I.D through I.G present the distribution of various household members through individual households. This distribution is broken down into four groups—total household members, male heads of household, guerrillas, and women. These calculations are averages based on the sample of households under analysis.

    I.D   Average number of total white members per household

          7.3

    I.E   Average number of male heads of household per household

          0.88

    I.F   Average number of guerrillas per household

          0.75

    I.G   Average number of rebel women per household

          1.88

Calculations I.H through I.J present the percentage of the rebel population made up by the male heads of household, guerrillas, and rebel women in the sample.

    I.H   Proportion of the rebel population made up of male heads of household

          13.54%

    I.I   Proportion of the rebel population made up of guerrillas

          11.68%

    I.J   Proportion of the rebel population made up of women

          28.69%

Appendix 2

All of the information in appendix 2 pertains solely to the Fristoe system of guerrilla war and the households analyzed in this study that have been identified as part of that network.

Calculations 2.A and 2.B demonstrate the total numbers of guerrillas and households. Additionally, these calculations record the number of related households, related guerrillas, and households related to guerrillas respectively, as well as the percentage of relations also organized in these three categories.

2.A   Total number of guerrillas involved in the Fristoe
system of guerrilla war
71
Number of guerrillas related to another guerrilla
26
Proportion of guerrillas related to another guerrilla
37%

2.B   Total number of households involved in the Fristoe
system of guerrilla war
82
Number of households related to another household
27
Proportion of households related to another household
34%

Number of households directly related to a guerrilla
65
Proportion of households directly related to a guerrilla
78%

Calculations 2.c through 2.m list the counties occupied by participants in the Fristoe system of guerrilla war and the respective number of households involved in the network that can be found in mentioned counties. It is to be noted as it was previously that the largest concentration of guerrillas and supporters involved in the Fristoe system of guerrilla war can be found in Jackson County.

2.c	Jackson County 60 households	2.d	Boone County 4 households
2.e	Cass County 4 households	2.f	Lafayette County 4 households
2.g	Clay County 2 households	2.h	Howard County 2 households
2.i	Johnson County 2 households	2.j	Buchanan County 1 household
2.k	Newton County 1 household	2.l	Ray County 1 household
		2.m	Breckenridge (ks) County 1 household

Appendix 3

The information provided in this section mirrors that of the second appendix, but the data presented here is reflective of the Holtzclaw system of guerrilla war instead of the Fristoe system.

Calculations 3.A and 3.B demonstrate the total numbers of guerrillas and households. Additionally, these calculations record the number of related households, related guerrillas, and households related to guerrillas respectively, as well as the percentage of relation also organized in these three categories.

3.A   Total number of guerrillas involved in the Holtzclaw system of guerrilla war: 22
Number of guerrillas related to another guerrilla
7
Proportion of guerrillas related to another guerrilla
32%

3.B   Total number or households involved in the Holtzclaw system of guerrilla war: 40
Number of households related to another household
4
Proportion of households related to another household
10%

Number of households related to a guerrilla
20
Proportion of households related to a guerrilla
50%

Calculations 3.C through 3.H list the counties occupied by participants in the Holtzclaw system of guerrilla war and the respective number of households involved in the network that can be found in the mentioned counties. It is to be noted, as it was previously, that the Holztclaw system of guerrilla war is rather evenly dispersed over several counties.

3.C   Chariton County
      23 households
3.D   Howard County
      9 households
3.E   Linn County
      5 households
3.F   Jackson County
      1 household
3.G   Newton County
      1 household
3.H   Holt County
      1 household

Appendix 4

Below are lists of the guerrillas from the Fristoe and Holtzclaw systems of guerrilla warfare that have been identified in the census. Please note that there was some crossover between the two groups.

FRISTOE GUERRILLAS

James M. Anderson

William T. Anderson

John Barker

Isaac Basham

William Basham

William B. Bledsoe

Arch (Archie) Clements

Riley Crawford

James A. Cummins

John Dickerson

Paul (Payne) Dickerson

Isaac Flannery

Wm. P. Gibson

Wm. Greenwood

William H. Gregg

Thomas B. Hale

Joseph Hall

Robt. H. Hall

William M. Haller

Thomas Hamilton

Joseph P. L. Hardin

Thomas B. Harris

James A. Hendricks

John D. Holt

William F. Hopkins

Robert Hudspeth

Rufus Hudspeth

William (Napoleon aka Babe) Hudspeth

William Hulse

Alexander (Frank) James

Jesse H. James

John Jarrette

Carroll Johnson

Oliver Johnson

J. W. Koger

George W. Langdon
James Little
John M. Little
Richard P. Maddox
William Maddox
John McCorkle
Jurcas (Jabez) McCorkle
Wm. F. McGuire
L .B. McMurtry
Jacob (John) Mead
Samuel Montgomery
James W. Morris
Benona Morrow
Henry Palmer
Allen Porter
William Clarke Quantrill
Thomas Rice
John T. Ross
F. F. Shepherd

G. W. Shepherd
Danl. B. Shull
James Stevenson
S. S. (Strawder) Stone
Richard Tally
Thomas Tally
C. F. Taylor
George Todd
Harrison Trow
James Tucker
Daniel Vaughn
James Vaughn
Robert Wells
George Wiggington
Samuel Wilcockson
Albert Wyatt
Richard F. Yager
Coleman Younger
James Younger

HOLTZCLAW GUERRILLAS

Robert A. Black
Benjamin Boydston
Thomas H. Bragg
Jackson Brooks
Watson Cotterall
Harrison Cross
Tennessee Cupp
William Dalton
Henry Gooch
Jenkins Gooch
Joseph Gooch

Silas Gordon
Chares S. Hackley
Clifton D. Holtzclaw
Christopher Peyton
L. C. Peyton
Ruben Y. Peyton
Stephen Phillips
James T. Plunkett
John Thrailkill
Thomas Tippett
Thomas Todd

Appendix 5

What follows is the raw census data from which the previous appendices are drawn. This is simply a reproduction of the household census information for all of the guerrillas, whose names appear in **bold** lettering, and guerrilla supporters, whose names are accompanied by an asterisk (*), who were positively identified in the Federal Manuscript Census of 1860. Not all of the guerrillas who appear in the text of this study are listed here; neither do all of the supporters. However, it is the hope that this collection of raw data will give the reader some insight into individual households as well as a general feel for the size and shape of guerrilla households, their wealth, where household members were born, who they lived near. The first portion is a listing of the households in the Fristoe network that were gleaned from the census. In the second are the households from the Holtzclaw network. The households do not appear in alphabetical order but are rather grouped by their physical location, both county and township. Ages of children under a year appear in a ratio of month to year or day to total days in a year and are marked by a double asterisk (**).

Fristoe Network Households

County, Township/ Name	Age	Gender	Occupation	Real Estate (in dollars)	Personal Estate (in dollars)	Place of Birth
Jackson County, Sniabar Township						
Levi S. Montgomery	54	m	Farmer	4,000	6,000	KY
Elizabeth	32	f				KY
Samuel	18	m	Farmhand			MO
Elias A.	17	m	Farmhand			MO
Lucy M.	15	f				MO
Susanf.	15	f				MO
Samantha E.	12	f				MO
Mary J.	10	f				MO
Sophia W.	9	f				MO
Amanda	6	f				MO
Ophelia	4	f				MO
James L.	2	m				MO
Mildred	2/12**	f				MO
Elizabeth A. Walker	27	f				KY
Benjamin Basham	40	m	Carpenter	700	150	VA
Elizabeth	36	f				KY
Maranda F.	14	f				KY
Sarah A.	12	f				KY
Charles	8	m				KY
Nancy J.	5	f				IA
George W.	1	m				MO
William	20	m	Coach driver			VA
Dudley	9	m				MO
Fleming	7	m				MO
Valantino	5	m				MO
David Johnson	40	m	Farmer	12,000	8,600	VA
Frances E.	34	f				KY
James H.	18	m	Farmhand			MO
Larkinf.	17	m	Farmhand			MO
Susanf.	15	f				MO
Carroll	14	m				MO
Harvey A.	12	m				MO
David D.	10	m				MO

County, Township/ Name	Age	Gender	Occupation	Real Estate (in dollars)	Personal Estate (in dollars)	Place of Birth
Leo	9	m				MO
Mary A.	8	f				MO
Thomas	8	m				MO
Sarahf.	7	f				MO
Luther O.	4	m				MO
Gusta A.	2	f				MO
Bammer	1	m				MO
Mary E. Owings	23	f				KY
Richard Hopkins	45	m	Farmer	1,400	600	VA
Charlotte	45	f				VA
William F.	20	m	Sawyer			VA
Nannit	14	f				MO
Rebecca	12	f				MO
George	11	m				MO
Daniel	10	m				MO
Ruth	7	f				MO
John	5	m				MO
James A.	4	m				MO
Green	2	m				MO
Jacob Gregg	58	m	Merchant	5,000	9,600	TN
Nancy	53	f				KY
Christopher	27	m	Merchant	0	2,100	MO
William H.	22	m	Farmer	800	250	MO
Samantha E.	18	f				MO
Jacob F.	16	m				MO
Nancy	13	f				MO
J. W. Koger	25	m	Farmer	1,440	350	MO
Elizabeth	23	f				MO
Sarah E.	2	f				MO
William F.	1	m				MO
Joel Patterson	43	m	Miller	800	300	NC
Sarah	47	f				NC
Jesse	23	m	Farmhand	0	50	NC

County, Township/ Name	Age	Gender	Occupation	Real Estate (in dollars)	Personal Estate (in dollars)	Place of Birth
Sarah	11	f				MO
Joel	9	m				MO
Lewis G.	7	m				MO
Mary	4	f				MO
James A. Hendricks	27	m	Merchant	1,000	500	KY
Rebecca N.	19	f				MO
James Ligget	25	m	Farmer	0	3,000	KY
Sophie	24	f				KY
John A.	2	m				MO
William R.	4/12**	m				MO
Francis Dunn	26	m	Farmhand			Ireland
James Little	16	m	Farmhand	0	70	MO
S. S. (Strawder) Stone*	51	m	Farmer	3,400	2,300	KY
Mary	41	f				KY
John	23	m	Farmhand	0	40	MO
Samuel	19	m	Farmhand			MO
Lee	17	m	Farmhand			MO
William	15	m				MO
Wilcher	13	m				MO
Susan	11	f				MO
Bettie	8	f				MO
Mary F.	6	f				MO
Nancy	5	f				MO
Strother S.	2	m				MO
Elizabeth Lobb	34	f		0	3,400	KY
William T. Lobb	10	m				MO
Susanf. Lobb	7	f				MO

Jackson County, KC, Division 35

John Jarrette	25	m	Carpenter	0	1,090	KY
Josephine	19	f	Housekeeper			MO
Jeptha Duncan	33	m	Farmer	0	2,350	KY
George N. Todd	51	m	Stone mason	500	300	Scotland
Margerit	54	f	Housekeeper			Scotland

County, Township/ Name	Age	Gender	Occupation	Real Estate (in dollars)	Personal Estate (in dollars)	Place of Birth
George	20	m	Stone mason			Canada
Margarit	17	f				Canada
Alex McDonald	29	m	Teamster	200	300	Scotland
Alfred Hornbuckle	66	m	Farmer	1,400	530	NC
Nancy	42	f	Housekeeper			VA
Julia A.	3	f				MO
Noble T.	1	m				MO
Wm F. McGuire	22	m	Teamster	400	3,000	MO
N. B. Curl	19	m	Laborer			MO
J. J. Curl	13	m				MO
Maria Curl	17	f				MO
Andrew Howell	22	m	Laborer			VA
Josiah Vaughn	50	m	Farmer	3,520	975	KY
Mary	43	f	Housekeeper			KY
Daniel	19	m	Laborer	0	50	MO
James	17	m	Laborer			MO
Margaret	12	f				MO
Susan E.	11	f				MO
Alexander	7	m				MO
Sarah S.	2	f				MO
Mary Vaughn	23	f				IL
Amozon (Morgan?) Hays	40	m	Farmer	15,000	8,000	MO
Mary B	35	f	Housekeeper			MO
James S.	16	m				MO
Sophie S.	5	f				MO
Mayf.	3	f				MO
L. B. McMurtry	19	m	Farmer			MO
Wm Overstreet	25	m	Farmer			KY
James Tucker	35	m	Laborer			Ireland
Catherine	27	f	Housekeeper			Ireland
James	7/12**	m				MO

County, Township/ Name	Age	Gender	Occupation	Real Estate (in dollars)	Personal Estate (in dollars)	Place of Birth
James B. Yager	50	m	Farmer	11,200	80	KY
Mary J.	47	f	Housekeeper			KY
Richard F.	21	m	Freighter			MO
Rachel M.	15	f				MO
Louisa M.	10	f				MO
John B. Kurtz	35	m	Schoolteacher	0	6,700	KY
Richard P. Maddox	26	m	Farmer	6,400	40	MO
William Maddox	29	m	Farmer	6,000	4,600	MO
Nancy	19	f	Housekeeper			IL
Anna E.	2	f				MO
Samuel Davis	24	m	Laborer			TN
Rebecca Detherage	20	f				IL
E. Y. Johnson	49	f	Housekeeper	4,480	11,345	TN
William	20	m	Farmer			MS
Oliver	18	m				MS
Margerit	16	f				MS
Josiah Vaughn	50	m	Farmer	3,520	975	KY
Mary	43	f	Housekeeper			KY
Daniel	19	m	Laborer	0	50	MO
James	17	m	Laborer			MO
Margerit	12	f				MO
Susan E.	11	f				MO
Alexander	7	m				MO
Sarah S.	2	f				MO
Mary Vaughn	23	f				IL
Thomas B. Hale	30	m	Druggist	1,500	15,000	KY
Mary	28	f	Housekeeper			KY
Margerit Carlins	20	f	Servant			Ireland
Belle M Burnett	21	f				KY

County, Township/ Name	Age	Gender	Occupation	Real Estate (in dollars)	Personal Estate (in dollars)	Place of Birth
Jackson County, Blue Township						
Williamson Stevenson	66	m	Farmer	3,000	3,500	KY
Mildred	57	f				KY
James	22	m	Farmhand	0	600	KY
Harriet Ross	38	f	Farm manager	19,000	7,400	KY
Charles N.	18	m				MO
John T.	16	m				MO
Ella	13	f				MO
James	10	m				MO
Silas Barker	63	m	Farmer	2,400	1,300	VA
Mary	18	f				MO
John	15	m				MO
Lucy F.	13	f				MO
Catherine Shepherd	60	f		0	140	VA
George W.	18	m	Farmhand	0	50	MO
Susan E.	7	f				MO
Margaret Baker	15	f				KY
J. L. Fristoe	47	m	Farmer	14,300	5,200	KY
Ann	20	f				MO
Charley	1	m				MO
L. R. Bell	29	m	Schoolteacher	7,000	160	KY
H. R. James	27	m	Stage driver	4,800	0	Canada
James Thompson	24	m	Stage driver			KY
Jurcas (Jabez) McCorkle	19	m	Farmhand			MO
Mark Fristoe	17	m	Farmhand			Mexico
Nancy McCorkle	52	f				KY
John	20	m	Farmhand	0	200	MO
Daniel C. Tally	49	m	Farmer	2,500	3,000	VA
Mary A.	41	f				MO

County, Township/ Name	Age	Gender	Occupation	Real Estate (in dollars)	Personal Estate (in dollars)	Place of Birth
Richard	17	m	Farmhand			MO
Thomas	16	m				MO
Genosha	14	f				MO
Polly J	12	f				MO
Chris H.	9	m				MO
Spencer	7	m				MO
Sally	5	f				MO
William	3	m				MO
Benj F.	40	m	Farmhand			KY
Isaac Basham	24	m	Farmer	300	125	VA
Angeline	22	f				KY
Henry R.	3/12	m				MO
Joseph P. L. Hardin	24	m	Farmer	0	500	TN
Sarah	25	f				TN
Mary B.	4/12	f				MO
William J. Morris	43	m	Farmer	6,000	1,100	KY
Martha	37	f				TN
Joseph	20	m	Farmhand			KY
James W.	18	m	Farmhand			KY
John A	12	m				MO
Lydia A.	9	f				MO
Sarah F.	7	f				MO
David M	5	m				MO
Edward	3	m				MO
Elvira J.	1	f				MO
S. J. Rice	38	m	Farmer	0	2,500	KY
Perlina	48	f				KY
Thomas	12	m				KY
Albert	9	m				KY
Augustus	4	m				KY
Elizabeth Wells	42	f				KY
Robert	18	m	Farmhand			MO
Lola	15	f				MO

County, Township/ Name	Age	Gender	Occupation	Real Estate (in dollars)	Personal Estate (in dollars)	Place of Birth
Mary A.	12	f				MO
Franklin	10	m				MO
James	3	m				MO
Isaac B. Wells	32	m	Farmer	2,000	900	VA
Sarah A.	34	f				VA
Isaac Flannery	16	m		400	200	MO
Missouri Wells	5	f				MO
Catherine	4	f				MO
Frank E.	2	m				MO
Mary R.	1	f				MO
Jackson County, Independence Township						
Jane Haller	42	f		8,200	1,000	PA
Oliver J.	13	m				PA
Sarah J.	6	f				MO
John C.	20	m		2,000	0	PA
William M.	19	m		2,000	0	PA
F. F. Yager	32	m	Master carpenter	2,500	7,500	KY
Susan M.	24	f				KY
Susan F.	2/12	f				MO
William B. Bledsoe	24	m	Carpenter's apprentice			TN
Frederick A. Brill	23	m	Carpenter	0	80	NY
James M. Murry	59	m		2,000	6,000	KY
Sarah	58	f				KY
Nat. R.	30	m	Lawyer	0	500	KY
C. F. Taylor	18	m	Printer's apprentice			MO
John Bruce	25	m	Lawyer			KY
Charlesfarr	23	m	Painter			NH
Thomas Dearman	24	m	Printer			KY
James A. Drummond	26	m	Plasterer			NJ
Isaac Palmer	49	m	Teamster	400	10	OH
Barbara	39	f				OH

County, Township/ Name	Age	Gender	Occupation	Real Estate (in dollars)	Personal Estate (in dollars)	Place of Birth
Lou	17	f				MO
Allen	13	m				MO
Minerva E.	10	f				MO
Thomas	7	m				MO
Mollie	5	f				MO
Edwin	2/12	m				MO
R. H. Porter	60	m	Merchant, trader	5,800	4,200	KY
Amelia M.	33	f				KY
Fred K.	13	m				KY
Sally McCormick	50	f				KY
Henry Porter	18	m				MO

Jackson County, Fort Osage Township

	Age	Gender	Occupation	Real Estate (in dollars)	Personal Estate (in dollars)	Place of Birth
John B. Hamilton	58	m	Farmer	5,600	6,400	KY
Parmelia	36	f				KY
Thomas	20	m	Farmhand			MO
John B.	18	m	Farmhand			MO
Mary E.	16	f				MO
James	14	m				MO
Samuel	12	m				MO
Nancy A.	10	f				MO
Martha A.	8	f				MO
Robert	2	m				MO
Jesse Morrow	50	m	Farmer	5,500	6,400	KY
Sylvia	53	f				KY
Tabitha	25	f				MO
Nathan	21	m	Farmer			MO
Mary L.	20	f				MO
William	18	m	Farmhand			MO
Benona	16	m				MO
Missouri	14	f				MO
George	12	m				MO
Rufus T. Bollen	10	m				MO

County, Township/ Name	Age	Gender	Occupation	Real Estate (in dollars)	Personal Estate (in dollars)	Place of Birth
Louise Hudspeth	31	f		1,200	2,500	MO
Michael Brown	9	m				MO
Rufus Hudspeth	21	m	Farmer	1,200	7,600	MO
William (Napoleon, aka Babe)	18	m		1,200	5,200	MO
Joseph	2	m		1,200	5,200	MO
George Hudspeth	40	m	Farmer	3,800	8,000	KY
Elizabeth	30	f				VA
Tabitha	1	f				MO
Harrison Trow	19	m	Farmhand			IL
Sarah Scott	13	f				MO

Boone County, Missouri Township

County, Township/ Name	Age	Gender	Occupation	Real Estate (in dollars)	Personal Estate (in dollars)	Place of Birth
Henry Langdon	44	m	Blacksmith	1,000	500	KY
Sarah P.	41	f				KY
James S.	21	m	Journ. Carpenter			KY
George W.	19	m	Farmhand			KY
Susanf.	13	f				KY
Laura M.	10	f				KY
Margarit A. McKay	3	f				MO
Thomas Matheny	3	m				MO
Charles B. Dunn	1/365**	m				MO

Boone County, Cedar Township

County, Township/ Name	Age	Gender	Occupation	Real Estate (in dollars)	Personal Estate (in dollars)	Place of Birth
John Sappington	58	m	Farmer	350	2,500	KY
Rebecca	50	f				KY
John W.	10	m				MO
Jane	48	f				MO
Rebecca	16	f				MO
John	13	m				MO
John C. Willcockson	20	m	Laborer			MO
Samuel Willcockson	62	m	Farmer	1,000	1,200	KY
Eliza J.	36	f				KY
Jno W.	18	m				MO
Conlon F.	23	m				MO
Emily A.	19	f				MO

County, Township/ Name	Age	Gender	Occupation	Real Estate (in dollars)	Personal Estate (in dollars)	Place of Birth
Cass County, Big Creek Township						
Joseph Hall	53	m	Farmer	3,000	1,820	KY
EB	51	f				KY
Margaret	16	f	Housekeeper			KY
Joseph	20	m	Laborer			KY
Robt H.	18	m	Laborer			KY
Jane (James) Clemens	49	m	Farmer	1,000	200	NC
Jane	30	f				NC
Wm	20	m				NC
Arch (Archie)	14	m				MO
Mary	8	f				MO
Handy	7	m				MO
Henry	5	m				MO
Cass County, Harrisonville						
H. W. Younger	50	m	Mayor	30,000	7,000	KY
Bershaby	44	f				KY
Coleman	15	m	Farmer			MO
Sallie	13	f				TN
James	12	m				MO
Jno	10	m				MO
Emily	8	f				MO
Robt	5	m				MO
Hennrietta	4	f				MO
Chris Slates	22	m	Laborer			IN
Geo Clayton	21	m	Sadler			MO
Caroline	18	f				MO
Cass County, Sugar Creek Township						
Nelson Shull	46	m	Sawyer	0	2,100	KY
Harriet	48	f				KY
Amanda	18	f				KY
Danl B.	17	m				KY
George	13	m				MO
James H.	11	m				MO
Charles	5	m				MO
Mary	7	f				MO

County, Township/ Name	Age	Gender	Occupation	Real Estate (in dollars)	Personal Estate (in dollars)	Place of Birth
Cass County, Dolan Township						
Reuben Mead	45	m	Farmer	2,400	1,100	KY
Martha J.	38	f				VA
Jacob (John)	20	m				KY
Eli	18	m				KY
Jane	14	f				KY
William	12	m				KY
Elizabeth	10	f				KY
John L.	7	m				MO
Louisa C.	5	f				MO
Reuben O.	2	m				MO
Frances M.	3/12**	m				MO
James Wearington	21	m				KY
Clay County, Washington Township						
Reuben Samuel	33	m	Farmer	5,000	6,125	KY
Zarilda	35	f				KY
Alexander (Frank) James	16	m				MO
Jesse H.	12	m				MO
Susan S	10	f				MO
Sarah Samuel	1	f				MO
Clay County, fishing River Township						
John D. Holt	34	m	Merchant	16,500	12,000	NC
Martha	28	f				MO
Eugene W.	9	m				MO
Laura Bell	6	f				MO
John E.	2	m				MO
Sarah M. Perry	18	f		3,000	3,000	MO
Howard County, City of fayette						
William R. Dickerson	55	m	Blacksmith	9,830	5,200	KY
Eliza	47	f	Domestic			KY
Marion	22	m	Blacksmith	0	130	MO
Grant	19	m	Farmer			MO
John	17	m	Blacksmith			MO
Payne (Paul)	15	m	Farmer			MO

County, Township/ Name	Age	Gender	Occupation	Real Estate (in dollars)	Personal Estate (in dollars)	Place of Birth
William	10	m				MO
Joseph	6	m				MO
Jefferson Lome	17	m	Apprentice			MO
Johnson County, Warrensburg Township						
Daniel H. Greenwood	57	m	Farmer	0	3,600	KY
Winifred E.	50	f				KY
Wm	22	m				MO
Susan E. P.	18	f				MO
Sarah L.	16	f				MO
George B.	14	m				MO
Daniel H. Jr.	12	m				MO
Edward L.	10	m				MO
John H.	8	m				MO
Johnson County, Jackson Township						
Wm. P. Gibson	22	m	Teacher	0	300	TN
Martha A.	22	f				MO
Charles S.	4/12	m				MO
Buchanan County, Marion Township						
Virginia Wyatt	49	f	Farmer	5,000	6,500	KY
Mary	20	f				KY
William W.	17	m				KY
Albert	16	m				KY
Charley	14	m				KY
Jefferson	10	m				KY
George	8	m				MO
Octavia	4	f				MO
Lucetta	3	f				MO
Ray County, Polk Township						
Annie Cummins	57	f	Farmer	900	600	NC
James A.	27	m	farm laborer			NC
Mary C.	23	f				NC
Nancy	18	f				MO
Lacuhi R.	15	f				MO
Jinnett	12	m				MO

County, Township/ Name	Age	Gender	Occupation	Real Estate (in dollars)	Personal Estate (in dollars)	Place of Birth
Jackson County, Sniabar Township						
Rhoda Harris	59	f	Farm manager	7,400	5,000	VA
Marion L.	17	m	Farmhand			MO
Thomas Vandever	41	m	Cattle driver	0	100	IN
Susan*	26	f				MO
Arminia	5	f				MO
Jeptha	3	m				MO
Thomas	1	m				MO
Laura	4/12	f				MO
Martin Bean	17	m	Carpenter	0	50	Ireland
John Leonard	22	m	Farmhand	0	50	Ireland
Armina (Annina) Silvey*	24	f		0	300	MO
Jeptha	6	m				VA
Lewis	4	m				MO
Rowland	2	m				MO
Jackson County, KC, Division Thirty-five						
David Tate*	53	m	Farmer	300	1,500	PA
Richard	22	m	Laborer	0	100	KY
Andrew L.	15	m	Laborer			KY
Francis M.	11	m				KY
Elizabeth	13	f				KY
Tilman	19	m	Laborer			KY
Jackson County, Blue Township						
Jack Basham*	47	m	Farmer	300	500	VA
Sophia	47	f				VA
Edmund	26	m	Farmhand			VA
Solomon	21	m	Farmhand			VA
Jack	19	m	Farmhand			VA
John	17	m				VA
Ann*	15	f				KY
William	13	m				KY
Armatha*	12	f				KY
Pauline	9	f				KY

County, Township/ Name	Age	Gender	Occupation	Real Estate (in dollars)	Personal Estate (in dollars)	Place of Birth
Daniel	7	m				KY
George W.	4	m				MO
Sarah	9/12**	f				MO
James R. Wood*	38	m	Farmer	5,000	5,000	VA
Nancy	32	f				VA
Jeremiah	16	m				MO
Elizabeth	6	f				MO
Nimrod	3	m				MO
Mary	1	f				MO
Rebecca Chrisman	50	f		0	3,000	VA
Joseph H. Twyman	29	m	0	0	500	MO
Robert H. Brown	41	m	Farmer	3,000	1,100	KY
William	18	m	Farmhand			KY
Elizabeth*	16	f				KY
Reuben	15	m				IN
Sarah	12	f				IN
John	11	m				IN
Thomas	8	m				IN
George	6	m				IN
John Prewitt*	59	m	Farmer	1,000	400	MD
Elizabeth	47	f				MD
Comfort	23	f				IL
Rebecca	21	f				MO
Ellen*	19	f				MO
Jane*	15	f				MO
Eliza	12	f				MO
Robert	9	m				MO
Steven	5	f				MO
Ruth	4	f				MO
Joseph Dillingham	31	m	Farmer	2,400	0	KY
Martha*	23	f				MO
Richard	5	m				MO
James	3	m				MO

County, Township/ Name	Age	Gender	Occupation	Real Estate (in dollars)	Personal Estate (in dollars)	Place of Birth
Elizabeth	1	f				MO
Elizabeth Haskins	19	f				MO
Amanda Millsap	16	f	House servant			MO
Jackson County, Fort Osage Township						
L. W. Twyman*	35	m	Physician	0	1,300	KY
Frances C.	31	f		2,000	350	MO
Julia	11	f				MO
William	7	m				MO
Thomas	6	m				MO
Leo	5	m				MO
Joseph	2	m				MO
Edward Blanchard	27	m	Farmhand			NY
Boone County, Perche Township						
Wm Gosling*	80	m	Farmer	4,000	1,575	NJ
Phebe	70	f				VA
Sylvester Gosling*	50	m	Farmer	7,000	7,350	KY
Abigal	46	f				KY
Franklin	22	m	Carpenter	0	125	MO
James	21	m	Student			MO
Lucinda	17	f				MO
Robert	15	m				MO
Jessell	13	m				MO
Jospeh	8	m				MO
Margaret	6	f				MO
Laura	4	m (?)				MO
Lafayette County, Middleton Township						
Joseph Chrisman*	62	m	Farmer	20,000	11,000	VA
Jane	52	f				VA
Henry	16	m				MO
Virginia	12	f				MO
Charles	10	m				MO
H. Taylor	8	m				MO

County, Township/ Name	Age	Gender	Occupation	Real Estate (in dollars)	Personal Estate (in dollars)	Place of Birth
William Fristoe*	56	m	Farmer	30,000	9,600	KY
Susan	45	f				KY
Malinda	26	f				MO
Wm Henry	19	m				MO
Franklin	15	m				MO
John	8	m				MO
Anna Wood	2	f				MO
Susan Carmeal	18	f				MO
Lafayette County, Clay Township						
Jonas Hines*	46	m	Farmer	3,000	500	TN
Pheobe T.	43	f				KY
Elmira	21	f				KY
Larry	18	m				MO
John	13	m				MO
Mary	9	f				MO
Wm, H. Church	28	m	Plasterer			WI
Jos. Hook*	40	m	Farmer	0	3,500	VA
Parthenia A.	39	f				KY
Elizabeth E.*	16	f				MO
Josephine	18	f				MO
Isabelle	8	f				MO
Parthenia	6	f				MO
James	10	m				MO
Howard County, Prairie Township						
Jefferson Payne*	56	m	Farmer	6,000	10,800	KY
Mary J.	39	f	Domestic			KY
Pollie*	18	f	Domestic			MO
Elizabeth	16	f	Domestic			MO
Leticia	15	f	Domestic			MO
Franklin	13	m				MO
Newton County, Shoal Creek Township						
John S. Redding*	43	m	Millwright	1,400	2,500	OH
Nancy	34	f				TN
Mathew	9	m				MO

County, Township/ Name	Age	Gender	Occupation	Real Estate (in dollars)	Personal Estate (in dollars)	Place of Birth
Sarah	6	f				MO
Charlotte	4	f				MO
Mary	2	f				MO
John	2/12**	m				MO
Francis M. Comb	19	m				IA
Rachel Coleman	17	f				MO
Edmund Redding*	33	m	Blacksmith	0	200	OH
Eli Roberts	31	m	Miller	0	100	IL
Jackson County, Sniabar Township						
James M. Walker*	66	m	Farmer	37,600	26,500	VA
Polly	58	f				KY
Zachariah	22	m	Farmhand			MO
John Carroll	12	m				MO
Jackson County, KC Division Thirtyfive						
John Wigington*	63	m	Farmer	3,000	2,215	KY
Mary A.	50	f	Housekeeper			KY
Mary*	17	f				MO
George	16	m				MO
Jackson County, Blue Township						
Reuben Harris	56	m	Farmer	3,000	2,200	VA
Laura	42	f				TN
Bathsheba	22	f				MO
Thomas B.	20	m	Farmhand			MO
Laura F.	18	f				MO
Nancy L.	16	f				MO
Richard A.	11	m				MO
Union	8	f				MO
Eliza	6	f				MO
Richard Sly	5	m				MO
Virginia Harris	3	f				MO
Freeman Hulse*	47	m	Farmer	0	1,200	KY

County, Township/ Name	Age	Gender	Occupation	Real Estate (in dollars)	Personal Estate (in dollars)	Place of Birth
Judeth	49	f				KY
Zadoch (idiotic)	20	m	Farmhand			KY
William	18	m	Farmhand			KY
Sallie*	16	f				KY
Betsy	14	f				MO
James	10	m				MO
Annie	8	f				MO
Richard	6	m				MO

Jackson County, Fort Osage Township

County, Township/ Name	Age	Gender	Occupation	Real Estate (in dollars)	Personal Estate (in dollars)	Place of Birth
William Hudspeth	81	m	Farmer	8,200	28,000	NC
Joel Hudspeth	42	m	Farmer	1,000	4,500	KY
Robert Hudspeth	39	m	Farmer	4,500	13,600	KY
Palalou Bell*	32	f		0	1,000	KY
Elaine Hudspeth	20	f		1,200	5,200	MO
Ada Hudspeth	9	f				AK
Samuel Little	50	m	Farmhand			KY
Cynthia Hudspeth	45	f	Farm manager	4,000	3,600	KY
Missouri	20	f		0	800	MO
Mary	18	f		0	800	MO
William	16	m		0	1,500	MO
Sarah	13	f		0	1,000	MO
Thomas*	11	m		0	1,000	MO
F. F. Shepherd	27	m	Farmhand	0	400	MO

Kansas, Breckenridge County

County, Township/ Name	Age	Gender	Occupation	Real Estate (in dollars)	Personal Estate (in dollars)	Place of Birth
William C. Anderson	40	m	Farmer	500	500	KY
Martha J.	36	f				KY
William T.	21	m		0	500	KY
James M.	17	m				IA
Mary E.*	14	f				MO
Josephine*	11	f				MO
Martha J.*	8	f				MO
Charles	1	m				KS

Holtzclaw Network Households

County, Township/ Name	Age	Gender	Occupation	Real Estate	Personal Estate	Place of Birth
Chariton County, Prairie Township						
Watson Cotterall	29	m	Farmer	0	137	VA
Mary J.	23	f				KY
Alexander Lane	20	m	Farm laborer			OH
Benjamin Griswold	13	m	Farm laborer			KY
Edmond	12	m				KY
Elizabeth M.	10	f				KY
Andrew J. Ray	39	m	Farmer	360	255	KY
Elizabeth	27	f				MO
Delitha E.	6	f				MO
Malissa J.	5	f				MO
William J.	2	m				MO
Sarah E.	7/12**	f				MO
Tennessee Cupp	30	m	Farm laborer			MO
George W. Boydston	46	m	Farmer	0	426	VA
Jane	42	f				KY
James	17	m	Farm laborer			MO
Benjamin	15	m	Farm laborer			MO
John	13	m				MO
Linda F. Payne	10	f				MO
Green W. Plunkett	52	m	Farmer	2,400	4,237	KY
Margaret	51	f				KY
James T.	20	m	Farmer			MO
William C.	18	m				MO
Nancy	15	f				MO
Charles A.	10	m				MO
Elizabeth Brooks	53	f	Farmer	1,200	329	VA
Jackson	30	m	Farmer			VA

County, Township/ Name	Age	Gender	Occupation	Real Estate	Personal Estate	Place of Birth
Chariton County, Keyteseville Township						
Polly A. Datton (or Dalton)	23	f	Farmer	3,000	410	MO
Virginia A.	7	f				MO
Ardelia	5	f				MO
Mathias Hines	54	m	Cooper	0	800	VA
Levina	52	f				VA
Frances	18	f				MO
Molinda	12	f				MO
Claborn	13	m				MO
William	14	m				MO
Howard County, Prairie Township						
John Cross	69	m	Farmer	3,200	7,145	VA
Sallie	62	f	Domestic			KY
Polly	42	f	Domestic			MO
Harrison	22	m	Teacher	0	325	MO
Lilly A.	17	f	Domestic			MO
John Taylor	17	m	Laborer			MO
Sallie Cross	50	f	Domestic			KY
Luvicy	58	f	Domestic			VA
Howard County, Chariton Township						
L. C. Peyton	43	m	Farmer	0	3,600	KY
Amanda	36	f	Domestic			KY
John G.	18	m	Laborer			KY
Sarah A.	15	f				KY
Ruben Y.	13	m				MO
Christopher	11	m				MO
James	8	m				MO
Senora	5	f				MO
George B.	2	m				MO
Isaac Day	19	m				VA

County, Township/ Name	Age	Gender	Occupation	Real Estate	Personal Estate	Place of Birth
Howard County, Richmond Township						
Neriah Todd	55	m	Farmer	20,000	10,200	KY
Minerva	27	m (f?)	Domestic			MO
William H.	27	m	Farmer	1,000	2,470	MO
Thomas	23	m	Bapt. Minister	1,000	720	MO
Eugene	21	m	Teacher	0	150	MO
James	20	m	Laborer	0	150	MO
Neriah	15	m	Laborer	0	100	MO
Bettie	14	f				MO
Rhenault	12	m				MO
Joseph D.	16	m	Laborer	0	100	MO
Thomas Todd Jr.	12	m		0	100	MO
Linn County, Township 59, Range 21						
Geo. W. Phillips	46	m	Farmer	1,600	839	KY
Lucy	42	f				KY
William	21	m	Schoolteacher			KY
Stephen	20	m	Laborer			MO
Margaret	17	f				MO
Susan	16	f				MO
Lucy	11	f				MO
Mary	9	f				MO
James	5	m				MO
Richard	4	m				MO
Emma	6/12**	f				MO
Rolen Gooch	47	m	Farmer	7,200	4,093	KY
Louisa	41	f				VA
Jenkins	18	m	Laborer			MO
Gideon	16	m	Laborer			MO
Mildred	13	f				MO
Rolen	9	m				MO
Nathaniel	6	m				MO
Joseph Gooch	22	m	Farmer	480	313	MO
Elizabeth	25	f				AL
William	3	m				MO
Mildred	2	f				MO
James	3/12	m				MO

County, Township/ Name	Age	Gender	Occupation	Real Estate	Personal Estate	Place of Birth
Linn County, Township 60, Range 22						
William N. Bragg	46	m	Farmer	3,600	1,152	AL
Hanah	47	f				AL
Thomas H.	19	m				MO
Benjamin H.	17	m				MO
Amanda	15	f				MO
Bethsheba	10	f				MO
Martha	8	f				MO
Jackson County, Sniabar Township						
Robert A. Black	44	m	Farmer	2,500	1,760	VA
Martha	42	f				VA
Henry	20	m	Carpenter			VA
Nancy J.	18	f				MO
Mary E.	16	f				MO
James	15	m				VA
Martha	13	f				MO
Aronlle	11	f				MO
Sallie A.	9	f				MO
Susanf.	7	f				MO
Robert M.	5	m				MO
Newton County, Granby Township						
Silas Gordon	31	m	Miner	0	230	MO
Millie	31	f				TN
Melissa	12	f				MO
Christopher Swindle	26	m	Miner			TN
Holt County, Lewis Township						
Geo R. Cooper	40	m		7,000	1,600	KY
Elizabeth	34	f				KY
Samuel T.	15	m				KY
Susan F.	13	f				MO
W. Robt	12	m				MO
Mary J.	10	f				MO
Elizabeth A.	7	f				MO

County, Township/ Name	Age	Gender	Occupation	Real Estate	Personal Estate	Place of Birth
John A.	4	m				MO
Phebe C.	2	f				MO
John Thrailkill	22	m		0	225	MO
Chariton County, Prairie Township						
Hiram Lewis*	38	m	Farmer	1,800	441	KY
Martha A.	18	f				MO
William	6/12**	m				MO
Nathaniel Butler*	64	m	Farmer	6,000	7,200	VA
Nancy	64	f				KY
Erastus	36	m				MO
Mary	33	f				MO
George M.	1	m				MO
George Swindler	16	m	farm laborer			MO
James Stark*	48	m	Farmer	1,600	1,415	KY
Mary J.	19	f				MO
Elizabeth	17	f				MO
James	14	m				MO
Laura	9	f				MO
Jacob Ash	21	m	Schoolteacher			VA
John Watson*	54	m	Farmer	1,380	17,205	VA
Andrew J.	23	m	Farmer	7,040	1,200	MO
William N.	21	m				MO
Frances A.	15	f				MO
John C.	6	m				MO
Moses Hurt*	52	m	Farmer	15,000	17,692	KY
Eliza J.	45	f				KY
Alphonse	16	m				MO
James	14	m				MO
Charles S.	12	m				MO
Grant	10	m				MO
Eliza J.	4	f				MO
Jane Bowlin	22	f	Seamstress			MO

County, Township/ Name	Age	Gender	Occupation	Real Estate	Personal Estate	Place of Birth
Chariton County, Keytesville Township						
Peter Fox	50	m	Farmer	1,280	1,270	NC
Isabell*	38	f				MO
America	18	f				MO
Melissa C.	13	f				MO
Fountain	10	m				MO
Josephine	8	f				MO
Jackson B.	5	m				MO
Elizabeth Baker	18	f				MO
Chariton County, Bee Branch Township						
Wm. E. McCart	28	m	Farmer	960	525	MO
Roselyne*	28	f				IN
David Andrew	5	m				MO
Sarah Matilda	3	f				MO
Maryfrances	1	f				MO
Sarah A. Hart	16	f				PA
John Chapman	47	m	Farmer	2,500	1,093	NY
Betsy*	43	f				OH
Edmond	19	m	Farmer			MI
Dennis Byron	17	m	Farmer			MI
Berkeley Bush	15	m	Farmer			MI
James Wm	13	m				MI
Mary	11	f				MI
John Chapman	9	m				MI
Emily	7	f				MI
Betsy	5	f				MI
David	4	m				MO
Edna A.	2	m (?)				MO
Olivia	5/12**	f				MO
Berry Owen	33	m	Farmer	900	500	MO
Thomas S.	31	f				MO
Elizabeth*	9	m				MO
Mary	3	f				MO

County, Township/ Name	Age	Gender	Occupation	Real Estate	Personal Estate	Place of Birth
William	1	m				MO
David A. Moore	25	m	Farmer	900	100	IN
Susan M.	17	f				MO
A. J. McCart	22	m	Farmer	600	240	MO
E. M. Elizabeth*	21	f				MO
Louisa E. McCart	12	f				MO
John Shoemaker	50	m	Farmer	400	0	NC
Mary Ann*	39	f				MO
Margaret	16	f				MO
Warren Shoemaker	3	m				MO
Peter Heartz	50	m	Farmer	200	200	PA
Sarah Ann	16	f				PA
Anna M Heartz	14	f				PA
Eliza Ann	13	f				PA
Hettie Ann	11	f				PA
Polly M.	9	f				PA
Elizabeth	8	f				PA
Sabina	7	f				PA
Wm P	4	m				PA
Ann Noble*	61	f				OH
Anna Heartz	3	f				IL
Jacob E. Brockman	53	m	Farmer	700	600	KY
Elizabeth*	47	f				KY
Ezekiel M.	18	m	Farmer			MO
Louis Owen	16	m	Farmer			MO
Mary E. J.	13	f				MO
Joseph B.	10	m				MO
James R.	7	m				MO
Henry Bevins	30	m	Farmer	0	50	MO
Mary Ann E.*	31	f				MO
Christopher	11	m				MO

County, Township/ Name	Age	Gender	Occupation	Real Estate	Personal Estate	Place of Birth
John	10	m				MO
James	7	m				MO
Giles Shelton	3	m				MO
Chariton County, Clark Township						
Elizabeth Fuller*	43	f	Farmer	400	525	NC
James	15	m				MO
Marion	13	m				MO
William	11	m				MO
Chariton County, Buffalo Lick Township						
Martin C. Hurt*	44	m	Tobacconist	10,560	20,384	KY
Permelia	34	f				MO
Horatio C.	18	m				MO
Florella A. B.	16	f				MO
Peyton L.	14	m				MO
Rubesta	12	f				MO
Cleora	7	f				MO
Lola	3	f				MO
Shelton Winn	27	m	Laborer			MO
Richard Owen	55	m	Schoolteacher	0	1,790	Wales
John Sharon	21	m				NJ
Barton Philpott	23	m				MO
Hawkinson	25	m				Sweden
Howard County, Prairie Township						
Layton S. Eddins*	55	m	Farmer	27,670	44,763	VA
Susan C.	42	f	Domestic			KY
Franklin Sutton	26	m	Overseer			VA
Sarah A. Hall	22	f	Domestic			MO
Howard County, Chariton Township						
Thos Morrison Jun.*	41	m	Farmer	5,200	1,720	MO
Elizabeth	44	f	Domestic			MO
Sarah J.	20	f	Domestic			MO
William J.	16	m	Laborer			MO
Mary	14	f				MO
Susan	12	f				MO

County, Township/ Name	Age	Gender	Occupation	Real Estate	Personal Estate	Place of Birth
James	10	m				MO
Elizabeth	8	f				MO
Thomas	4	m				MO
Henry	1	m				MO
Ias Warner	22	m	Laborer			MO
Thos. Morrison Sen.	71	m	Farmer	1,200	5,600	KY
Lucinda	65	f	Domestic			KY
Howard County, Boonslick Township						
Henry B. Miller*	37	m	Farmer	5,260	3,665	VA
Permelia	29	f	Domestic			MO
Frances F.	11	f				MO
Sarah R.	9	f				MO
Thos G.	6	m				MO
Henry B.	3	m				MO
Nathanial	11/12**	m				MO
Martha Brown	59	f	Domestic			TN
Howard County, Bonefemme Township						
Robt. W. Fann	23	m	Farmer	200	180	MO
Rebecca	22	f	Dom			IN
Eliza Jane	1	f	MO			MO
Nathaniel Pitney*	54	m	Farmer	2,000	4,300	OH
Jane	54	f	Dom			KY
William S.	18	m	Farmer			MO
Olsen S.	14	m				MO
Chariton County, Prairie Township						
Thomas Tippett*	34	m	Farmer	1,400	425	KY
Matilda	32	f				MO
Thomas	13	m				MO
Sarah E.	7	f				MO
James A.	4	m				MO
John W.	2	m				MO
James Holsclaw*	60	m	Farmer	6,720	9,380	KY
Lucinda*	59	f	Domestic			KY
Clifton D.	32	m	Farmer	0	150	MO

County, Township/ Name	Age	Gender	Occupation	Real Estate	Personal Estate	Place of Birth
Elizabeth*	30	f	Domestic			MO
James P.	28	m	Student			MO
William A.	27	m	Clerk	0	200	MO
Eliza J.*	26	f	Seamstress			MO
Frances A.*	24	f	Domestic			MO
Benj F.	22	m	Laborer	0	100	MO
Sarah M.*	15	f	Domestic			MO
John M.	14	m	Laborer			MO
Howard County, Boonslick Township						
Wm. E. Hackley*	49	m	Farmer	2,200	1,165	KY
Lucie	49	f	Domestic			TN
Nancy J.	20	f	Domestic			MO
Wm F.	18	m				MO
Lucie B.	16	f				MO
Charles S.	14	m				MO
Ann	11	f				MO
Martha	10	f				MO
Jefferson	8	m				MO
James	6	m				MO
Boyd S.	3	m				MO
Linn County, Township 60, Range 22						
Nancy Gooch*	46	f	Farm Owner	4,500	7,189	KY
James	24	m	Laborer			MO
John	22	m	Laborer			MO
Henry	19	m	Laborer			MO
Daniel	17	m	Laborer			MO
Joseph	16	m	Laborer			MO
Rolen	13	m				MO
Terry Gooch	20	m	Schoolteacher			OH

Notes

LIST OF ABBREVIATIONS

DCM   District of Central Missouri
EL   Ellis Library
FMC   Federal Manuscript Census
NARA   National Archives and Records Administration
OR   *The War of the Rebellion: A Compilation of the Official Records of the Union and Confederate Army*, 130 vols. (Washington: Government Printing Office, 1880–1902).
PM   Union Provost Marshals' File of Papers Relating to Individual Citizens
RG   Record Group

INTRODUCTION

1. Within the body of literature dedicated to manhood during the Civil War, there are two major groups: Northern and Southern. Inside of these major groups men have been further divided into class and race categories. Despite wide variety of men identified and analyzed by scholars, the guerrilla seems to be singular in his regional identity, his appearance, his relationship to women, and his wartime actions. For a survey of the important works that investigate manhood during the Civil War era, see Whites, *Civil War as a Crisis in Gender*; Silber, *Romance of Reunion*; Berry, *All That Makes a Man*; Greenberg, *Manifest Manhood*; Foote, *Gentlemen and the Roughs*; Miller, *John Bell Hood*.

2. *The War of the Rebellion: A Compilation of the Official Records of the Union and Confederate Armies* (hereafter *OR*), ser. 1, vol. 41, pt. 2, 75–77.

3. Edwards, *Noted Guerrillas*; Connelley, *Quantrill and the Border Wars*; Brownlee, *Gray Ghosts of the Confederacy*; Castel, *William Clarke Quantrill*. For fuller analysis of Edwards's role in the mythmaking, see Hulbert, "Constructing Guerrilla Memory," For more on Connelley and his attempts at constructing a history that demonized the guerrillas, see Beilein, "'Nothing but Truth is History.'"

4. Fellman, *Inside War*; Sutherland, *A Savage Conflict*. For scholars whose work speaks to these same themes, see Mackey, *Uncivil War*; Myers, *Executing Daniel Bright*.

5. Fellman, *Inside War*; Sutherland, *A Savage Conflict*; Mackey, *Uncivil War*; Myers, *Executing Daniel Bright*; Edwards, *Noted Guerrillas*; Connelley, *Quantrill and the Border Wars*; Brownlee, *Gray Ghosts of the Confederacy*; Castel, *William Clarke Quantrill*. It is also important to note that while this book is about men, it does not preclude women from being guerrillas or participating in the guerrilla war. At the forefront of scholarship of guerrilla women is LeeAnn Whites. See Whites, "Forty Shirts and a Wagonload of Wheat"; Whites, "Tale of Three Kates." Professor Whites is also working on a biography of Kate Clark, aka Kate King.

6. Here we take Aristotle as a guide, who reminds us that "it is by looking at how things develop naturally from the beginning that one may best study them," in Aristotle, *Politics*, 2; Berry, *All That Makes a Man*, 12; Franklin, *Militant South*. See also Wyatt-Brown, *Southern Honor*.

7. Berry, *All That Makes a Man*, 12; Franklin, *Militant South*; Wyatt-Brown, *Southern Honor*; Linderman, *Embattled Courage*; Whites, *Civil War as a Crisis in Gender*.

8. Linderman, *Embattled Courage*; Whites, *Civil War as a Crisis in Gender*. For the role of white men in Southern society as the enforcers of social structure and order, see Franklin, *Militant South*.

9. Castel, *William Clarke Quantrill*; Brownlee, *Gray Ghosts of the Confederacy*.

10. For a survey of guerrilla writings, see Watts, *Babe of the Company*; Hildebrand, *Autobiography*; McCorkle, *Three Years with Quantrill*; Gregg, "A Little Dab of History"; Younger, *Confessions of a Missouri Guerrilla*; James Cummings, *Jim Cummins*; Walker, *Recollections of Quantrill's Guerrillas*; Trow, *Charles W. Quantrell*; Jackman, *Behind Enemy Lines*; Bailey, *Confederate Guerrilla*.

11. Watts, *Babe of the Company*, 6, 9.

12. Ibid., 9; *OR*, ser. 1, vol. 41, pt. 2, 75–77; Hildebrand, *Autobiography*, 51; Younger, *Confessions of a Missouri Guerrilla*, 2; McCorkle, *Three Years with Quantrill*, 23.

13. Gregg, "A Little Dab of History," 6; Walker, *Recollections of Quantrill's Guerrillas*, 15.

14. *OR*, ser. 1, vol. 41, pt. 2, 75–77.

15. Walker, *Recollections of Quantrill's Guerrillas*, 1; McCorkle, *Three Years with Quantrill*, 52; Hildebrand, *Autobiography*, 74.

16. *Confederate Veteran*, May 1907, 279; *Kansas City Times*, Aug. 20, 1910. Younger, *Confessions of a Missouri Guerrilla*, 57.

17. While this work seeks to offer a more nuanced description of guerrilla identity, Robert Mackey's work is helpful for its definitions of various types of "irregular" fighters and as an aid for distinguishing between the various types. See Mackey, *Uncivil War*, 6–9.

18. Hermann Hesse, *Glass Bead Game*, 169.

1. Household War

1. Gregg, "A Little Dab of History," 49.

2. *OR*, ser. I, vol. 22, pt. 2, 428; *OR*, ser.ser. I, vol. 13, pt. 1, 446.

3. Whites and Long, *Occupied Women*. The essays in this anthology work to reframe the discussion of the war on the level of the household.

4. Fox-Genovese, *Within the Plantation Household*. For other works on the household, see McCurry, *Masters of Small Worlds*; Faust, *Mothers of Invention*; Wood, *Masterful Women*; Bercaw, *Gendered Freedoms*; Bynum, *Unruly Women*; Whites, *Civil War as a Crisis in Gender*; Whites, *Gender Matters*.

5. 1860 US Federal Manuscript Census (hereafter FMC), Jackson County, MO, 176 (EL). To see the census data for the Gregg household and the households of many of the other men who appear in this book, see app. 5.

6. 1860 US FMC, Jackson County, MO, 176 (EL); Bowen, "Guerrilla War in Western Missouri."

7. McCurry, *Masters of Small Worlds*; Dunkelman, *Brothers One and All*, 25.

8. Slave Schedule, 1860 US FMC (EL); Faust, *Mothers of Invention*, 63. See also Faus, *James Henry Hammond*; Proctor, *Bathed in Blood*.

9. Mutti-Burke, *On Slavery's Border*. For extended discussions of the conflict along the Kansas-Missouri border during the 1850s, see Oertel, *Bleeding Borders*; Etcheson, *Bleeding Kansas*; Earle and Mutti-Burke, *Bleeding Kansas, Bleeding Missouri*.

10. Mutti-Burke, *On Slavery's Border*; Oertel, *Bleeding Borders*; Etcheson, *Bleeding Kansas*; Earle and Mutti-Burke, *Bleeding Kansas, Bleeding Missouri*; Ponce, *Kansas's War*, 144.

11. Household scholarship is informative in understanding the motivations for going to war; see Silber, *Gender and the Sectional Conflict*.

12. Gregg, "A Little Dab of History," 49.

13. Mrs. Gregg, "Can Forgive"; Frank, "Bedrooms as Battlefields."

14. Gregg, "A Little Dab of History," 1.

15. Ben Loan to Samuel Curtis, Oct. 3, 1862, DCM, Letters Sent 1862–1865, entry 3372, vols. 225–26, RG 393, pt. 2, NARA. Another example of guerrillas as "sons," can be seen in the report from the headquarters of the District of Central Missouri to Governor Hamilton Gamble, Oct. 8, 1862, DCM, Letters Sent 1862–1865, entry 3372, vols. 225–26, RG 393, pt. 2, NARA. Also, in a public letter to Union officers in Missouri, "Bloody" Bill Anderson, the infamous guerrilla captain, refers time and again to the guerrillas as the "sons" of Missouri, in *OR*, ser. I, vol. 41, pt. 2, 75–77. Watts, *Babe of the Company*, 6. Bowen figures an average age of guerrillas in Jackson County as 20.5 years of age in his article "Guerrilla War in Western Missouri," 30–51. In "Quantrill, James, Younger, et. al.," Bowen shows the median age of guerrilla captains to be more than three years older than followers; in "Who Were the Bushwhackers" (17), Kenneth Noe found the average age of guerrillas captured in western Virginia and held at Camp Chase, Ohio, to be thirty-four but offers little other than speculation as to why these guerrillas were so much older

than other guerrillas; Bell Wiley, *Life of Billy Yank*, 303 (Wiley does not offer an average age of the Confederate soldier in *Life of Billy Yank* but states that 80 percent of the soldiers were between the ages of eighteen and twenty-nine in *Life of Johnny Reb*, 330–31); Earl Hess, *Union Soldier in Battle*, 144–45. See also app. 1 (1.B).

16. OR, ser. I, vol. 13, pt. 1, 446–47. For a discussion of Union strategy against rebel men in occupied areas, see Grimsley, *Hard Hand of War*; Ash, *When the Yankees Came*; Fellman, *Inside War*, 81–97, 115–17. Within the guerrilla community, the average age of male heads of households in 1860 was forty-five. See Appendix 1 (1.A).

17. For an in-depth analysis of the system of assessments, see Smith, "An Experiment in Counterinsurgency." The combined value of real and personal property for the average Missouri family was $3,398.81. See *Statistics of the United States in 1860*, 307, 346.

18. Smith, "An Experiment in Counterinsurgency"; Mrs. Gregg, "Can Forgive," 26–29; Stiles, *Jesse James*, 83, 89–91, 112–13, 140–1; Gregg, "A Little Dab of History," 49. The plight of Dr. Reuben Samuels, Jesse James's stepfather, is representative of the experience of older white men in this conflict, and Stiles does a good job of contextualizing his wartime experience.

19. Geiger, *Financial Fraud and Guerrilla Violence*.

20. Ibid.

21. Edwards, *Noted Guerrillas*, 284; Britton, *Memoirs of the Rebellion*, 246–47, 395. The partnership between rebel women and their men in the brush stands in sharp contrast to at least one study of Southern women's experience in the Civil War. An influential work from Drew Gilpin Faust, *Mothers of Invention*, looks into the experience of planter-class white women in the South during the war. Faust contends that the war and the absence of their male kin placed an incredible strain on white, slaveholding women across the South. These new circumstances forced these women to create a variety of survival strategies. In the end, however, the war was too much for these women, as it threatened something that they valued much more than a real Confederate nation: it threatened to take away their class status atop society. Ironically, white planter-class women called their men home from a war that was intended to create a country ruled by the planter class, for the planter class. See Faust, *Mothers of Invention*, 3–8. Other scholars suggest that Southern women were more proactive in assisting their men during the war. Victoria Bynum's *Unruly Women*, study of yeoman class and poor white and black women in North Carolina before and during the war, depicts women shaping the war. Bynum shows, at a particular point during the war, a segment of these women acting in support of their men. While Bynum's larger thesis draws comparisons between the prewar actions of so-called disorderly women with those of women who acted out in public spaces against the Confederacy, she also shows that women protected those men of theirs who had deserted from the army. She explains that "the very duties ascribed to nineteenth-century women—nurturance of family and maintenance of hearth and home"—led these women to defy

Confederate authority and provide their men with aid and shelter after they had deserted the Confederate army. As women they understood that they had twin tasks—to be nurturing their men and holding the household together—tasks that made women full partners in their husbands' wartime activities. Bynum, *Unruly Women*, 132, 130–50.

22. Mrs. Gregg, "Can Forgive," 27; McCorkle, *Three Years With Quantrill*, 149. It is unclear from where Miss Wayman came from. She was not a part of the Hook household in 1860 but was was likely a family member uprooted by General Order No. 11 (discussed later in this chapter). Despite the loss of old men and the departure of young white men into the brush, rebel homes remained locations of production because of the skills and the age, on the young side, of their occupants. In the antebellum period, white female labor was critical to the success of the household and the independence of white men. It took relatively young bodies to adjust to the increased requirements of wartime labor, however. While their ages ranged from twelve to seventy, the average age of the women was just under thirty years in 1860. The relative youth of these rebel women illustrates, if nothing else, a capability for providing the labor necessary to maintain their households in a time of war just as they had in times of peace. See Appendix 1 (1.C).

In *Masters of Small Worlds*, her study of yeoman households in antebellum South Carolina, Stephanie McCurry explains that yeoman farmers "could aspire to self-sufficiency in large measure because, in addition to grain, virtually everything else their families ate was grown or raised, preserved, and cooked by women, and virtually everything they wore was spun and woven, dyed and sewed by women (72)." McCurry concludes that, "a farm household without a farm wife was a disadvantaged one, indeed (75)." For another description of farm women's productive abilities, see Faragher, *Sugar Creek*, 118.

23. Union Provost Marshals' File of Papers Relating to Individual Citizens (hereafter PM), Cases Against Eliza, Jane, and Harriet Spencer. Kristin Wood, in *Masterful Women*, offers analysis of the leadership of women in guiding their households during the antebellum South, her major argument being that widowed women—anywhere from 11 to 20 percent of the slaveholding population—were more than capable of managing their plantations in the absence of men.

24. Correspondence from Captain Joseph Peak to Central District Headquarters, June 16, 1864, DCM, Letters Received 1862–1865, entry 3379, RG 393, pt. 2, NARA; Correspondence from Jonathon Philips to Major J. W. Barnes, Feb. 22, 1865, DCM, Letters Received 1862–1865, entry 3379, RG 393, pt. 2, NARA; Benecke, *Historical Sketch*, 25.

25. For the question of total war, see Forster and Nagler, eds., *On the Road to Total War*. In *The Civil War and the Limits of Destruction*, Mark Neely argues that total war did not exist in the Civil War and that forces on both sides restrained their destructive efforts. The debate over total war tends to be framed at the level of the nation-state. Here, however, the household is the frame of analysis. If the debate over total war were to be elevated (or reduced, depending on your perspective) to a

discussion that focused on the primary social unit, it would seem that the guerrilla households did experience war in total. That is not to argue that destruction had no limits, only to say that everyone in the household was involved in war making and could expect to feel the effects of war.

26. Britton, *Memoirs of the Rebellion*, 118.

27. Grimsley, *Hard Hand of War*. Despite quite a bit of evidence to the contrary, John Fabian Witt contends that the Lieber Code was not really grounded in counterinsurgency or a hard war that targeted noncombatants. Instead, he argues that abolitions was at the root of General Order No. 100. Given the course of events—Halleck's uneasiness in combating the guerrilla system of war in Missouri, his request of Lieber, Lieber's response, and the subsequent publication of General Order No. 100—as well as the substance of General Order No. 100, which tends to serve as a guidebook for who can be killed, who should be shown mercy, whose property can be seized, and whose possessions deserve protection, it seems that any attempts at abolition were an afterthought. See Witt, *Lincoln's Code*.

28. *OR*, ser. I, vol. 22, pt. 2, 428, 460–61; Whites, "Forty Shirts and a Wagonload of Wheat." Whites's article is the first to truly demonstrate the significance of women in the guerrilla conflict on the border. She returns women to their rightful place at the center of the guerrilla conflict, demonstrates their power with driving the war, and explores the ways in which the Union's targeting of women led to the raid on Lawrence and the subsequent issuance of General Order No. 11. See also Harris, "Catalyst for Terror"; Brownlee, *Gray Ghosts of the Confederacy*, 121; Castel, *William Clarke Quantrill*, 119–20.

29. Gregg, "A Little Dab of History," 46, 48, 49, 52; Walker, *Recollections of Quantrill's Guerrillas*, 1.

30. Reverend Richard Cordley, letter to the congressional record, found at http://www.kancoll.org/books/cordley_massacre/quantrel.raid.html; Goodrich, *Black Flag*, 77–95.

31. *OR*, ser. I, vol. 26, pt. 2, 382–83; Goodrich, *Black Flag*, 96–97; Bass, "Recollections of Quantrill," *Reminiscences of the Civil War*, 233–38.

32. An apt example of the sort of cultural interface that takes place between the guerrillas and their enemies can also be seen in Native American and European American conflicts. See Grenier, *First Way of War*.

33. "The War in Kansas—Fearful Massacre at Lawrence by Quantrill's Guerrillas," *Frank Leslie's Illustrated Newspaper*, Sept. 12, 1863.

34. Ibid.; Collins, *Jim Lane*. For a similar read on imagery and myth in the Civil War, albeit going in the opposite direction, see Silber, "Intemperate Men, Spiteful Women."

35. "The Destruction of the City of Lawrence, Kansas and the Massacre of Its Inhabitants by the Rebel Guerrillas," *Harper's Weekly*, Sept. 5, 1863.

36. Bordo, "Feminism, Postmodernism."

37. *OR*, ser. I, vol. 22, pt. 2, 428; Mrs. Frances Fristoe Twyman, "Reminiscences of the War," *Reminiscences*, 263–67; Mrs. Gregg, "Can Forgive," 27; Brownlee, *Gray Ghosts of the Confederacy*, 126–27; Castel, *William Clarke Quantrill*, 144–48; Castel,

Civil War Kansas, 142–53; Fellman, *Inside War,* 96. The District of the Border was defined as "the State of Kansas north of the 38th parallel, and the two western tiers of counties of Missouri north of the same parallel and south of the Missouri River will constitute the District of the Border, and will be commanded by Brigadier General Thomas Ewing, jr.; headquarters at Kansas City." See *OR,* ser. I, vol. 22, pt. 2, 315.

38. For the success of Order No. 11 in eliminating guerrilla activity from the border, and preventing future raids into Kansas, see Castel, *Civil War Kansas,* 152–53. The guerrillas did not leave Jackson County right away, but by October 1 the guerrillas of the border, under the command of Quantrill, left for Texas and would not return in any notable way. See Brownlee, *Gray Ghosts of the Confederacy,* 127.

39. Trow, *Charles W. Quantrell,* 77–93.

40. McCorkle, *Three Years With Quantrill,* 116–17.

41. *Harper's Weekly,* Dec. 16, 1865.

42. The birth of children out of wedlock offers proof of these intimate relations. For example, according to the census, there were two children found in the Fox households in 1870 who were born during the war, and the legitimacy of one was questionable. Peter, who was seven years of age in 1870, was probably fathered by Peter Fox senior—Isabella's late husband—before he was killed in 1864, assuming of course that she and not one of her daughters was the boy's mother. The other child, named Susan Terrill, who was six years old in 1870, was not living in a household with anyone who shared her surname. The census placed her under Nancy Fox, implying that she was the child's mother. Nancy, however, was only twenty years old in 1870, which raises some questions about the child's origins. Some women explicitly admitted to the birth of a bastard child. Mary Cull, who was twenty-two at the time her statement was taken in September of 1864, was an unwed mother. Her child was "about 14 months old." The father of the child was a guerrilla named Frank Parker, to whom she had been engaged before the war began. Although Cull observed him to be "a bad man," she also said that "he never used force" with her. See PM, Case Against Isabella Fox; PM, Case Against the Culls; 1870 US FMC, Saline County, MO (EL). Whites, *Gender Matters,* 65–67.

43. *OR,* ser. 1, vol. 34, pt. 3, 349.

44. *OR,* ser. 1, vol. 41, pt. 1, 65–67.

45. Fellman implies that the love that bound men and women together before the war was nothing but a myth during the war itself. See Fellman, *Inside War,* 193–230.

46. McCorkle, *Three Years with Quantrill,* 179–80; Gregg, "A Little Dab of History," 96; Mrs. Gregg, "Can Forgive," 29.

47. Mrs. Gregg, "Can Forgive," 29–30; McCorkle, *Three Years with Quantrill,* 180. The exact number of guerrillas that rode to Texas with the wedding party is unknown, but it is said to have been as many as fifty guerrillas. A number of guerrillas recount going South with Gregg, Hendricks, and Mattox and the wives of the latter three men. Others, including McCorkle, rode toward Kentucky with Quantrill but also observe that these men went to Texas. See Cummings, *Jim Cummins* 55; Trow, *Charles W. Quantrell,* 223; Gregg, "A Little Dab of History," 99–102; Edwards, *Noted Guerrillas,* 328.

2. REBEL KIN

1. PM, Testimony of W. H. Sidner, July 24, 1863 (emphasis added).

2. Wyatt-Brown, *Southern Honor*, 252. Cousinry is a reoccurring topic in *Southern Honor* that clearly demonstrates how fundamental extended family was to the experiences of Southerners.

3. The rebel households that make up the system of guerrilla warfare on the border, known in this chapter as the Fristoe system of guerrilla war, were gleaned from guerrilla memoirs, such as McCorkle, *Three Years with Quantrill*; Gregg, "A Little Dab of History"; Watts, *Babe of the Company*; Cummings, *Jim Cummins*; Walker, *Recollections of Quantrill's Guerrillas*; and Trow, *Charles W. Quantrell*. Data was compiled for each of these households from the 1860 US FMC, Boone, Buchanan, Cass, Clay, Howard, Jackson, Johnson, Lafayette, Newton, and Ray Counties, MO (EL). Rebel households making up the second system of warfare, known here as the Holtzclaw system of guerrilla war, were found primarily in the Provost Marshals' records, but also in *History of Howard and Chariton Counties* and *History of Linn County, Missouri*. Data for each household in the system was compiled from the 1860 US FMC, Chariton, Holt, Howard, Jackson, Linn, and Newton Counties, MO (EL). The names of guerrillas and supporters from both systems of warfare will appear with their census data and tables in an appendix at the end of this work.

4. Fellman, *Inside War*, 23; Sutherland, *A Savage Conflict*, ix–x; Myers, *Executing Daniel Bright*, 133; Mackey, *Uncivil War*; Castel, *William Clarke Quantrill*; Castel, *Civil War Kansas*; Castel and Goodrich, *Bloody Bill Anderson*.

5. Myers, *Executing Daniel Bright*, 146. Even though Myers contends that the community of Pasquotank was destroyed by guerrilla warfare, Myers's analysis of the various definitions of the word "community" was useful in the development of my own definition. Fellman's "community" is more or less Missouri, and he even takes liberties with those self-imposed boundaries. A classic example of this frame is the first sentence of his introduction, on p. xv: "The attack came at any Missouri farmyard, any night." While he asserts that "communities" within the state were divided, he offers little by way of definition or size. For works that discuss the importance of kinship in the antebellum South, see Cashin, *A Family Venture*; Baptist, *Creating an Old South*; Kenzer, *Kinship and Neighborhood*; Burton, *In My Father's House*; Censer, *North Carolina Planters*.

6. Edwards, *Noted Guerrillas*, 16. See also Fellman, *Inside War*, 249–51.

7. McCorkle, *Three Years with Quantrill*, 57–61.

8. While I see kinship being important to both men and women, in *A Family Venture* Joan Cashin makes a compelling argument that kinship was thought to be more important to women.

9. See apps. 4 and 5.

10. McCandless, *A History of Missouri*, 37. According to the 1850 US FMC, 71 percent of the free population originated from slave states to the East. For a complete description of antebellum settlement of Missouri, see 31–66; also see app. 5.

For more general descriptions of the migration of Southerners from the East to the frontier, see Cashin, *A Family Venture*, 3–8; Baptist, *Creating an Old South*, 1–15; Oakes, *Ruling Race*, 76, 77–95; McCoy, *Elusive Republic*, 196–208.

11. The Fristoe family had a legacy of prominent marriages. Richard's father married the sister of Supreme Court justice Marshal. Richard's wife, Polly, was the niece of future general and president Zachary Taylor. Richard's younger brother married the daughter of his mentor and the man for whom he was aide-de-camp, Andrew Jackson. For a survey of the history of marriage before the Civil War, see Cott, *Public Vows*, 9–104.

12. 1860 US FMC, Jackson County, MO (EL), 114.

13. Castel, *William Clarke Quantrill*, 1–21; Etcheson, *Bleeding Kansas*; McPherson, *Battle Cry of Freedom*, 145–69. For a general history of slave patrols, see Hadden, *Slave Patrols*.

14. McCorkle, *Three Years With Quantrill*, 57–61; Walker, *Recollections of Quantrill's Guerrillas*, 31–33, 98; Gregg, "A Little Dab of History," 1; Hale, *We Rode With Quantrill*, 161.

15. McCorkle, *Three Years With Quantrill*, 57–61; Brownlee, *Gray Ghosts of the Confederacy*, 61–62.

16. 1860 US CC, Jackson County, MO, 207, 208, 209, 224 (EL); Eakin and Hall, *Branded As Rebels*.

17. Although it is a study of men that fought in a formal army, Mark Dunkleman's *Brothers One and All* looks at a single Civil War regiment from western New York and cites the high percentage of men with kin in the regiment to argue that familial bonds play an important role in the success of the regiment. Dunkleman also contends that ethnic homogeneity and strong ties to family at home facilitated success on the battlefield. In *Heroes and Cowards*, Costa and Kahn state that "Ties between kin and ties between comrades of the same ethnicity" were the strongest ties soldiers could have. See Dunkelman, *Brothers One and All*, 22, 26, 31; Costa and Kahn, *Heroes and Cowards: The Social Face of War* (Princeton: Princeton University Press, 2008), xviii, 6. See also app. 2 (2.A).

18. Edwards, *Noted Guerrillas*, 17–18. Edwards said of promotion through merit that "respect for personal prowess begat discipline."

19. McCorkle, *Three Years With Quantrill*, 57–61; 1860 FMC, Cass and Jackson Counties, MO (EL); Edwards, *Noted Guerrillas*, 55, 136–37.

20. Streater, "'She-Rebels' on the Supply Line," 11, 88–89; Whites, "Forty Shirts and A Wagon Load of Wheat." There is an important distinction to draw between the "domestic supply line," discussed by both Streater and Whites, and what I am calling the rebel supply line. Whites and Streater emphasize the support provided by women like that discussed in the first chapter of this work. I am emphasizing the "line" of rebel supply line, or what can be understood as the connections between women in these different households.

21. Mauss, *Gift*, 13.

22. Ibid.

23. Ibid.

24. Walker, *Recollections of Quantrill's Guerrillas*, 44; McCorkle, *Three Years With Quantrill*, 84.

25. See app. 2 (2.B).

26. Slave Schedule, 1860 US FMC, Jackson County, MO, 11 (EL); Keckley, *Behind the Scenes*, 47.

27. Slave Schedule, 1860 US FMC, Jackson County, MO, 11 (EL); Keckley, *Behind the Scenes*, 47; 1860 US FMC, Jackson County, MO, 121 (EL).

28. Letters from Gregg to Connelley, May 14, 1903, Nov. 26, 1904, Quantrill (William Clarke) Research Collection, McCain Library and Archives. King, *Stolen Childhood*, 45–46. See esp. King's discussion of Elizabeth Keckley and her questioning of the law that made children of mixed race black as opposed to white. Noland clearly did not think of himself as black but considered himself to be much more than a color predicated on an arbitrary law. For a powerful analysis of the way in which the memory of African American participation in the war has been used, see Levin, *Remembering the Battle*.

29. Letters from Gregg to Connelley, May 14, 1903, Nov. 26, 1904, Quantrill (William Clarke) Research Collection, McCain Library and Archives.

30. Ibid; the B. James George Collection (EL) has a copy of an image in which Noland appears with the Quantrill men.

31. *OR*, ser. I, vol. 22, pt. 2, 473.

32. For an example of the migration from the western part of the state to the central part of the state by the guerrillas of the Fristoe system, see McCorkle, *Three Years with Quantrill*, 145–213. Both Castel and Brownlee argue that the war was all but played out on the border, in Castel, *Civil War Kansas*, 152–53, and Brownlee, *Gray Ghosts of the Confederacy*, 127.

33. *History of Howard and Chariton Counties*, 274, 275; Edwards, *Noted Guerrillas*, 304; *History of Linn County*, 351 (emphasis added).

34. PM, Trial against Harry Truman, Report by Truman to Col. Baker, May 16, 1865.

35. In addition to Holtzclaw, Jim Jackson, the Gooch brothers, and their brother-in-law were all veterans of the "regular" war. See the Missouri State Archives, Soldiers' Records: War of 1812–World War I, which is accessible online at http://sos.mo.gov/archives/soldiers.

36. Harry Truman's assaults against Missourians sympathizing with the South is the best such example of antagonism by pro-Union men and Union soldiers. See PM, Trial against Harry Truman, for his reports and charges and testimony against him.

37. *OR*, ser. 1, vol. 41, pt. 2, 564; *History of Linn County*, 351.

38. PM, Testimony of James Callaway, July 25, 1863, Testimony of Eliza Jane Stewart, July 25, 1863; *OR*, ser. 1, vol. 41, pt. 1, 178.

39. 1860 US FMC, Chariton, Howard, and Linn Counties, MO (EL). See app. 3 (3A–3I).

40. PM, Testimony of Henry S. Gooch, Testimony of W. H. Sidner; *OR*, ser. 1, vol. 48, pt. 1, 1096, and ser. 1, vol. 48, pt. 2, 25, 46; *History of Linn County*, 351, 354, 355; see Missouri State Archives, Soldiers' Records: War of 1812–World War I (www.

sos.mo.gov/archives/soldiers). I have deduced that "Howard" Bragg is Benjamin H. Bragg, who served with the Gooch brothers in the 2nd Missouri out of Linneaus, Linn County.

41. PM, Testimony of Eliza Jane Stewart, July 25, 1863, Testimony of Roland Gooch, Testimony of Henry Gooch, July 29, 1863.

42. 1860 US FMC, Chariton County, MO (EL). For information on Starks, see PM, Case Against Harry Truman. For a description of a fight that occurred at Butler's house while he was aiding Holtzclaw's band, see OR ser. 1, vol. 41, pt. 1, 178.

43. PM, Testimony of Henry S. Gooch, July 29, 1863.

44. PM, Case Against Isabella Fox.

45. Hattaway and Jones, *How the North Won*, 705–720; Jones, *Civil War Command*, 39–55, 99–109.

46. Holtzclaw's band was always able to escape and never fought a decisive battle in which they lost. This is a credit to the large area over which they freely ranged.

47. PM, Parole Document for Clifton D. Holsclaw, June 29, 1865.

48. Ibid.

49. PM, Testimony of W. H. Sidner.

3. The Hired Hand

1. Walker, *Recollections of Quantrill's Guerrillas*, 95, 3–9. Of the reports on the events that occurred at the Walker farm in early December of 1860, Andrew Walker's carries the most credibility. He was the only actual participant who left an account of the events, although it was not paid attention to in any official way by the earliest historians of the war. All other accounts of Quantrill's earliest days are secondhand retellings of the events.

2. Schob, *Hired Hands*, 1–4, 209–33.

3. For examples of the Quantrill biographies of the moralizing variety, see Connelley, *Quantrill and the Border Wars*; Castel, *William Clarke Quantrill*; Schultz, *Quantrill's War*. Pro-guerrilla analysis can be found in Edwards, *Noted Guerrillas*; Leslie, *Devil Knows How to Ride*.

4. Schob, *Hired Hands*, 228. Most modern scholars of the guerrilla war avoid direct analysis of Quantrill as much as possible. For instance, see Fellman, *Inside War*; Sutherland, *A Savage Conflict*.

5. Jeffrey McClurken, *Take Care of the Living*, 101, 99–117. A well-known exception comes in the form of Edward Isham. See Bolton and Culclasure, *Confessions of Edward Isham*.

6. Don R. Bowen, "Guerrilla War in Western Missouri"; Trow, *Charles W. Quantrell*; Gregg, "A Little Dab of History," 87–88. US 1860 FMC, Jackson County, MO (EL).

7. Walker, *Recollections of Quantrill's Guerrillas*, 11–12. It is possible that Walker's claim to have been Quantrill's confidant is false. It would be an attractive notion to be the one man who had not been duped. Walker does not claim that Quantrill

told him the whole truth, only that he was from Ohio; he never revealed that the tale of revenge concerning Quantrill's fictional brother being gunned down was a lie as well. If Walker wanted to construct a narrative about being the man in the know, certainly he would have included the other half of Quantrill's lie. Connelley, *Quantrill and the Border Wars*, 54–151; Castel, *William Clarke Quantrill*, 22–63; Schultz, *Quantrill's War*, 1–66.

8. Connelley, *Quantrill and the Border Wars*, 6, 34, 81, 166–73; Beilein, "'Nothing but Truth is History.'" It is important to note here that the present chapter is reliant upon the men who were present with Quantrill and left first-hand accounts: Andrew Walker and William H. Gregg. I believe that this gives us the best view of the guerrilla chieftain, at the same time offering the guerrilla perspective and perhaps being less critical of the guerrillas or their war. The goal of this chapter is to better understand Quantrill's position and role within the guerrilla war effort, not debate whether or not the guerrilla war was a legitimate undertaking.

9. Edward Ayers has long been fighting the power of hindsight. He has in his different works reminded readers that the years before the Civil War were not written like a script and our historical subjects were not actors moving and speaking on cue, all looking toward playing out the great national tragedy. Instead, he suggests we attempt to see the world as the men and women we study might have seen it so that we can understand their motivations and actions in the complex context of the ever-changing conditions on the ground. For one example of this way of thinking, see Ayers, "What Caused the Civil War?"

10. Fellman, *Inside War*, 141. Fellman says of this letter from Quantrill that "it is tempting to dismiss these sentiments as the maunderings of an ordinary young man steeped in watered-down literary romanticism. However, something in Quantrill's writing is quite authentic and disturbing." He concludes from these lines that Quantrill "might, if the occasion permitted, turn savagely on life with . . . the 'Mephistophelan cry that all created things deserve to be destroyed.'" Here Fellman is grasping. The letters of Edward Fitch are instructive as a comparison. Fitch was a migrant from New England and an abolitionist who settled in the Kansas Territory in the mid-1850s and would later be killed in the slaughter at Lawrence. His prewar correspondence is not as full of the romantic flourish as Quantrill's, but it demonstrates the multitude of challenges faced by these young men who moved out West. Also, Fitch's letters are full of references to violence, seem to show a near obsession with firearms, and are sprinkled with violent threats towards his enemies. Of course, hindsight has created a much more forgiving framework through which we read these letters. See Fitch and Fitch, *Postmarked*.

11. Connelley, *Quantrill and the Border Wars*, 103–39.

12. Walker, *Recollections of Quantrill's Guerrillas*, 4–8.

13. 1860 US FMC, Jackson County, MO, 205 (EL). Jim Liggett was twenty-five years old, making him a contemporary of Andrew Walker. Liggett was also descended from a wealthy father, William Liggett, making the backgrounds of Jim Liggett and Andrew Walker very similar.

14. For works discussing the Southern household, and the roles, relations, and identities of people in antebellum households, see: Fox-Genovese, *Within the Plantation Household*. See also Whites, *Civil War as a Crisis in Gender*; Whites, *Gender Matters*; Bynum, *Unruly Women*; McCurry, *Masters of Small Worlds*; Faust, *Mothers of Invention*; Wood, *Masterful Women*; Bercaw, *Gendered Freedoms*. For a discussion on the seasonal aspects of a hired hand's life, see Schob, *Hired Hands*, 3–4, 150–72.

15. Walker, *Recollections of Quantrill's Guerrillas*, 9.

16. Ibid., 10; For a reference to the involvement of troops under Mayes in the Battle of Wilson's Creek, see Piston and Hatcher , *Wilson's Creek*, 92. See also James L. Huston's entry for Quantrill in the *Encyclopedia of Oklahoma History and Culture*: http://digital.library.okstate.edu/encyclopedia/entries/q/quoo2.html.

17. Gregg, "A Little Dab of History," 10, 49. Gregg frequently talks about Union soldiers and Kansans killing and plundering in the name of the Union. He said of Doc Jennison, a known jayhawker, that "although government officials said Jennison was not a U.S. officer and had no authority, yet he carried the U.S. flag, and, was often assisted in his forays by troops stationed at Independence and, other stations in Jackson and adjoining counties." For overviews of the Kansas-Missouri "Border War," see Castel, *William Clarke Quantrill*, 1–21; McPherson, *Battle Cry of Freedom*, 145–69; Etcheson, *Bleeding Kansas*. For sources concerning the antebellum militia and slave patrols, see Westover, "Evolution of the Missouri Militia," 32 (for discussion of the 1804 militia act); Franklin, *Militant South*; Rowe, *Bulwark of the Republic*; Hadden, *Slave Patrols*.

18. Walker, *Recollections of Quantrill's Guerrillas*, 13–14.

19. Ibid., 15, 97.

20. Ibid., 14–15.

21. Ibid., 15.

22. See the household literature for the centrality of the household, note 9 above. Walker, *Recollections of Quantrill's Guerrillas*, 2, 11–12. Besides the fact that the two men were a part of the same household, Walker claims he trusted Quantrill from the outset. Further, Quantrill shared more with Walker than any of the other guerrillas, including the truth about his background.

23. Walker, *Recollections of Quantrill's Guerrillas*, 17–18.

24. William E. Connelley interview with William H. Gregg, July 14, 1916. William E. Connelley Collection, RH MS 2, Box 1. Spencer Research Library, Lawrence, KS.

25. Whites, "Tale of Three Kates"; Letters, Fletch Taylor to W. W. Scott, File 3, Box 1, ser. 1, William Elsay Connelley Collection, Denver Public Library; McCorkle, *Three Years with Quantrill*, 144; Gregg, "A Little Dab of History," 86–88.

26. PM, Case against Isabella Fox; Case against Mahala Drew; *OR*, ser. I, vol. 48, pt. 1, 290. Harrison Trow also mentions leaving camp to visit a lady friend. Having a woman made survival possible on a number of levels, in Trow, *Charles W. Quantrell*, 93. "Love" is being used for the lack of a better word. It is difficult if not impossible to know what sort of emotions historical actors felt, especially given their silence

on the subject. It is fair to question how genuine Jackson's feelings were: was this love, lust, or some feigned affection through which he might gain support for the war? I don't pretend to know. Instead I am using love as a catchall—affections that ran one or both ways, however temporary or lasting these feelings might have been, that facilitated female-male support in this household war.

27. OR, ser. 1, vol. 8, pt. 1, 57–58.

28. Gregg, "A Little Dab of History," 10–11.

29. Ibid., 89–90. There is no disputing that a man had to be capable of violence to become a guerrilla chief and maintain his hold over his men. A comparison comes by way of the buccaneers Quantrill and his men were often compared to. Colin Woodard, a journalist by trade, has performed some of the most serious research on piracy in the late seventeenth and early eighteenth century and has generated some fascinating conclusions. One of the most interesting and illuminating observations in terms of our understanding of the relationship between pirate leaders and violence is Woodard's that in the historical record there is no evidence that Blackbeard was ever personally violent toward his victims until his final moments, when he was killed during a fight with the assassins sent to bring him down. Woodard, *Republic of Pirates*. See also Woodard, "Last Days of Blackbeard."

30. Gregg, "A Little Dab of History," 23, 35, 45.

31. Younger, *Story of Cole Younger*, 19.

32. Gregg, "A Little Dab of History," 45–46.

33. Ibid., 46, 48, 49, 52.

34. Ibid., 46–47.

35. Ibid., 59–60; Connelley, *Quantrill and the Border Wars*, 298–99, 308–9.

36. Gregg, "A Little Dab of History," 53, 59; McCorkle, *Three Years with Quantrill*, 125.

37. Gregg, "A Little Dab of History," 47, 59–60, 76; For a more developed discussion of household-centered warfare, see Streater, "'She-Rebels' on the Supply Line," 11, 88–89.

38. OR, ser. I, vol. 22, pt. 2, 473; Edwards, *Noted Guerrillas*, 210; Gregg, "A Little Dab of History," 78–79; Walker, *Recollections of Quantrill's Guerrillas*, 23.

39. Stiles, *Jesse James*, 100; Castel and Goodrich, *Bloody Bill Anderson*, 31–33.

40. Gregg, "A Little Dab of History," 86.

41. Schultz, *Quantrill's War*, 282.

42. Wyatt-Brown, *Southern Honor*, 350–61; Bowen, "Quantrill, James, Younger, et al, 42–48.

43. See chapter 4 for the logistical variables that required guerrilla bands remain ten or smaller in their number.

44. Schultz, *Quantrill's War*, 282–84.

45. Ibid., 282–300.

46. Ibid.

47. Ibid, 298–300.

48. Ibid, 111; Leslie, *Devil Knows How to Ride*, 129, 346; Trow, *Charles W. Quantrell*.

49. William Clarke Quantrill to his mother, Feb. 8, 1860, as reprinted in Connelley, *Quantrill and the Border Wars*, 94–96.

4. REBEL FOODWAYS

1. Hildebrand, *Autobiography*, 9–10.

2. Ibid., 110.

3. OR, ser. 3, vol. 2, pt. 1, 302, 301–9 (emphasis added); Fellman, *Inside War*, 24, 29. Fellman clearly believes that the guerrillas only received aid by taking it from helpless civilians. See the chapter "Terror and a Sense of Justice: Civilians in Guerrilla War," *Inside War*, 23–80.

4. OR, ser. 3, vol. 2, pt. 1, 302, 301–9; Fellman, *Inside War*, 24, 29. See also Gary Gallagher, *Confederate War*, 140–44.

5. Wyatt-Brown, *Southern Honor*.

6. Hildebrand, *Autobiography*, 4–5. While it is done in an effort to prove that antebellum Southerners were inherently lazy and therefore inherently Celtic—perhaps a leap in reasoning—Grady McWhiney does prove the pervasive nature of free-ranging hogs in the antebellum South in *Cracker Culture*, 51–79; Hurt, *Agriculture and Slavery*, 127–30.

7. Hildebrand, *Autobiography*, 4–5. For the origins of the uniquely Southern way of raising "domestic" livestock, see Anderson, "Animals into the Wilderness." Certainly, by the mid-nineteenth century even Southerners had begun to fence some of their animals in, but the practice of free grazing remained prevalent.

8. Hildebrand, *Autobiography*, 4–5.

9. 1860 US Federal Agricultural Census, MO (EL); Hurt, *Agriculture and Slavery*, 127–30.

10. Hurt, *Agriculture and Slavery*, 127–30.

11. McPherson, *Battle Cry of Freedom*, 291.

12. Compiled statistics of the Slave Schedule of the 1860 US FMC (EL); see also chapter 2, which illustrates the interrelated nature of Southern communities in Missouri.

13. Hurt, *Agriculture and Slavery*, 111–14. See also Astor, *Rebels on the Border*, 15–32.

14. Benecke, *Historical Sketch*, 7, 15–16, 24.

15. Fellman, *Inside War*, 70, 65–73.

16. Stephanie McCurry, *Masters of Small Worlds*, 72, 75. For another description of farm women's productive abilities, see Faragher, *Sugar Creek*, 118; Jensen, *Loosening the Bonds*, 34, 35, 53, 54, 97–105. To see how Southern women managed their households during the war, see Wood, *Masterful Women*, 159–92. The practice of letting hogs roam free created a situation that facilitated guerrilla warfare. Grady McWhiney argues in *Cracker Culture* that white Southerners were essentially Celtic, and he claims that "herding" was a long-standing practice among Celtic peoples. He makes another contention, however, and that is that "black slavery and the open-range system of grazing livestock . . . made it possible for most white southerners to practice a leisurely lifestyle." While McWhiney had no intention of making any worthwhile statements about women or gender in the Old South, one can use gender analysis to build on his assertion about "the open-range system of grazing livestock." Herding required next to no labor, and according to McWhiney, if Southerners got hungry "they simply stuck another hog." Therefore, it seems that

harvesting pork was a job that could be done by anyone in the household, man or woman. McWhiney, *Cracker Culture*, 51, 75, 51–79.

17. 1860 US Federal Agricultural Census, MO (EL).

18. Watts, *Babe of the Company*, 25.

19. Wiley, *Life of Johnny Reb*, 90, 94, 97, 134.

20. While it was certainly common knowledge among those with a basic education of the Western world's recent history, military scholars wrote about Napoleon's failure in Russia. These scholars' works were digested and taught at places like West Point, therefore influencing the military elite of the United States and Confederate governments and militaries. See Von Clausewitz, *On War*, 245. For experiences with logistical issues during the Mexican-American War, see Winders, *Mr. Polk's Army*, 20, 118–26. While it is not entirely or evenly mostly centered on the ability of the US Government to feed their army in Mexico, Paul Foos's work describes in detail the fairly difficult existence of soldiers in the US Army during the Mexican-American War in *A Short, Offhand, Killing Affair*.

21. Taylor, *The Supply for Tomorrow Must Not Fail*, 11–14.

22. Wiley, *Life of Billy Yank*, 224, 225–29, 246.

23. Britton, *Memoirs of the Rebellion*, 194, 195.

24. *OR*, ser. I, vol. 48, pt. I, 1223.

25. PM, Case Against Isabella Fox.

26. See app. 3.

27. 1860 US Federal Agricultural Census, MO (EL).

28. Joanne Chiles Eakin, *Tears and Turmoil*, 5; *OR*, ser. I, vol. 41, pt. 2, 424. Captains Holtzclaw, Jackson, Anderson, and Rider (and others like Thrailkill and Perkins) are often identified together with a band of fifty or sixty guerrillas. Sometimes a notable guerrilla, such as one of those listed above, is mentioned as the leader of a conglomerate guerrilla band with one or two less influential guerrilla captains mentioned as well.

29. Hildebrand, *Autobiography*, 89; Walker, *Recollections of Quantrill's Guerrillas*, 24–25.

30. Gregg, "A Dab of History" (supplement), 9; Hildebrand, *Autobiography*, 84.

31. Letter to Capt. Wallis, Apr. 22, 1863, Letters Received 1863–1864, DCM, RG 393, pt. 2, 3379, NARA.

32. PM Records, Case Against Holtzclaw.

33. Ibid.; *History of Linn County*, 352; *OR*, ser. I, vol. 41, pt. 2, 564.

34. Thomas, *Confederacy*, 99; In *Battle Cry of Freedom* (848), James McPherson writes that Lee intended "to try a breakout attack" on April 9, but "the gray scarecrows" were greatly outnumbered, and clearly starved.

35. Alexander, *Fighting for the Confederacy*, 531.

36. Ibid., 532.

37. Ibid.

38. Gallagher, *Confederate War*, 142.

39. McPherson, *Battle Cry of Freedom*, 848; Hildebrand, *Autobiography*, 2, 110, 112.

5. The Rebel Style

This chapter was originally published in *Civil War History* 58:2 (June 2012) as "The Guerrilla Shirt: A Labor of Love and the Style of Rebellion in Civil War Missouri" and appears courtesy of the Kent State University Press.

1. *OR*, ser. 1, vol. 41, pt. 4, 334, 354, 726–27; Castel and Goodrich, *Bloody Bill Anderson*, 126–30.

2. *OR*, ser. 1, vol. 41, pt. 4, 334, 354, 726–27; Castel and Goodrich, *Bloody Bill Anderson*, 126–30.

3. Castel and Goodrich, *Bloody Bill Anderson*, 126–30. For an example of the manner in which Union officers described the guerrillas, see *OR*, ser. 1, vol. 41, pt. 2, 719. There is important work emerging at the intersection of masculinity and material culture. See esp. Weicksel, "Fabric of War; Trainor, "Beard Goes to War." See also Kristen Tegtmeier Oertel, who contends that from the outset of settlement in Kansas, a conflict arose within bleeding Kansas between Northerners and Southerners over "what kind of men they were." Ortel, *Bleeding Borders*, 85–108. Throughout her work, Oertel also shows the influence of Native Americans, directly or indirectly, in the shaping of the sectional crisis along the border. For other scholarship that shows the war as a conflict between differing gender systems see Silber, *Romance of Reunion*, and Silber, *Gender and the Sectional Conflict*.

4. Wiley, *Life of Billy Yank*, 58–62. Unlike the North, whose uniformity on the battlefield reflected its ever industrialized, modernized, and bureaucratized character, the Confederacy wished to be all these things and fight a conventional war that would reflect this, but it fell short. See Wiley, *Life of Johnny Reb*, 108–22. For studies concerning manhood within the conventional armies during the war, see Foote, *Gentlemen and the Roughs*. Also, see Linderman, *Embattled Courage*.

5. Franklin, *The Militant South*; Dickson Bruce, *Violence and Culture*; Wyatt-Brown, *Southern Honor*; Bailey, *Confederate Guerrilla*, 39–40; Walker, *Recollections of Quantrill's Guerrillas*, 22; Bowen, "Guerrilla War in Western Missouri," 30–51; Bowen, "Quantrill, James, Younger, et al.," 42–48.

6. Wiley, *Life of Johnny Reb*, 19, 108–22; Wiley, *Life of Billy Yank*, 21–22; Whites, *Civil War as a Crisis in Gender*, 47–48; Faust, *Mothers of Invention*, 9–29.

7. Brownlee, *Grey Ghosts of the Confederacy*, 104; Walker, *Recollections of Quantrill's Guerrillas*, 22. See also Etcheson, *Bleeding Kansas*. In respect to regional playing a role in the identity of these men, one of Don Bowen's undercited studies of guerrilla warfare in Jackson County shows that not only relative-depravation was the motivating factor in wages a guerrilla war among the sons of slaveholders but that the majority of the guerrillas were born and raised in Missouri (62.4 percent). Of the 28.4 percent who were born elsewhere in the South and the remaining 10 percent or so, it is likely that many would have moved to Missouri long before the war. See Bowen, "Guerrilla War in Western Missouri," 30–51, 39.

8. Connelley, *Quantrill and the Border Wars*, 317–18.

9. Faragher, *Daniel Boone*, 20–21; Nicolas Proctor, *Bathed in Blood*, 8–9.

10. Streater, "'She-Rebels' on the Supply Line," 88–89; McCurry, *Masters of Small Worlds*, 72. For works that discuss the household in respect to mid-nineteenth century farm work, see Faragher, *Sugar Creek*; Jensen, *Loosening the Bonds*; Hurt, *Agriculture and Slavery*. See 1860 US Federal Agricultural Census for Howard, Chariton, and Linn Counties, MO (EL). According to one Union soldier, Wiley Britton, in *Memoirs of the Rebellion* (246), Southerners grew "small patches" of cotton on their farms, perhaps too small to be of any consequence for the census taker. There are countless accounts in military reports of clothes being captured following a raid on a guerrilla camp or the home of a guerrilla supporter. For one example, see *OR*, ser. 1, vol. 22, pt. 1, 686.

11. John McCorkle, *Three Years with Quantrill*, 183. McCorkle talks about gathering clothes and blankets for the winter months. It was evidently a major concern.

12. Connelley, *Quantrill and the Border Wars*, 317–18; Wiley, *Life of Johnny Reb*, 111; Hurt, *Agriculture and Slavery*, 135–38; *Agriculture of the United States in 1860*, 88, 92. Statewide, the 1.1 million Missourians owned 937,445 sheep, making the ration nearly one sheep for each person residing in the state.

13. PM Records, Case Against Mollie Grandstaff, Testimony of John C. Bender, Sept. 17, 1863. This story is central to Whites, "Forty Shirts and a Wagonload of Wheat," 56–78. In *Babe of the Company* (8), Hamp Watts claimed that his guerrilla shirt was made of velvet. While I cannot be sure who Grandstaff's sweetheart was who posthumously gave her up, it may have been Daniel Boone Schull (who went by Boone and was a relative of the famous frontiersman). According to McCorkle in *Three Years with Quantrill* (68), he was killed in June of 1863, around the time Grandstaff's likeness was pulled off the body of a dead guerrilla.

14. Stiles, *Jesse James*, 88. Gregg, "A Little Dab of History," 64–69. Gregg offers a brief account of the escape out of Kansas after the Lawrence raid when sixty guerrillas held up thousands of Union soldiers, clearly illustrating the significance of easily accessible ammunition.

15. McMorris, *Crazy Quilts*, 63; *The Language and Poetry of Flowers*, 9, 18, 21, 25; Beverly Seaton, *Language of Flowers*; *Reminiscences*, 24–27; Walker, *Recollections of Quantrill's Guerrillas*, 22.

16. McMorris, *Crazy Quilts*, 63; *The Language and Poetry of Flowers*, 9, 18, 21, 25; Beverly Seaton, *Language of Flowers*; *Reminiscences*, 24–27; Walker, *Recollections of Quantrill's Guerrillas*, 22; Castel and Goodrich, *Bloody Bill Anderson*, 126.

17. Berry, *All That Makes a Man*, 12. The presence of photographs of a number of guerrillas, while not overwhelming in number, nevertheless proves the popularity of this ritual.

18. 1860 US FMC, Breckenridge County, KS Terr. (EL); Castel and Goodrich, *Bloody Bill Anderson*, 11–18.

19. *OR*, ser. I, vol. 22, pt. 2, 428, 460–61. General Order No. 10 came out on Aug. 18, 1863 but the subsequent passage of the more radical General Order No. 11 on Aug. 25 would make it null and void. See *OR*, ser. I, vol. 22, pt. 2, 473. In "Forty Shirts and a Wagonload of Wheat," Whites offers helpful analysis of the timeline of the arrest of the women who were imprisoned in the building that collapsed.

See also Harris, "Catalyst for Terror; Brownlee, *Gray Ghosts of the Confederacy*, 121; Castel, *Quantrill*, 119–20; Mark Grimsley, *Hard Hand of War*, 142–51. For analysis of Confederate policies that allowed women to be targeted and their bodies assaulted in the pursuit of counterinsurgent policies, see Myers, "Dissecting the Torture."

20. McCorkle, *Three Years with Quantrill*, 122–23; Gregg, "A Little Dab of History," 46, 53–54; Harris, "Catalyst for Terror," 290–306; Brownlee, *Gray Ghosts of the Confederacy*, 121; Castel, *Quantrill*, 119–20; Myers, "Dissecting the Torture."

21. John Grenier, *First Way of War*; Malone, *Skulking Way of War*. See Chet, *Conquering the American Wilderness*. As Grenier contends in *The First Way of War*, there was a tradition of uniquely American warfare that combined unlimited war and traditional petite guerre and was built on three pillars: "extirpative war, ranging and scalp hunting." Guy Chet challenges the idea that Native American tactics ruled the day during colonial conflicts, and, more important, he asserts that the European forces in the New World earned victory through the mastering and execution of their own well-established tactics that favored the tactical defensive. It does seem, though, that the raiding and petite guerre that characterized combat between and among the white and Indian settlements was nevertheless a distinctive part of American warfare, especially when the white forces in the conflict were made up of primarily frontiersmen, militia, or other "irregular" troops. Perhaps more important than the reality of their recent past, men of the Civil War generation idealized the guerrilla or "frontier" warfare waged by their predecessors during the colonial, revolutionary, and antebellum period. For more on the latter, see Sutherland, *A Savage Conflict*, 9–25. Clay Mountcastle illustrates the use of so-called "punitive war" by the Union Army, some of which can be seen in Ewing's policies, in *Punitive War*, 8–20.

22. Goodrich and Castel, *Bloody Bill Anderson*, 29.

23. Ibid, 35, 36; Castel, *Quantrill*, 164–65. Castel asserts that Bush Smith was a prostitute, but his notes do not substantiate this claim. He says "Frank Smith . . . explicitly states that Bush Smith . . . was Anderson's mistress, and that he never married her." While this does not preclude Smith from being a prostitute, there is nothing else in the sources that assert her occupation.

24. Walker, *Recollections of Quantrill's Guerrillas*, 22; Castel and Goodrich, *Bloody Bill Anderson*, 126; Bailey, *Confederate Guerrilla*, 48; PM, Case against Miss Mary Spencer, testimony of Miss Hattie Spencer, Sept. 5, 1864. John McCorkle describes the scene of a similar guerrilla wedding between William H. Gregg and Lizzie Hook, in McCorkle, *Three Years with Quantrill*, 179–80.

25. Walker, *Recollections of Quantrill's Guerrillas*, 22. There is one photograph of a guerrilla wearing a Union jacket: George Todd, who wears the enemy uniform in his portrait.

26. Walker, *Recollections of Quantrill's Guerrillas*, 25–26.

27. Ibid.; Proctor, *Bathed in Blood*, 57–60.

28. Correspondence from Major B. K. Davis to Colonel Chester Harding at Lexington, MO, May 7 1865, DCM, Letters Sent 1862–1865, entry 3372, vols. 225–26, RG 393, pt. 2, NARA.

29. *OR*, ser. 1, vol. 34, pt. 2, 458; ibid., pt. 4, 34.

30. Within the guerrillas' memoirs there are plenty of examples of individual men and groups of guerrillas coming together, but there is no mention of the dress of these men being a factor in their meeting, which may further the point that they had little or no trouble distinguishing between friend and foe. See Gregg, "A Little Dab of History"; McCorkle, *Three Years with Quantrill*; Watts, *Babe of the Company*; Cummings, *Jim Cummins*; Walker, *Recollections of Quantrill's Guerrillas*; Trow, *Charles W. Quantrell*. Gregg makes the claim at the end of his first supplement chapter that Scholl and Wyatt had been killed by their own men, though McCorkle, in *Three Years with Quantrill* (103), who was there, refutes it, saying that Scholl had ridden through the Union line by accident and been shot in the back by the Union soldiers once he got behind them.

31. According to queer theorist Amy Robinson, when two members of the "in-group"—both passing—come into contact with each other, they "are privy to the visual codes that evade the duped spectators of the pass." By "collapsing intuition and identity so that the in-group itself becomes synonymous with a certain way of seeing, these subjects insist on an ineffable epistemological framework unavailable to an outside reader." The act of one group of white men—the guerrillas—passing themselves off as another otherwise indistinguishable group of white men—the Union soldiers—without losing the ability to identify their own kind seems to be essentially the same as homosexual men and women passing as their straight counterparts. The interaction between the passer (guerrilla) and dupe (Union trooper) was "a hostile encounter between two ways of reading, to pass offers competing rules of recognition in the place of discrete essences of 'natural' identities." Robinson, "It Takes One to Know One," 715, 716, 719, 721, 715–36. Francis Lieber's historical and legal description of the guerrilla and guerrilla war offers some insight into how people located within the conventional army culture interpreted others. *OR*, ser. 3, vol. 2, pt. 1, 301–9. According to Lieber, one aspect of the guerrilla's "irregularity" is "the idea of the danger with which the spy surrounds us, because he that to-day passes you in the garb and mien of a peaceful citizen, may to-morrow, as a guerrillaman, fire your house or murder you from behind the hedge."

32. Trow, *Charles W. Quantrill*, 79–82.

33. Silber, "Intemperate Men, Spiteful Women."

34. Robinson, "It Takes One to Know One."

35. Walker, *Recollections of Quantrill's Guerrillas*, 23.

36. McCorkle, *Three Years with Quantrill*, 79. Sean Trainor asserts that in the antebellum period facial hair could indicate the intensity of a man's political views. In particular, beard growth indicated extreme political views—either radical or reactionary—and more beards appeared on the faces of men as the North and South pulled farther apart and the nation moved closer to war. Trainor, "Beard Goes to War."

37. *St. Louis Tri-Weekly Republican*, Oct. 28, 1864, as cited in Castel and Goodrich, *Bloody Bill Anderson*, 113–14, 154n.

38. *OR*, ser. 1, vol. 41, pt. 2, 75–77; Fellman, *Inside War*, 139. Fellman believes the letter demonstrates Anderson's "infantile narcissism and a sense of omnipotence," but I think that when read closely it offers quite a bit more, especially in respect to why the guerrillas fought and fought as they did. I think that we must read what the guerrillas did with the same measure of empathy we would grant the sources produced by a person whose morals better resemble our own. In this I follow the advice of James Axtell, who exhorts us "to judge each society by its own standards and values, not those of today. We can compare individual choices of action with those made by other people in the same or similar circumstances or with other choices possible for *that* society at *that* time," as well as to "strive to be scrupulously fair to all parties, which is possible only after immersing ourselves so deeply in the historical sources of each society that we are as much or more at home in their time and place than in our own." Axtell, *European and the Indian*, 210.

39. *OR*, ser. 1, vol. 41, pt. 2, 76.

40. Ibid., 75, 76.

41. Ibid., 719.

42. Ibid., pt. 1, 443; ibid., pt. 3, 456, 489.

43. *St. Louis Tri-Weekly Republican*, Oct. 28, 1864, as cited in Castel and Goodrich, *Bloody Bill Anderson*, 113–14, 154n.

44. *Missouri Statesman*, Aug. 5, 1864, as cited in Fellman, *Inside War*, 189, 297n; Castel and Goodrich, *Bloody Bill Anderson*, 47.

45. Castel and Goodrich, *Bloody Bill Anderson*, 126; Proctor, *Bathed in Blood*, 57–60; Berry, *All That Makes A Man*, 12–13.

46. *OR*, ser. 1, vol. 41, pt. 1, 442; ibid., pt. 4, 334, 354, 726–27; Castel and Goodrich, *Bloody Bill Anderson*, 126–30; Proctor, *Bathed in Blood*, 57–60.

6. The Rebel Horseman

1. Connelley, *Quantrill and the Border Wars*, 466–67.

2. Watts, *Babe of the Company*, 9. Famously, Mark Twain, himself something of a guerrilla or partisan or some other unconventional soldier in Missouri, wrote that "Sir Walter had so large a hand in making Southern character, as it existed before the war, that he is in great measure responsible for the war." See Twain, *Life on the Mississippi*, 376. For other examples of societies in which the horse was fundamental to culture, see Hamalainen, *Comanche Empire*, and DeLay, *War of a Thousand Deserts*.

3. Armistead, *Horses and Mules*. For works on the guerrilla conflict that give scant analysis to the role of the horse in the war, see Fellman, *Inside War*; Sutherland, *A Savage Conflict*; Mackey, *Uncivil War*; Castel, *William Clarke Quantrill*; Castel, *Civil War Kansas*; Castel and Goodrich, *Bloody Bill Anderson*; Brownlee, *Grey Ghosts of the Confederacy*. For works of military history that discuss the horse in combat, see Jones, *Civil War Command*, 27; Nosworthy, *Bloody Crucible of Courage*, 42,

280–309, 472–95; Beringer, Hattaway, Jones, and Still, *Why the South Lost the Civil War*, 14. For a work of cultural history that looks directly at the role of the horse in the war, see Anderson, *Blood Image*, 17–67. Other works of cultural history that suggest the importance of the horse in vague, nonmaterial ways are Wyatt-Brown, *Southern Honor*; Franklin, *Militant South*; Bruce, *Violence and Culture*. See also Onuf, "Thoroughbred Horses."

4. Anderson, "Animals into the Wilderness." For a discussion of Southern migration patterns and the extension of Southern social practices from east to west, see Baptist, *Creating an Old South*; Bynum, *Free State of Jones*; Carroll, *Homesteads Ungovernable*; Cashin, *A Family Venture*; Clark and Guice, *Old Southwest*; Oakes, *Ruling Race*; Hurt, *Agriculture and Slavery*.

5. Anderson, "Animals into the Wilderness," 382–84.

6. Grenier, *First Way of War*, 35–36. In *Albion's Seed*, David Hackett Fischer claims that the horse was a part of Virginia culture in a way it wasn't elsewhere in the English colonies. His conclusions mostly originate from T. H. Breen in his article "Horse and Gentlemen." The Boonslick region was essentially the area of land along the Missouri River in what is now the state of Missouri. This same area would become known as "Little Dixie." See Hurt, *Nathan Boone*, 59, 84–87, 93–94, 101, 135.

7. Hadden, *Slave Patrols*, 121.

8. Brown, *Good Wives*, 278–79; Breen, "Horse and Gentlemen." The article, "The Great Race," in the *Liberty Tribune*, May 19, 1854 (vol. 9, no. 6) describes a Missouri-style horse race: "A few days since a race came off which is decidedly the greatest treat of the season, in the way of horse-racing. The bet was made by Dr. J.C. Tiffin and W.H. Ballard, of Knoxville, Ray County. The Doctor bet two hundred dollars to one hundred and fifty dollars that his mare could beat the horse of Mr. Ballard's to Kingston, a distance of fifteen miles; and also bet a horse against the one Mr. B rode that when he got to Kingston Ballard would not be in sight; and Mr. W. Thompson also bet with Mr. Ballard on Dr. Tiffin's mare. Each gentlemen rode his own horse, and on the conclusion of the bets, mounted their respective steeds and off they dashed, running very closely together until near the end of the distance, when Mr. Ballard led off ahead and won the race by some fifty yards. The race was run through the distance of fifteen miles or thereabouts without stoppage, in about fifty minutes. We understand neither nag was injured much, is any; manifesting a little stiffness only after the race. Can any of our neighbors beat this? The cream of the matter is that the Doctor had sent some one ahead to prepare water for him, but Mr. B. was so close with him that he had no time for stopping." Bailey, *Confederate Guerrilla*, 40.

9. 1860 US FMC for MO and VA (EL); *Compiled Returns of Agriculture Census*, 92, 161.

10. *Agriculture of the United States in 1860*, 88, 92, 154; Anderson, *Blood Image*, 22. For all of Anderson's thoughts on the importance of the horse in Southern culture, see 17–67. See General Thomas Ewing's Aug. 3, 1863. assessment of the rebellious quality of the population in his District of the Border in *OR*, ser. I, vol. 22, pt. 2, 428.

11. Data procured from the 1860 US FMC for MO (EL), and the 1860 US Federal Agriculture Census for MO (EL).

12. Armistead, *Horses and Mules*, 26–28. Depending on the time and place, and of course the quality of the mount, horses cost anywhere from $150 to several hundred dollars.

13. Walker, *Recollections of Quantrill's Guerrillas*, 13–14.

14. In *Jesse James* (101), Stiles discusses the equipment Jesse James required to become a guerrilla in the same casual tone that a mother might use to discuss a checklist of supplies for her son's first day of school: "Then he needed pistols, a horse, and a saddle." The way that Stiles writes this passage conveys the matter-of-fact attitude that Missouri guerrillas and their supporters had about the essential quality of the horse in guerrilla warfare. See also Dalton, *Under the Black Flag*, 24; Bailey, *Confederate Guerrilla*, 35.

15. Walker, *Recollections of Quantrill's Guerrillas*, 22–23.

16. Gregg, "A Little Dab of History," 10–11, 40.

17. Trow, *Charles W. Quantrell*, 40; *OR*, ser. I, vol. 22, pt. 1, 584.

18. *OR*, ser. I, vol. 8, pt. 1, 463–64, 611–12.

19. Walker, *Recollections of Quantrill's Guerrillas*, 14–15.

20. Gregg, "A Little Dab of History," 11–12.

21. Armistead, *Horses and Mules*, 5–38.

22. Gregg, "My War Horse Scroggins," Quantrill (William Clark) Research Collection, McCain Library and Archives.

23. Gregg, "A Little Dab of History" (2nd addendum)," 10; Bailey, *Confederate Guerrilla*, 43.

24. Bailey, *Confederate Guerrilla*, 43, 54.

25. He does not include Missouri in his study of the occupied South, but Stephen Ash offers a great description of the garrisoned towns and their purpose in Union occupation. *When the Yankees Came*, 76–107.

26. Ibid; Fellman, *Inside War*, 132–92.

27. For accounts of telegraph lines being cut and railroads being destroyed by guerrillas, see Watts, *Babe of the Company*, 24. A Union report discussing the actions of Holtzclaw and his guerrilla band said of a particular Union outpost that "they will be very fortunate indeed if they can hold the post and keep up the military telegraph lines, which are being cut daily." *OR*, ser. I, vol. 41, pt. 2, 657. A similar discussion appears in ibid., 860; see also ibid., 705, and ibid., pt.1, 418.

28. Ibid., vol. 34, pt. 1, 1028.

29. Ibid. One of the pro-Union citizens who was robbed by the guerrillas was the father of the future Spanish-American War and World War I general John "Black Jack" Pershing. General Pershing got his nickname "Black Jack" because he led black soldiers during the Spanish-American War. There's likely a connection between his father's Union sentiments and his decision to lead black soldiers in the segregated United States Army.

30. Ibid.

31. Ibid.

32. Ibid.

33. Ibid., vol. 41, pt. 2, 719.

34. Report from Colonel Levian Martin to Captain L. G. Lamrant, May 20, 1865; report from Colonel George Hall to Captain James Steger, Dec. 30, 1863, Letters Received, DCM, RG 393, pt. 2, entry 3379, NARA; report of Brigadier General E. B. Brown to Major O. D. Green, Jan. 7, 1864, Letters Sent, vol. 225, 226, RG 393, pt. 2, entry 3372, NARA.

35. Britton, *Memoirs of the Rebellion,* 54, 156.

36. PM, Case Against Clifton Holtzclaw.

37. McCurry, *Masters of Small Worlds,* 62.

38. Britton, *Memoirs of the Rebellion,* 446.

39. 1860 U.S. Federal Agriculture Census.

40. Jackman, *Behind Enemy Lines,* 111.

41. PM, Case Against Harry Truman.

42. Edwards, *Noted Guerrillas,* 28.

7. THE REBEL GUN

1. Younger, *Confessions of a Missouri Guerrilla,* 17–19; McCorkle, *Three Years with Quantrill,* 70, 68–71; Walker, *Recollections of Quantrill's Guerrillas,* 19–21; Gregg, "A Little Dab of History," 11–12.

2. In the form of a footnote, for which he has a special propensity, Connelley offers an extensive description of the Colt revolver. He says, "In the warfare of the border it was the principle weapon, and the guerrillas and other irregular forces rarely carried any other arm. Quantrill and his men never used anything but the Colt's navy, and their superior marksmanship came from the mastery and application of its principles. The pride to-day of the survivor of the Civil War is the Colt's navy revolver carried by him through that period of strife." Connelley, *Quantrill and the Border Wars,* 320–22.

3. For older works on the subject, see Edwards, *Noted Guerrillas,* 14; Connelley, *Quantrill and the Border Wars,* 320–22; Brownlee, *Gray Ghosts of the Confederacy,* 104; Castel, *William Clarke Quantrill,* 113–14. More recent works on guerrilla warfare include Fellman, *Inside War;* Sutherland, *A Savage Conflict;* Mackey, *Uncivil War.* Works that contribute to the history of firearms in the Civil War more broadly are Jones, *Civil War Command,* 134, 273, 274; Beringer, Hattaway, Jones, and Still, *Why the South Lost the Civil War,* 13, 14, 15, 48–49, 114, 117, 130–31, 458–81; Nosworthy, *Bloody Crucible of Courage,* 28, 30–34, 36–37, 44–45, 181, 189, 307, 309, 374, 376, 474–78, 609–28, 645; McWhiney and Jamieson, *Attack and Die,* 48, 49, 56–58, 78, 79, 82, 97, 144, 146; Griffith, *Battle Tactics ,* 73–90, 184–88; Hess, *Rifle Musket.*

4. Franklin, *Militant South,* 14–32; Wyatt-Brown, *Southern Honor,* 149–74; Bruce, *Violence and Culture,* 62, 63–64, 89–91, 94–97, 196–211.

5. Younger, *Confessions of a Missouri Guerrilla,* 2.

6. Franklin, *Militant South,* 18; Proctor, *Bathed in Blood.*

7. Stephanie McCurry, *Masters of Small Worlds,* 5–36. McCurry opens her work with a scuffle between a planter and a yeoman in which the yeoman draws on and

fires his pistols at the planter. While this particular planter was too arrogant to think this thing a possibility, many others including the planter's father would have known differently.

8. Greenberg, *Manifest Manhood*; Foos, *A Short, Offhand, Killing Affair.*

9. Castel, *William Clarke Quantrill*, 1–21; Etcheson, *Bleeding Kansas*; McPherson, *Battle Cry of Freedom*, 145–69.

10. Younger, *Confessions of a Missouri Guerrilla*, 4.

11. Hosley, *Colt*; Tucker and Tucker, *Industrializing Antebellum America*, 1–91.

12. Castel, *William Clarke Quantrill*, 1–21; Etcheson, *Bleeding Kansas*; James M. McPherson, *Battle Cry of Freedom*, 145–69.

13. Walker, *Recollections of Quantrill's Guerrillas*, 11; McCorkle, *Three Years with Quantrill*, 57; Hildebrand, *Autobiography*, 21.

14. McCorkle, *Three Years with Quantrill*, 59; Hildebrand, *Autobiography*, 23.

15. Hildebrand, *Autobiography*,104, 45.

16. Walker, *Recollections of Quantrill's Guerrillas*, 22; Younger, *Confessions of a Missouri Guerrilla*, 16; McCorkle, *Three Years with Quantrill*, 62–63.

17. Griffith, *Battle Tactics*, 75, 193.

18. Wiley, *Life of Johnny Reb*, 286–307; Hess, *Rifle Musket.*

19. Dave Grossman, *On Killing*, 134–35. It does not take much to jump from the well-founded connection between sex and killing to get to the connection between the tools of both activities.

20. Griffith, *Battle Tactics*, 79, 193.

21. Linderman, *Embattled Courage*, 134–55.

22. Edwards, *Noted Guerrillas*, 55.

23. Ibid.

24. Jackman, *Behind Enemy Lines*, 59; Britton, *Memoirs of the Rebellion, 1863*, 120; McCorkle, *Three Years with Quantrill*, 135.

25. Gregg, "A Little Dab of History," 8; McCorkle, *Three Years with Quantrill*, 156.

26. PM, Case Against Samuel Caldwell, Testimony of Virginia, Apr. 1862; Walker, *Recollections of Quantrill's Guerrillas*, 41–42. Andrew Walker also recalled hiding fourteen barrels of gunpowder, which they stole from a Federal arsenal at Liberty, Missouri, in a haystack on his father's farm.

27. Younger, *Confessions of a Missouri Guerrilla*, 14–15.

28. Ibid; Edwards, *Noted Guerrillas*, 55.

29. Britton, *Memoirs of the Rebellion, 1863*, 383.

30. Griffith, *Battle Tactics*, 75, 193. In *Rifle Musket* (52, 58), Earl Hess has offered the final word in this matter. He says, "There were weapons available during the Civil War that were far more advanced than the rifle musket," which were repeaters. While he believes that there needs to be "further study to determine exactly what tactical effect [repeaters] had on a variety of different battlefields," it seems evident that he is in agreement with Griffith.

31. Walker, *Recollections of Quantrill's Guerrillas*, 25–26.

32. Gregg, "A Little Dab of History," 65, 66.

33. *History of Linn County*, 354–55.

34. For a great description of the landscape of "irregular" warfare in the occupied South, see Ash, *When the Yankees Came*, 76–107.

35. Gregg, "A Little Dab of History," 96–97.

36. PM, Affidavit of James H. Callaway, July 25, 1863, Testimony of James Phillips, July 28, 1863, Testimony of W. H. Sidner, July 24, 1863.

37. *OR*, ser. 1, vol. 41, pt. 2, 490; Letter from AAG J. H. Stegar to Chief of Ordinance, Lt. F. H. Baker, May 23, 1864, Letter from BWP Mooney to Colonel Chester Harding, May 27, 1865, Letter from Captain J. A. Lucien to Colonel John F. Phillips, Aug. 26, 1863 (all Letters Sent, Letter Received, DCM, RG 393, NARA).

38. Louis Benecke, a skilled practitioner of counterinsurgency measures, felt the need to purchase Spencer repeaters because the army was still supplying men with muzzle-loading rifles even after the debacle at Centralia. See Benecke, *Historical Sketch*, 25.

39. See Grossman's "Killing and Physical Distance: From a Distance, You Don't Look Anything Like a Friend," in Grossman, *On Killing*, 97–137.

40. Hildebrand, *Autobiography*, 28.

41. Ibid.

42. Grossman, "Non-Firers Through History."

43. Grossman, "Killing and Physical Distance."

44. Younger, *Story of Cole Younger*, 53–54.

45. Ibid., 50–52.

46. Stiles, *Jesse James*, 196–98.

47. Grossman, "Killing and Physical Distance."

8. THE REBEL BUSHWHACKER

1. *OR*, ser. 1, vol. 41, pt. 1, 440–41.

2. Ibid. Masculine identity has become an important topic of study as historians attempt to understand the war on ever more intimate levels. For the most prominent works, see Berry, *All That Makes a Man*; Foote, *Gentlemen and the Roughs*.

3. Hobbes, *Leviathan*, 83, 81–85. For an image of the guerrillas as the destroyers of civilization, see Fellman, *Inside War*. In *A Savage Conflict* (ix–x), Daniel Sutherland expands on Fellman's argument and asserts that it was the guerrillas' collective turn on Southern society that led to Confederate surrender.

4. Watts, *Babe of the Company*, 5; Linderman, *Embattled Courage*; Berry, *All That Makes a Man*; Miller, *John Bell Hood*. Perhaps the best example of the expectations placed on men fighting in the conventional war comes from the eponymous tale of Thomas "Stonewall" Jackson. See William Hettle, *Inventing Stonewall Jackson*.

5. Watts, *Babe of the Company*, 25; Linderman, *Embattled Courage*.

6. Hurt, *Agriculture and Slavery*, 1–23.

7. *OR*, ser. 1, vol. 34, pt. 2, 779.

8. Most of the guerrillas grew up on farms. See Bowen, "Guerrilla War in Western Missouri." Even today, heading toward that infamous, blood-drenched field a few miles from Centralia, a curious scholar can find the brush overwhelming. The farmers' fields are cut into the wood, but the trees creep into the fields as if they are trying to take back what was once theirs. The first time you can imagine the guerrillas, astride their horses, lurking about the bottoms, is when the road to the battlefield crosses over Young's Creek. Here you get your first fleeting glimpse of the world inside the brush. It is obvious why things grow here, being so low, so close to the water. Then, when you get to the battlefield and enter the guerrillas' old rendezvous, you truly understand. It is surprisingly dark; the forest canopy nearly blocks out the sun. Much of the underbrush has been cut away from a path through the guerrilla haunt, but to either side it grows chest high, and if a person were to go off the path, they would find that the underbrush is thick enough to conceal one's feet. The creek bed is at least eight feet deep, so that hundreds of horses could move about and drink in the creek and remain invisible.

9. *OR*, ser. 1, vol. 41, pt. 1, 416.

10. Walker, *Recollections of Quantrill's Raiders*, 14, 97.

11. *OR*, ser. 1, vol. 8, pt. 1, 57, 347; Connelley, *Quantrill and the Border Wars*, 223.

12. *OR*, ser. 1, vol. 8, pt. 1, 463, 463–64, 611–12. Fellman, *Inside War*, 253. Beilein and Hulbert, *Civil War Guerrilla*, 1–12.

13. Gregg, "A Little Dab of History," 9–10; *OR*, ser. 3, vol. 2, pt. 1, 301–9; *OR*, ser. 1, vol. 8, pt. 1, 463–64, 611–12; ser. 3, vol. 3, pt. 1, 148–64. For a larger discussion of Union policy as it was directed at men and women off the formal field of battle, see Grimsley, *Hard Hand of War*.

14. Gregg, "A Little Dab of History," 28; McCorkle, *Three Years with Quantrill*, 97.

15. Gregg, "A Little Dab of History," 27, 29–30. *St. Louis Tri-Weekly Missouri Republican*, Aug. 1, 1862.

16. *OR*, ser. 1, vol. 13, pt. 1, 131.

17. Ibid., vol. 34, pt. 4, 300–1.

18. McCorkle, *Three Years with Quantrill*, 65–66.

19. Walker, *Recollections of Quantrill's Guerrillas*; McCorkle, *Three Years with Quantrill*; Gregg, "A Little Dab of History."

20. PM, file 1583.

21. *OR*, ser. 1, vol. 41, pt. 1, 425–26; Gerteis, *Civil War St. Louis*.

22. Fellman, *Inside War*, 112, 174–75.

23. Grimsley, *Hard Hand of War*. One measure of the fear felt by Union troopers and the realization that the countryside was not under their control was in the movement toward a hard war.

24. PM, Case Against Isabella Fox, Testimony of Marilla Carmen, Jan. 23, 1865 (Carmen's husband Robert—one of two Union men in the town—was executed after the surrender of Keytesville); *OR*, ser. I, vol. 41, pt. 1, 425, 429.

25. Ibid., 432; McCorkle, *Three Years with Quantrill*, 159.

26. *OR*, ser. 1, vol. 41, pt. 1, 415.

27. Ibid. For analysis of a more infamous massacre of African American men by Confederate soldiers that took place in the context of the conventional war, see Cimprich, *Fort Pillow*.

28. Trow, *Charles W. Quantrell*, 57. For a more in-depth discussion on how men like Trow "re-remember" their war so that black men could simultaneously fit into two contrasting stereotypes—the "savage" slave-turned-rapist and the loyal Uncle Remus—in the minds of white men decades after the war, see Hulbert, "Guerrilla Memory," 84–122.

29. Hulbert, "Guerrilla Memory," 84–122.

30. Axtell, *European and the Indian*, 207–41. According to Axtell, "scalplocks, braided and decorated with jewelry, paint, and feathers, represented a person's 'soul' or living spirit (ibid., 213–14)." Although dealing with American servicemen in World War Two, Simon Harrison demonstrates that taking the skulls of dead Japanese soldiers was inspired by hunting practices and was appreciated within the context of the soldiers' community. However, when these men returned to the United States, they either found an explicit rejection of the objects by their loved ones and peers or felt an implicit shame that caused them to hide the skulls or throw them away. It is unknown how the guerrillas' kin felt about their scalps, but it is possible that there was only a limited acceptance of the trophies. See Harrison, "Skull Trophies of the Pacific War." I owe a special thanks to Craig Warren for turning me on to Harrison's work.

31. Younger, *Autobiography*, 44.

32. *Columbia Missouri Statesman*, Aug. 5, 1864. Fellman, 189; Proctor, *Bathed in Blood*, 57–60; Beilein, "Guerrilla Shirt," 173–79. For a searchable online version of the *OR*, see https://ehistory.osu.edu/books/official-records.

33. Gregg, "A Little Dab of History," 7; McCorkle, *Three Years with Quantrill*, 78; Walker, *Recollections of Quantrill's Guerrillas*, 22.

34. Hadden, *Slave Patrols*.

35. Gregg, "A Little Dab of History," 88–89. Fellman, *Inside War*, 213–14. For a description of Colorado troopers at their most infamous, see Kelman, *A Misplaced Massacre*. I am not drawing a direct connection between the treatment of Native Americans by Colorado troopers and their treatment of the guerrillas; however, there are clear parallels between the tactics used against both groups.

36. Castel and Goodrich, *Bloody Bill Anderson*, 79–86. See also Hulbert, "Business of Guerrilla Memory."

37. Castel and Goodrich, *Bloody Bill Anderson*, 87–98; Stiles, *Jesse James*, 119–27.

38. *St. Louis Globe Democrat*, Oct. 10, 1882; Stiles, *Jesse James*, 379.

39. Walter Williams's description of Centralia with statements of Frank James, William E. Connelley Collection, Denver Public Library.

40. Ibid.

41. *OR*, ser. 1, vol. 41, pt. 2, 75–77.

CODA

1. McCorkle, *Three Years with Quantrill*, 99–100.

2. Ibid.

3. Ibid. There has been a great deal of publishing on the topic of death in the Civil War. Mark Schantz contends that mid-nineteenth-century Americans held complicated but generally optimistic views on dying, death, and the afterlife that ultimately facilitated the incredible amount of bloodletting in the Civil War. The comfort through which the guerrillas approached their mortality is certainly a reflection of this idea. Drew Gilpin Faust supposes that "in the Civil War the United States, North and South, reaped what many participants described as a 'harvest of death.'" Certainly, whatever the number of total killed was and the even greater number of total people affected by these deaths, there is no doubt that it was more than four years marked by dying and dealing with death. That being said, the process through which guerrillas died and the way that the people around them dealt with both the physical sanctification of the bodies and their disposal, as well as the emotional and psychological coping, was more in line with prewar practices rather than some new anomalous work of death. See Schantz, *Awaiting the Heavenly Country*; Faust, *This Republic of Suffering*, xiii. See also Neff, *Honoring the Civil War Dead*; Berry, *All That Makes a Man*, 174.

4. Leslie, *Devil Knows How to Ride*, 406–20.

5. Ibid.

6. Ibid.

7. Ibid. Whites, *Gender Matters*, 35–36; Silber, *Daughters of the Union*, 1.

8. Ibid.

9. Ibid.

10. McCorkle, *Three Years with Quantrill*, 99–100.

11. Ibid.

Bibliography

PRIMARY MATERIALS

Unpublished Materials
Denver Public Library, Denver, Colorado
    William Elsey Connelley Papers
Ellis Library and State Historical Society of Missouri, Columbia, Missouri
    B. James George Collection, 1887–1975, (C3564)
    Gregg, William H., "A Little Dab of History Without Embellishment," [1906],
    (C1113)
    Microfilm, Special Collections
    Union Provost Marshals' File of Papers Relating to Individual Citizens
    US Federal Manuscript Census
    US Federal Manuscript Agricultural Census
    US Federal Manuscript Census: Slave Schedules
Filson Historical Society, Louisville, Kentucky
McCain Library and Archives, University of Southern Mississippi, Hattiesburg,
    Mississippi
    Quantrill (William Clarke) Research Collection
National Archives
    Record Group 393, Part 2, Entry 3379, District of Central Missouri, Letters
    Received, 1862–1865
    Record Group 393, Part 2, Entry 3372, District of Central Missouri, Letters
    Sent, Vol. 225, 226
    Record Group 393, Part 2, Entry 3376, District of Central Missouri, Telegrams
    Sent and Received, April 64–July 65, Vols. 245–46

Record Group 393, Pt. 2, Entry 3530, District of Central Missouri, Letters Sent, August 1862–June 65, Vol. 287
Spencer Research Library, Lawrence, Kansas
    William E. Connelley Collection

Newspapers
Confederate Veteran, 1907
Frank Leslie's Illustrated Newspaper 1861–1865
Harper's Weekly 1861–1865
Kansas City Times, 1910
Liberty Tribune 1861–1865
Missouri Statesman, 1864
Rolla Express 1861–1863
St. Louis Globe-Democrat 1852–1986
St. Louis Tri-Weekly Republican, 1864

Published Memoirs and Early Histories
Agriculture of the United States in 1860, compiled from the original returns of the eighth census by Joseph C. G. Kennedy, superintendent of the census. Washington, DC: Government Printing Office, 1864.
Alexander, Edward Porter. *Fighting for the Confederacy: The Personal Recollections of General Edward Porter Alexander.* Edited by Gary Gallagher. Chapel Hill: University of North Carolina Press, 1989.
Bailey, Joseph. *Confederate Guerrilla: The Civil War Memoir of Joseph M. Bailey.* Edited by T. Lindsay Baker. Fayetteville: University of Arkansas Press, 2007.
Benecke, Lewis. *Historical Sketch of the "Sixties" in Chariton County, Missouri.* Brunswick, MO, 1909.
Britton, Wiley. *Memoirs of the Rebellion on the Border, 1863.* Chicago: Cushing, Thomas, 1882.
Connelly, William Elsey. *Quantrill and the Border Wars.* Cedar Rapids: Torch Press, 1910.
Cummings, James. *Jim Cummins, The Guerrilla.* Excelsior Springs, MO: Daily Journal, 1908.
Dalton, Kit. *Under the Black Flag.* Memphis: L. J. Tobert, 1995.
Eakin, Joanne Chiles, and Donald Hale. *Branded as Rebels: A List of Bushwhackers, Guerrillas, Partisan Rangers, Confederates, and Southern Sympathizers from Missouri During the War Years.* N.p., 1993.
Edwards, John N. *Noted Guerrillas, or the Warfare of the Border.* St. Louis: H. W. Brand, 1879.
Fitch, Edward, and Fitch, Sarah. *Postmarked: Bleeding Kansas, Letters from the Birthplace of the Civil War, Pioneer Dispatches from Edward and Sarah Fitch.* N.p.: Purple Duck Press, 2013.

Goodman, Thomas M. *A Thrilling Record: Founded on Facts and Observations Obtained During Ten Days' Experience with Colonel William T. Anderson*. Des Moines: Mill and Co., Steam Book and Job Printing House, 1868.

Gregg, Mrs. "Can Forgive, But Never Forget." In *Reminiscences of the Women of Missouri During the Sixties*, compiled by Missouri Division, United Daughters of the Confederacy, 26–30. Dayton: Morningside Press, 1988.

Hale, Donald. *We Rode With Quantrill: Quantrill and the Guerrilla War as Told by the Men and Women Who Were with Him*. Independence, MO, 1975.

Hildebrand, Samuel. *Autobiography of Samuel S. Hildebrand*, edited by Kirby Ross. Fayetteville: University of Arkansas Press, 2005.

History of Howard and Chariton Counties: Written and Compiled from the most Official Authentic and Private Sources. St. Louis: National Historical Company, 1883.

The History of Linn County, Missouri: An Encyclopedia of Useful Facts, etc. Kansas City: Birdsall and Dean, 1882.

Jackman, Sidney Drake. *Behind Enemy Lines: The Memoirs and Writings of Brigadier General Sidney Drake Jackman*. Springfield, MO: Oak Hills, 1997.

Keckley, Elizabeth. *Behind the Scenes: Or, Thirty Years a Slave, and Four Years in the White House*. New York: G. W. Carleton., 1868.

The Language and Poetry of Flowers. Boston: De Wolfe, Fisk, 1877 (?).

McCorkle, John. *Three Years with Quantrill: A True Story*, written by O. S. Barton. Notes by Albert Castel. Norman: University of Oklahoma Press, 1992.

Monks, William. *A History of Southern Missouri and Northern Arkansas; Being an Account of the Early Settlements, the Civil War, the Ku-Klux, and Times of Peace*, edited by John F. Bradbury Jr. and Lou Wehmer. Fayetteville: University of Arkansas Press, 2003.

Reminiscences of the Women of Missouri During the Sixties, compiled by Missouri Division, United Daughters of the Confederacy. Dayton: Morningside Press, 1988.

Statistics of the United States in 1860; Compiled from the Original Returns and Being the Final Exhibit of the Eighth Census. Washington, DC: Government Printing Office, 1866.

Trow, Harrison. *Charles W. Quantrell: A True History of His Guerrilla Warfare on the Missouri and Kansas Border During the Civil War of 1861 to 1865*, edited and written by J. P. Burch. Vega, TX: J. P. Burch, 1923.

Twain, Mark. *Life on the Mississippi*. New York: P. F. Collier, 1917.

Walker, A. J. *Recollections of Quantrill's Guerrillas: as Told by A. J. Walker of Weatherford, Texas, to Victor E. Martin in 1910*. Edited by Joanne Chiles Eakin. Independence, MO: Two Trails, 1996 [1910].

The War of the Rebellion: A Compilation of the Official Records of the Union and Confederate Armies. 128 vols. Washington, DC, 1880–1902.

Watts, Hamp B. *The Babe of the Company. an unfolded leaf from the forest of never-to-be-forgotten years*. Fayette, MO: Democrat-Leader Press, 1913.

Younger, Thomas Coleman. *Confessions of a Missouri Guerrilla: The Autobiography of Cole Younger*. Reprint. St. Paul: Minnesota Historical Society Press, 2000.

———. *The Story of Cole Younger, by Himself*. Chicago: Henneberry Company, 1903.

Secondary Materials

Published (Books and Periodicals) and Unpublished Materials

Anderson, Fred. *A People's Army: Massachusetts Soldiers and Society in the Seven Years' War.* New York: W. W. Norton, 1984.

Anderson, Paul C. *Blood Image: Turner Ashby in the Civil War and the Southern Mind.* Baton Rouge: Louisiana State University Press, 2002.

Anderson, Virginia DeJohn. "Animals into the Wilderness: The Development of Livestock Husbandry in the Seventeenth-Century Chesapeake." *William and Mary Quarterly* 59, no. 2 (April 2002): 377–408.

Aristotle. *Politics.* Translated by Carnes Lord. Chicago: University of Chicago Press, 2013.

Armistead, Gene C. *Horses and Mules in the Civil War: A Complete History with a Roster of More Than 700 War Horses.* Jefferson, NC: McFarland, 2013.

Ash, Stephen. *When the Yankees Came: Conflict and Chaos in the Occupied South.* Chapel Hill: University of North Carolina Press, 1995.

Astor, Aaron. *Rebels on the Border: Civil War, Emancipation, and the Reconstruction of Kentucky and Missouri.* Baton Rouge: Louisiana State University Press, 2012.

Axtell, James. *The European and the Indian: Essays in the Ethnohistory of Colonial North America.* New York: Oxford University Press, 1981.

Ayers, Edward. "What Caused the Civil War?" In Edward Ayers, *What Caused the Civil War? Reflections on the South and Southern History,* 131–44. New York: W. W. Norton, 2005.

Bailey, Anne, and Daniel Sutherland, eds. *Civil War Arkansas: Beyond Battles and Leaders.* Fayetteville: University of Arkansas Press, 2000.

Baptist, Edward. *Creating an Old South: Middle Florida's Plantation Frontier Before the Civil War.* Chapel Hill: University of North Carolina Press, 2002.

Beilein, Joseph M., Jr. "The Guerrilla Shirt: A Labor of Love and the Style of Rebellion in Civil War Missouri," *Civil War History* 58, no. 2 (June 2012): 151–79.

———. "Household War: Guerrilla-Men, Rebel Women, and Guerrilla Warfare in Civil War Missouri." PhD dissertation. University of Missouri, 2012.

———. "'Nothing but Truth Is History': William E. Connelley, William H. Gregg, and the Pillaging of Guerrilla History." In Beilein and Hulbert, *Civil War Guerrilla,* 207–30.

Beilein, Joseph M., Jr. and Matthew Hulbert, eds. *The Civil War Guerrilla: Unfolding the Black Flag in History, Memory, and Myth.* Lexington: University Press of Kentucky, 2015.

Bercaw, Nancy. *Gendered Freedoms: Race, Rights, and the Politics of the Household in the Delta, 1861–1875.* Gainesville: University Press of Florida, 2003.

Beringer, Richard, Herman Hattaway, Archer Jones, and William Still. *Why the South Lost the Civil War.* Athens: University of Georgia Press, 1986.

Berry, Stephen. *All That Makes a Man: Love and Ambition in the Civil War South.* New York: Oxford University Press, 2003.

———, ed. *Weirding the War: Stories from the Civil War's Ragged Edges.* Athens: University of Georgia Press, 2011.

Blassingame, John. *The Slave Community: Plantation Life in the Antebellum South.* New York: Oxford University Press, 1979.

Bolton, Charles, and Scott Culclasure, eds. *The Confessions of Edward Isham: A Poor White Life of the Old South.* Athens: University of Georgia Press, 1998.

Bordo, Susan. "Feminism, Postmodernism, and Gender-Scepticism." In *Feminism/ Postmodernism,* edited by Linda J. Nicholson, 133–56. New York: Routledge, 1990.

Bowen, Don R. "Counterrevolutionary Guerrilla War: Missouri, 1861–1865." *Conflict* 8 (1988): 69–78.

———. "Guerrilla War in Western Missouri: 1862–1865: Historical Extensions of the Relative Deprivation Hypothesis." *Comparative Studies in Society and History* 19 (January 1977): 30–51.

———. "Quantrill, James, Younger, et al.: Leadership in a Guerrilla Movement, Missouri, 1861–1865." *Military Affairs* 41 (February 1977): 42–48.

Boydston, Jeanne. *Home and Work: Housework, Wages, and the Ideology of Labor in the Early Republic.* New York: Oxford University Press, 1990.

Breen, T. H. "Horse and Gentlemen: The Cultural Significance of Gambling among the Gentry of Virginia." *WMQ* 34, no. 2 (April 1977): 239–57.

Breihan, Carl. *The Killer Legions of Quantrill.* Seattle: Hangman Press, 1971.

Brown, Kathleen. *Good Wives, Nasty Wenches and Anxious Patriarchs: Gender, Race, and Power in Colonial Virginia.* Chapel Hill: University of North Carolina Press, 1996.

Brownlee, Richard S. *Gray Ghosts of the Confederacy: Guerrilla Warfare in the West, 1861–1865.* Baton Rouge: Louisiana State University Press, 1958.

Bruce, Dickson. *Violence and Culture in the Antebellum South.* Austin: University of Texas Press, 1979.

Burton, Orville. *In My Father's House Are Many Mansions: Family and Community in Edgefield, South Carolina.* Chapel Hill: University of North Carolina Press, 1985.

Bynum, Victoria. *The Free State of Jones: Mississippi's Longest Civil War.* Chapel Hill: University of North Carolina Press, 2001.

———. *Unruly Women: The Politics of Social and Sexual Control in the Old South.* Chapel Hill: University of North Carolina Press, 1992.

Camp, Stephanie. *Closer to Freedom: Enslaved Women and Everyday Resistance in the Plantation South.* Chapel Hill: University of North Carolina Press, 2004.

Carroll, Mark. *Homesteads Ungovernable: Families, Sex, Race and the Law in Frontier Texas, 1823–1860.* Austin: University of Texas Press, 2001.

Cashin, Joan. *A Family Venture: Men and Women on the Southern Frontier.* Baltimore: Johns Hopkins University Press, 1991.

———. *Civil War Kansas: Reaping the Whirlwind.* Lawrence: University Press of Kansas, 1997.

Castel, Albert. "Quantrill's Bushwhackers: A Case Study in Partisan Warfare." *Civil War History* 13 (March 1967): 40–50.

———. *William Clarke Quantrill: His Life and Times.* New York: F. Fell, 1962.

Castel, Albert, and Thomas Goodrich. *Bloody Bill Anderson: The Short, Savage Life of a Civil War Guerrilla.* Lawrence: University Press of Kansas, 1998.

Censer, Jane Turner. *North Carolina Planters and Their Children: 1800–1860*. Baton Rouge: Louisiana State University Press, 1984.

Chet, Guy. *Conquering the American Wilderness: The Triumph of European Warfare in the Colonial Northeast*. Amherst: University of Massachusetts Press, 2003.

Cimprich, John. *Fort Pillow, a Civil War Massacre, and Public Memory*. Baton Rouge: Louisiana State University Press, 2005.

Clark, Thomas, and John Guice. *The Old Southwest, 1790–1830: Frontiers in Conflict*. Norman: University of Oklahoma Press, 1996.

Clinton, Catherine, and Nina Silder, eds. *Divided Houses: Gender and the Civil War*. New York: Oxford University Press, 1992.

Collins, Robert. *Jim Lane: Scoundrel, Statesman, Kansan*. Gretna, LA: Pelican Publishing Co., 2007.

Connell, Evan. *Son of the Morning Star*. San Francisco: North Point Press, 1984.

Connelly, Thomas Lawrence, and Archer Jones. *The Politics of Command: Factions and Ideas in Confederate Strategy*. Baton Rouge: Louisiana State University Press, 1973.

Costa, Doria, and Matthew Kahn. *Heroes and Cowards: The Social Face of War*. Princeton, NJ: Princeton University Press, 2008.

Cott, Nancy. *Public Vows: A History of Marriage and the Nation*. Cambridge, MA: Harvard University Press, 2000.

Creighton, Margaret S. *The Colors of Courage: Gettysburg's Forgotten History, Immigrants, Women, and African Americans in the Civil War's Defining Battle*. New York: Basic Books, 2005.

Davis, David Brion. *The Slave Power Conspiracy and the Paranoid Style*. Baton Rouge: Louisiana State University Press, 1969.

DeLay, Brian. *War of a Thousand Deserts: Indian Raids and the U.S.–Mexican War*. New Haven, CT: Yale University Press, 2008.

Delfino, Susanna, and Michele Gillespie, eds. *Neither Lady Nor Slave: Working Women of the Old South*. Chapel Hill: University of North Carolina Press, 2002.

Dorsey, Bruce. *Reforming Men and Women: Gender in the Antebellum City*. Ithaca, NY: Cornell University Press, 2002.

Dunkelman, Mark. *Brothers One and All: Esprit de Corps in a Civil War Regiment*. Baton Rouge: Louisiana State University Press, 2004.

Durrill, Wayne K. *War of Another Kind: A Southern Community in the Great Rebellion*. New York: Oxford University Press, 1990.

Eakin, Joanne Chiles. *Tears and Turmoil: Order #11*. Independence, MO: Blue and Grey Book Shoppe, 1996.

Earle, Jonathan, and Diane Mutti Burke. *Bleeding Kansas, Bleeding Missouri: The Long Civil War on the Border*. Lawrence: University of Kansas Press, 2013.

Escott, Paul. *Military Necessity: Civil-Military Relations in the Confederacy*. Westport: Praeger, 2006.

Etcheson, Nicole. *Bleeding Kansas: Contested Liberty in the Civil War Era*. Lawrence: University Press of Kansas, 2004.

Faragher, John Mack. *Daniel Boone: The Life and Legend of an American Pioneer*. New York: Macmillan, 1993.

———. *Sugar Creek: Life of the Illinois Prairie.* New Haven, CT: Yale University Press, 1986.

Faust, Drew. *James Henry Hammond and the Old South: A Design for Mastery.* Baton Rouge: Louisiana State University Press, 1985.

———. *Mothers of Invention: Women of the Slaveholding South in the American Civil War.* New York: Vintage Books, 1996.

———. *This Republic of Suffering: Death and the American Civil War.* New York: Vintage Books, 2009.

Feis, William. "Jefferson Davis and the 'Guerrilla Option': A Reexamination." In *The Collapse of the Confederacy,* edited by Mark Grimsley and Brooks D. Simpson. Lincoln: University of Nebraska Press.

Fellman, Michael. *Inside War: The Guerrilla Conflict in Missouri During the American Civil War.* Oxford: Oxford University Press, 1990.

Fischer, David Hackett. *Albion's Seed: Four British Folkways in America.* New York: Oxford University Press, 1991.

Fisher, Noel. *War at Every Door: Partisan Politics and Guerrilla Violence in East Tennessee, 1860–1869.* Chapel Hill: University of North Carolina Press, 1997.

Foos, Paul. *A Short, Offhand, Killing Affair: Soldiers and Social Conflict During the Mexican American War.* Chapel Hill: University of North Carolina Press, 2002.

Foote, Lorien. *The Gentlemen and the Roughs: Violence, Honor, and Manhood in the Union Army.* New York: New York University Press, 2010.

Ford, Lacy. *Origins of Southern Radicalism: The South Carolina Upcountry, 1800–1860.* New York: Oxford University Press, 1988.

Forster, Stig, and Jorg Nagler, editors. *On the Road to Total War: The American Civil War and the German Wars of Unification, 1861–1871.* New York: Cambridge University Press, 1997.

Fox-Genovese, Elizabeth. *Within the Plantation Household: Black and White Women of the Old South.* Chapel Hill: University of North Carolina Press, 1988.

Frank, Lisa Tendrich. "Bedrooms as Battlefields: The Role of Gender Politics in Sherman's March." In *Occupied Women: Gender, Military Occupation, and the American Civil War,* edited by LeeAnn Whites and Alecia P. Long, 33–48. Baton Rouge: Louisiana State University Press, 2009.

Franklin, John Hope. *The Militant South, 1800–1861.* Urbana: University of Illinois Press, 1956.

Fredrickson, George M. *Why the Confederacy Did Not Fight a Guerrilla War After the Fall of Richmond: A Comparative View.* Gettysburg, PA: Gettysburg College, 1996.

Freehling, William. "The Divided South, Democracy's Limitations, and the Causes of the Peculiarly North American Civil War." In William W. Freehling, *The Reintegration of American History,* 176–219. New York: Oxford University Press, 1994.

———. *The Road to Disunion: Secessionists at Bay, 1776–1854.* New York: Oxford University Press, 1990.

Freeman, Joanne. *Affairs of Honor: National Politics in the New Republic.* New Haven, CT: Yale University Press, 2001.

Gallagher, Gary. *The Confederate War.* Cambridge, MA: Harvard University Press, 1997.

Geiger, Mark W. *Financial Fraud and Guerrilla Violence in Missouri's Civil War, 1861–1865.* New Haven, CT: Yale University Press, 2010.

Gerlach, Russel. *Settlement Patterns in Missouri: A Study of Population Origins, With a Wall Map.* Columbia: University of Missouri Press, 1986.

Gerteis, Louis. *Civil War St. Louis.* Lawrence: University of Kansas Press, 2001.

Glatthaar, Joseph. *Forged in Battle: The Civil War Alliance of Black Soldiers and White Officers.* New York: Free Press, 1990.

Goldstein, Joshua S. *War and Gender: How Gender Shapes the War System and Vice Versa.* Cambridge: Cambridge University Press, 2001.

Goodrich, Thomas. *Black Flag: Guerrilla Warfare on the Western Border, 1861–1865.* Bloomington: Indiana University Press, 1999.

Greenberg, Amy. *Manifest Manhood and the Antebellum American Empire.* New York: Cambridge University Press, 2005.

Grenier, John. *The First Way of War: American War Making on the Frontier, 1607–1814.* New York: Cambridge University Press, 2005.

Griffith, Paddy. *Battle Tactics of the Civil War.* New Haven, CT: Yale University Press, 1989.

Grimsley, Mark. *The Hard Hand of War: Union Military Policy Toward Southern Civilians, 1861–1865.* Cambridge: Cambridge University Press, 1995.

Grossman, Dave. "Killing and Physical Distance: From a Distance, You Don't Look Anything Like a Friend." In Grossman, *On Killing,* 97–137.

———. "Non-Firers Through History." In Grossman, *On Killing,* 17–28.

———. *On Killing: The Psychological Cost of Learning to Kill in War and Society.* Boston: Little, Brown, 1996.

Hadden, Sally. *Slave Patrols: Law and Violence in Virginia and the Carolinas.* Cambridge, MA: Harvard University Press, 2001.

Hale, Donald. *We Rode With Quantrill: Quantrill and the Guerrilla War as Told by the Men and Women Who Were with Him.* Independence, MO, 1975.

Hamalainen, Pekka. *The Comanche Empire.* New Haven, CT: Yale University Press, 2008.

Harris, Charles F. "Catalyst for Terror: The Collapse of the Women's Prison in Kansas City." *Missouri Historical Review* 83, no. 3 (April 1995): 290–306.

Harrison, Simon. "Skull Trophies of the Pacific War: Transgressive Objects of Remembrance." *Journal of the Royal Anthropological Institute* 12, no. 4 (December 2006): 817–36.

Hattaway, Herman, and Archer Jones. *How the North Won: A Military History of the Civil War.* Champaign: University of Illinois Press, 1991.

Hess, Earl. *Field Armies and Fortifications in the Civil War: The Eastern Campaigns, 1861–1864.* Chapel Hill: University of North Carolina Press, 2005.

———. *The Rifle Musket in Civil War Combat: Reality and Myth.* Lawrence: University Press of Kansas, 2008.

———. *The Union Soldier in Battle: Enduring the Ordeal of Combat.* Lawrence: University Press of Kansas, 1997.

Hesse, Hermann. *The Glass Bead Game: A Novel*. New York: Macmillan, 1943.

Hettle, William. *Inventing Stonewall Jackson: A Civil War Hero in History and Memory*. Baton Rouge: Louisiana State University Press, 2011.

Higonnet, Margaret Randolph, Jane Jenson, Sonya Michel, and Margaret Collins Weitz, eds. *Behind the Lines: Gender and the Two World Wars*. New Haven, CT: Yale University Press, 1987.

Hobbes, Thomas. *Leviathan*. Edited by Marshall Missner. New York: Pearson, 2008.

Hosley, William. *Colt: The Making of an American Legend*. Amherst: University of Massachusetts Press, 1996.

Hulbert, Matthew. "The Business of Guerrilla Memory: Selling Massacres and the Captivity Narrative of Sergeant Thomas M. Goodman." In Beilein and Hulbert, *Civil War Guerrilla*, 123–44.

———. "Constructing Guerrilla Memory: John Newman Edwards and Missouri's Irregular Lost Cause." *Journal of the Civil War Era* 2, no. 1 (March 2012): 58–81.

———. "Guerrilla Memory: Irregular Recollections from the Civil War Borderlands." PhD diss., University of Georgia, 2015.

Hurt, R. Douglas. *Agriculture and Slavery in Missouri's Little Dixie*. Columbia: University of Missouri Press, 1992.

———. *Nathan Boone and the American Frontier*. Columbia: University of Missouri Press, 2000.

Jensen, Joan. *Loosening the Bonds: Mid-Atlantic Farm Women, 1750–1850*. New Haven, CT: Yale University Press, 1986.

Jones, Archer. *Civil War Command and Strategy: The Process of Victory and Defeat*. New York: Free Press, 1992.

Jones, Virgil. *Gray Ghosts and Rebel Raiders: The Daring Exploits of the Confederate Guerrillas*. New York: Henry Holt, 1956.

Kalyvas, Stathis. *The Logic of Violence in Civil War*. New York: Cambridge University Press, 2006.

Kelman, Ari. *A Misplaced Massacre: Struggling Over the Memory of Sand Creek*. Cambridge, MA: Harvard University Press, 2014.

Kenzer, Robert. *Kinship and Neighborhood in a Southern Community: Orange County, North Carolina, 1849–1881*. Knoxville: University of Tennessee Press, 1987.

King, Wilma. *Stolen Childhood: Slave Youth in Nineteenth-Century America*. Bloomington: Indiana University Press, 2011.

Leslie, Edward. *The Devil Knows How to Ride: The True Story of William Clarke Quantrill and his Confederate Raiders*. New York: Da Capo Press, 1998.

Levin, Kevin. *Remembering the Battle of the Crater: War as Murder*. Lexington: University Press of Kentucky, 2012.

Linderman, Gerald. *Embattled Courage: The Experience of Combat in the American Civil War*. New York: Free Press, 1987.

Link, William. *Roots of Secession: Slavery and Politics in Antebellum Virginia*. Chapel Hill: University of North Carolina Press, 2003.

Lowry, Thomas. *The Story the Soldiers Wouldn't Tell: Sex in the Civil War*. Mechanicsburg, PA: Stackpole Books, 1994.

Mackey, Robert. *The Uncivil War: Irregular Warfare in the Upper South, 1861–1865.* Norman: University of Oklahoma Press, 2004.

Malone, Patrick M. *The Skulking Way of War: Technology and Tactics Among the New England Indians.* New York: Madison Books, 1991.

Mauss, Marcel. *The Gift: The Form and Reason for Exchange in Archaic Societies.* New York: W. W. Norton, 1990 [1950].

McCandless, Perry. *A History of Missouri.* Vol. 2, *1820–1860.* Columbia: University of Missouri Press, 1972.

McClurken, Jeffrey. *Take Care of the Living: Reconstructing Confederate Veteran Families in Virginia.* Charlottesville: University of Virginia Press, 2009.

McCoy, Drew. *The Elusive Republic: Political Economy in Jeffersonian America.* Chapel Hill: University of North Carolina Press, 1980.

McCurry, Stephanie. *Masters of Small Worlds: Yeoman Households, Gender Relations, and the Political Culture of the Antebellum South Carolina Low Country.* New York: Oxford University Press, 1995.

McMorris, Penny. *Crazy Quilts.* New York: E. P. Dutton, 1984.

McMurry, Richard. *The Fourth Battle of Winchester: Toward a New Civil War Paradigm.* Kent, OH: Kent State University Press, 2002.

McPherson, James. *Battle Cry of Freedom: The Civil War Era.* New York: Ballantine Books, 1988.

McWhiney, Grady. *Cracker Culture: Celtic Ways in the Old South.* Tuscaloosa: University of Alabama Press, 1989.

McWhiney, Grady, and Perry Jamieson. *Attack and Die: Civil War Military Tactics and the Southern Heritage.* Tuscaloosa: University of Alabama Press, 1982.

Miller, Brian. *John Bell Hood and the Fight for Civil War Memory.* Knoxville: University of Tennessee Press, 2010.

Monaghan, Jay. *Civil War on the Western Border, 1854–1865.* Lincoln: University of Nebraska Press, 1955

Moore, Barrington. "The American Civil War: The Last Capitalist Revolution." In Barrington Moore, *Social Origins of Dictatorship and Democracy: Lord and Peasant in the Making of the Modern World,* 111–55. Boston: Beacon Press, 1966.

Mountcastle, Clay. *Punitive War: Confederate Guerrillas and Union Reprisals.* Lawrence: University Press of Kansas, 2009.

Mutti-Burke, Diane. *On Slavery's Border: Missouri's Small-Slaveholding Households, 1815– 1865.* Athens: University of Georgia Press, 2010.

Myers, Barton. "Dissecting the Torture of Mrs. Owens: The Story of a Civil War Atrocity." In *Weirding the War: Stories from the Civil War's Ragged Edges,* edited by Stephen Berry, 144–65. Athens: University of Georgia Press, 2011.

———. *Executing Daniel Bright: Race, Loyalty, and Guerrilla Violence in a Coastal Carolina Community, 1861–1865.* Baton Rouge: Louisiana State University Press, 2009.

Neely, Mark. *The Civil War and the Limits of Destruction.* Cambridge, MA: Harvard University Press, 2007.

Neff, John. *Honoring the Civil War Dead: Commemoration and the Problem of Reconciliation.* Lawrence: University Press of Kansas, 2005.

Nichols, Bruce. *Guerrilla Warfare in Civil War Missouri, 1862.* Jefferson, MO: McFarland, 2004.

Nicholson, Linda J., ed. *Feminism/Postmodernism.* New York: Routledge, 1990.

Noe, Kenneth. "Who Were the Bushwhackers? Age, Class, Kin, and Western Virginia's Confederate Guerrillas, 1861–1862." *Civil War History* 49 (2003): 5–26.

Nosworthy, Brent. *The Bloody Crucible of Courage: Fighting Methods and Combat Experience of the Civil War.* New York: Carroll and Graf, 2003.

Oakes, John. *The Ruling Race: A History of American Slaveholders.* New York: W. W. Norton, 1998.

Oertel, Kristen Tegtmeier. *Bleeding Borders: Race, Gender, and Violence in Pre-Civil War Kansas.* Baton Rouge: Louisiana State University Press, 2009.

Onuf, Rachel. "Thoroughbred Horses and the Rejuvenation of the Chesapeake Gentry, 1825–1835." Thesis, University of Virginia, 1997.

Paludan, Phillip S. "The American Civil War Considered as a Crisis in Law and Order." *AHR* 77 (June 1972).

Pierson, Michael. *Free Hearts and Free Homes: Gender and American Antislavery Politics.* Chapel Hill: University of North Carolina Press, 2003.

Piston, William, and Richard W. Hatcher III. *Wilson's Creek: Second Battle of the Civil War and the Men Who Fought It.* Chapel Hill: University of North Carolina Press, 2000.

Ponce, Pearl T. *Kansas's War: The Civil War in Documents.* Athens: Ohio University Press, 2011.

Proctor, Nicolas. *Bathed in Blood: Hunting and Mastery in the Old South.* Charlottesville: University Press of Virginia, 2002.

Rafuse, Ethan. "McClellan and Halleck at War: The Struggle for Control of the Union War Effort in the West, November 1861–March 1862." *Civil War History* 49 (January 2003): 32–51.

Robinson, Amy. "It Takes One to Know One: Passing and Communities of Common Interest." *Critical Inquiry* 20, no 4 (Summer 1994): 715–36.

Rowe, Ellen. *Bulwark of the Republic: The American Militia in Antebellum West.* Westport, CT: Praeger, 2003.

Royster, Charles. *The Destructive War: William Tecumseh Sherman, Stonewall Jackson and the Americans.* New York. Vintage Books, 1993.

Seaton, Beverly. *The Language of Flowers: A History.* Charlottesville: University Press of Virginia, 1995.

Schantz, Mark. *Awaiting the Heavenly Country: The Civil War and America's Culture of Death.* Ithaca, NY: Cornell University Press, 2008.

Schob, David. *Hired Hands and Plow Boys: Farm Labor in the Midwest, 1815–1860.* Champaign: University of Illinois Press, 1975.

Schultz, Duane. *Quantrill's War: The Life and Times of William Clarke Quantrill, 1837–1865.* New York: St. Martin's Press, 1996.

Schultz, Jane. *Women at the Front: Hospital Workers in Civil War America.* Chapel Hill: University of North Carolina Press, 2004.

Shea, William, and Earl Hess. *Pea Ridge: Civil War Campaign in the West.* Chapel Hill: University of North Carolina Press, 1992.

Sheehan-Dean, Aaron. *Why Confederates Fought: Family and Nation in Civil War Virginia*. Chapel Hill: University of North Carolina Press, 2007.

Silber, Nina. *Daughters of the Union: Northern Women Fight the Civil War*. Cambridge, MA: Harvard University Press, 2005.

———. *Gender and the Sectional Conflict*. Chapel Hill: University of North Carolina Press, 2008.

———. "Intemperate Men, Spiteful Women, and Jefferson Davis." In *Divided Houses: Gender and the Civil War*, edited by Catherine Clinton and Nina Silber, 283–305. New York: Oxford University Press, 1992.

———. *The Romance of Reunion: Northerners and the South 1865–1900*. Chapel Hill: University of North Carolina Press, 1993.

Smith, Merrill, ed. *Sex and Sexuality in Early America*. New York: New York University Press, 1998.

Smith, Wayne. "An Experiment in Counterinsurgency: The Assessment of Confederate Sympathizers in Missouri." *Journal of Southern History* 35 (August 1969): 361–80.

Stamp, Kenneth, ed. *The Causes of the Civil War*. New York: Touchstone, 1991.

———. *The Imperiled Union: Essays on the Background of the Civil War*. New York: Oxford University Press, 1980.

Stanley, Amy Dru. *From Bondage to Contract: Wage Labor, Marriage, and the Market in the Age of Slave Emancipation*. New York: Cambridge University Press, 1998.

Stiles, T. J. *Jesse James: Last Rebel of the Civil War*. New York: Vintage Books, 2003.

Streater, Kristen. "'She-Rebels' on the Supply Line: Gender Conventions in Civil War Kentucky." In *Occupied Women: Gender, Military Occupation, and the American Civil War*, edited by LeeAnn Whites and Apecia P. Long, 88–102. Baton Rouge: Louisiana State University Press, 2009.

Sutherland, Daniel. *American Civil War Guerrillas: Changing the Rules of Warfare*. New York: Praeger, 2013.

———. *A Savage Conflict: The Decisive Role of Guerrillas in the American Civil War*. Chapel Hill: University of North Carolina Press, 2009.

———. "Sideshow No Longer: A Historigraphical Review of the Guerrilla War." *Civil War History* 46 (March 2000): 5–23.

Taylor, Lenette. *"The Supply for Tomorrow Must Not Fail": The Civil War of Captain Simon Perkins Jr., a Union Quartermaster*. Kent, OH: Kent State University Press, 2004.

Thomas, Emory. *The Confederacy as a Revolutionary Experience*. Englewood Cliffs, NJ: Prentice-Hall, inc., 1971.

Trainor, Sean. "The Beard Goes to War: Men's Grooming and the American Civil War." Paper Presented at the Biannual Meeting of the Society of Civil War Historians, Baltimore, MD, June 12–14, 2014.

Tucker, Barbara, and Kenneth Tucker Jr. *Industrializing Antebellum America: The Rise of Manufacturing Entrepreneurs in the Early Republic*. New York: Palgrave Macmillan, 2008.

Von Clausewitz, Carl. *On War*. Edited and translated by Michael Howard and Peter Paret. New York: Alfred A. Knopf, 1993.

Weber, Jennifer. *Copperheads: The Rise and Fall of Lincoln's Opponents in the North.* New York: Oxford University Press, 2006.

Weber, Rebekah. "'It Is For You That We Fight': Gender and the Civil War in Saline County, Missouri." Master's thesis, University of Missouri, Columbia, 2000.

Weicksel, Sarah Jones. "The Fabric of War: Clothing, Culture, and Violence in the American Civil War Era." PhD diss., University of Chicago, forthcoming.

Weitz, Mark. *A Higher Duty: Desertion Among Georgia Troops During the Civil War.* Lincoln: University of Nebraska Press, 2000.

Westover, John. "The Evolution of the Missouri Militia, 1804–1919." PhD diss., University of Missouri, Columbia, 1948.

Whites, LeeAnn. *The Civil War as a Crisis in Gender: Augusta, Georgia, 1860–1890.* Athens: University of Georgia Press, 1995.

———. "Forty Shirts and a Wagonload of Wheat: Women, the Domestic Supply Line, and the Civil War on the Western Border." *Journal of the Civil War Era* 1 (March 2011): 56–78.

———. *Gender Matters: Civil War, Reconstruction, and the Making of the New South.* New York: Palgrave MacMillan, 2005.

———. "The Tale of Three Kates: Outlaw Women, Loyalty, and Missouri's Long Civil War." In *Weirding the War: Stories from the Civil War's Ragged Edges,* edited by Stephen Berry, 73–94. Athens: University of Georgia Press, 2011.

Whites, LeeAnn, and Alecia P. Long, eds. *Occupied Women: Gender, Military Occupation, and the American Civil War.* Baton Rouge: Louisiana State University Press, 2009.

Wiley, Bell Irvin. *The Life of Billy Yank: The Common Soldier of the Union.* New York: Doubleday 1971.

———. *The Life of Johnny Reb: The Common Soldier of the Confederacy.* New York: Doubleday, 1971.

Wilson, Harold. *Confederate Industry: Manufacturers and Quartermasters in the Civil War.* Jackson: University Press of Mississippi, 2002.

Wilson, Mark. *The Business of the Civil War: Military Mobilization and the State, 1861–1865.* Baltimore: Johns Hopkins University Press, 2006.

Winders, Richard. *Mr. Polk's Army: The American Military Experience in the Mexican War.* College Station: Texas A&M University Press, 1997.

Witt, John Fabian. *Lincoln's Code: The Laws of War in American History.* New York: Free Press, 2013.

Wood, Kirsten E. *Masterful Women: Slaveholding Widows from the American Revolution Through the Civil War.* Chapel Hill: University of North Carolina Press, 2004.

Woodard, Colin. "The Last Days of Blackbeard." *Smithsonian Magazine,* volume 44, issue 10, February 2014, 32–41.

———. *The Republic of Pirates: Being the True and Surprising Story of the Caribbean Pirates and the Man who Brought them Down.* Orlando: Harcourt Books, 2007.

Wyatt-Brown, Bertram. *Southern Honor: Ethics and Behavior in the Old South.* New York: Oxford University Press, 1982.

Websites

Ancestry.com. http://www.ancestry.com.

eHISTORY: The Ohio State University. http://ehistory.osu.edu/osu/sources/
records.

Encyclopedia of Oklahoma History and Culture. http://digital.library.okstate.edu/
encyclopedia/entries/q/quo02.html.

Kansas Collection Books. http://www.kancoll.org/books/cordley_massacre/
quantrel.raid.htm.

Missouri State Archives, Soldiers' Records. http://www.sos.mo.gov.records/soldiers.

Index